A Critical History of Economics

A Critical History of Economics

Economics

John Mills

palgrave
macmillan

First published in hardcover 2002

First published in paperback 2003 by
PALGRAVE MACMILLAN
Houndmills, Basingstoke, Hampshire RG21 6XS and
175 Fifth Avenue, New York, N. Y. 10010
Companies and representatives throughout the world

PALGRAVE MACMILLAN is the global academic imprint of the Palgrave Macmillan division of St. Martin's Press, LLC and of Palgrave Macmillan Ltd. Macmillan® is a registered trademark in the United States, United Kingdom and other countries. Palgrave is a registered trademark in the European Union and other countries.

ISBN 0–333–97130–2 hardback
ISBN 1–4039–1892–9 paperback

This book is printed on paper suitable for recycling and made from fully managed and sustained forest sources.

A catalogue record for this book is available from the British Library.

A catalogue record for this book is available from the Library of Congress

10   9   8   7   6   5   4   3   2   1
12   11   10   09   08   07   06   05   04   03

Printed and bound in Great Britain by
Antony Rowe Ltd, Chippenham and Eastbourne

Contents

Preface

In 1960, John F. Kennedy ran for president of the USA on a promise of 5% per annum growth in the American economy.[1] This was even higher than the 4% promised during the British general election of 1964 by both the major parties, but especially by Harold Wilson, whose Labour Party won. While for both the USA and Britain these targets were ambitious in relation to previous records they had achieved, they appeared by no means outlandish. During the 1950s and 1960s, the economies of continental Europe had managed to achieve cumulative growth rates of about 5% per annum. Japan was doing even better, with almost 10%.[2]

The results actually achieved, however, fell short of the promises. During the 1960s, the cumulative growth rate was nevertheless a reasonably respectable 4.2% in the USA and a rather more disappointing 2.9% in Britain. These growth rates, however, looked spectacularly successful compared to what happened over the decades to follow. Between 1973 and 1994, the growth rate in the USA, despite a large increase in the population, fell to 2.5%, and in Britain to a miserable 1.7%.[3] Nor, over these decades, was the position in continental Europe significantly better. There, the 5% and 6% average growth rates of the 1950s and 1960s sank to just under 2.5% per annum.[4] Expansion in Japan continued over this period, albeit at a slower rate than previously, but even there, by the 1990s, growth had almost disappeared.[5]

These depressing figures, however, mask a remarkable phenomenon. While for the vast bulk of the population in all these countries lower growth rates betokened more sluggish or – in many cases – non-existent increases or even falling living standards, for the well off across the Western world, no such thing happened. For them, the pledges made by President Kennedy and Prime Minister Harold Wilson came close to being fulfilled. Their real incomes – and wealth – rose exponentially. Across the whole of the Western developed world, credit creation was used to a much greater extent than previously to finance the purchase of existing capital assets, as price inflation pushed up their value, rather than paying for new investment.[6] As a result of a combination of disproportionately high increases in salaries, reductions in taxation, and rises in the value of real assets such as equity shares and property, those who were already rich became far better off. In the USA, between 1970 and 1998, the average increase in income, before tax, for the most wealthy 5% of the population rose cumulatively by 3.2% per annum,[7] pushing up their revenues to almost two and a half times their level in 1970, while reductions in taxation on the most well off probably pushed the total up to nearly 4% net of tax. In the European Union (EU), much the same occurred.

Inevitably, the increasingly greater proportion of the national income absorbed by the most wealthy was reflected in much harsher experiences for everyone else. In the USA, over the same three decades from 1970 to 1998, real wages per hour across the whole of the labour force, far from increasing, actually fell marginally,[8] an outcome which, in 1960, would have been dismissed as being off the spectrum of probabilities. For those out of work, the position was worse still, especially during the Reagan and Bush eras. Between 1980 and 1992 the real incomes of those in the lowest 20% of the US population fell by 6%.[9] In Europe, the same trends were mirrored in a rather different way. There, the standard of living for hourly paid workers, provided they had jobs, broadly speaking kept pace with the rise in national Gross Domestic Product, while the huge transfer of real income to those who were best off came from a major fall in living standards sustained by those who ceased working. In 1973, almost everyone in Western Europe who wanted a job had one. By the mid-1990s, average registered unemployment in the EU was 11%,[10] though even this figure hugely underestimated the real problem. International Labour Organisation figures show that in 1998 the total number of people in the EU who were not registered as unemployed but who would have been willing to work if suitable jobs had been available, if counted in, would have added about another 50% to the unemployment total.[11]

Nor are these trends ones which operated only within countries. They also occurred between them and, in particular, between different categories of countries in varying parts of the world. There were some great success stories, particularly the Tiger economies of Hong Kong, Singapore, South Korea and Taiwan. Around much of the Pacific Rim, including China, and only excluding Japan in the 1990s, huge growth rates were achieved throughout the period, when the economies of the West were doing so relatively poorly. At the other end of the spectrum, however, there were some desperate failures. Much of Africa, especially south of the Sahara Desert, saw no advance at all in living standards, as whatever rises in national income were achieved were more than swallowed up by exceptionally high increases in the size of the population.

Why did all this happen? Why did growth rates falter to the extraordinary extent that they did right across the Western, developed world? Why did unemployment in many countries become such a major problem? Why is there still an obsession with inflation, even though price rises are currently so low? Why has the distribution of both income and wealth across the world become so much more uneven? This book, like others I have written, sets out to explain how and why these developments were allowed to occur. It also suggests what should have been done instead in the past, and what needs to be done in the future, to stop the same trends continuing to materialise. My previous books have concentrated on economic history, using it to provide a context in which to explain why events and trends developed in the way they did. This book tackles the same agenda, but from a different angle. This time the concentration is not so much on events, but on ideas. Its objective is not so much to chronicle what actually happened, but to describe and to analyse, within the changing and varying framework of beliefs and concepts in which judgements were formed, what was happening to ideas about economics. How did informed opinion view what was going on? How did the participants come to believe that particular policies ought to be pursued? Why did they think that these policies, rather than others, were desirable, important and likely to be effective?

The chapters which follow therefore consist of a history of economic ideas, but within a critical context. Every attempt is made to express as fairly as possible the views set out by all those whose thinking has had a major impact on the development of economics as a discipline, but to do so in a way which does not just assess the impact each of these thinkers and writers achieved. There is also an evaluation as to whether, in the long sweep of history, what each of them – and especially the more major and influential figures – had to say has turned out to be right or wrong, judged by the particular criteria I believe should be used. These criteria are clearly central to the whole of the thesis which follows, and therefore need to be explained.

The starting point is that in very important respects, in my view, economics, as a discipline, is not in good shape. While having, inevitably, much to say about detailed matters, this book argues that they ought not to be its major focus. On the contrary, the principal role of economics ought to be to provide answers to the central questions faced by policy-makers on growth, employment and inflation, the alleviation of poverty, and making sure that there is a sustainable future. How do you achieve whatever rate of economic growth is decided to be desirable? How is full employment to be maintained? How, if the first two objectives are attained, is inflation to be held within acceptable bounds? How is the incidence of poverty and destitution to be kept at bay? How can we arrange matters so that the world economy has a viable future? The plain fact is that economics, as presently studied and taught, does not answer these questions, and never has done. Though the issues thus raised have been of great importance to most of those who have heavily influenced the way in which economics has evolved, no generally accepted theory embracing how to achieve all these goals together has been developed. Because – as this book will also explain – I believe that there should be ways to achieve all of them together, the criteria for judging the way in which economic thinking has developed fall into place. The test to be applied is the extent to which the contributions made by all those who have played a major part in the way in which economics has developed has brought us closer to finding answers to the core questions listed above.

Tackling this agenda has involved a number of major challenges, leaving aside for the moment the major issue as to whether, to provide the benchmark needed, there really are answers to the questions raised in the previous paragraph. The reader will have to make his or her own judgement when the arguments for believing that they exist are set out in the next chapter. In particular, there is the question of establishing a reasonably balanced view about the relative impact and importance of different thinkers on economics since, as a system of ideas, the discipline began to take shape. I wish I were in a position to claim that I had read everyone's works in the original. Alas, though I have read quite a number of them, of course I cannot claim to have read anything like all the vast amount of material available. I have therefore had to rely more, really, than I would have preferred, on secondary sources. Those which have been most helpful have included the short, concise and typically entertaining *A History of Economics – the Past as the Present* by John Kenneth Galbraith.[12] More comprehensive coverage is provided by Eric Roll's *A History of Economic Thought*,[13] Mark Blaug's *Economic Theory in Retrospect*[14] and Henry William Spiegel's *The Growth of Economic Thought*.[15] A much more recent book, with much more sympathy for monetarist ideas than I have is Mark Skousen's *The Making of Modern Economics*.[16] Much more critical of current economic thinking is Steve Keen's *Debunking Economics*.[17] Other publications which have been extremely useful include *The New Palgrave – A Dictionary of Economics*,[18] which contains a vast treasury of reference material, and Joseph A. Schumpeter's *Ten Great Economists*.[19] At the other end of the spectrum is another book by Joseph A. Schumpeter – his *History of Economic Analysis*[20] which is over 1,200 pages long. Reviewing this monumental work in 1954, shortly after it was first published, Jacob Viner expressed the view that there is

> much in this book which is redundant, irrelevant, cryptic, strongly biased, paradoxical, or otherwise unhelpful or even harmful to understanding. When all this is set aside, there still remains enough to constitute, by a wide margin, the most constructive, the most original, the most learned, and the most brilliant contribution to the history of the analytical phases of our discipline which has ever been made.

I am inclined to agree even more strongly with the first part than the second of this assessment of a nevertheless truly remarkable work.

While these are the main sources on which I have relied in choosing which economists to feature as being most influential, there are many other books and articles I have read which have shaped the assessments I have made, and the more significant of these, to my mind, are listed in the bibliography to be found starting on page 214. I also need to mention *The Economist* magazine which I have read almost every week since my days as an undergraduate in the late 1950s and early 1960s. These sources have been particularly important in trying to help me to decide which economists seem to have been most influential in the latter half of the twentieth century. In this respect, I have been much less able to rely on the opinions of others, as I know of no general attempt made recently to cover this ground, which is, in any event of course, bound to be more speculative. More time will have to elapse before it will be possible to come close to a definitive view about who have been the most significant thinkers of the period, though it is already clear who some of them will be.

As to the wider context which has enabled me to tackle the subjects covered in this book, I am extremely fortunate to have had a wide range of contacts over a long period, all of whom in various ways have shared my interest in the ideas which this book reflects, and who have thus influenced and contributed to the material which it contains. Among this group of people, Shaun Stewart, who sadly died in 1997, was the most important mentor. I have always had to struggle to emulate the standards of thoroughness, analytical ability and detailed knowledge which he set. Together with Bryan Gould, now returned to his native New Zealand, we wrote a book which was published in 1982,[21] and a long succession of pamphlets, bulletins and articles. Among those who have shared some of the views on economic policy expressed in the chapters which follow are several senior Labour politicians who are, or were, in the House of Lords, including Douglas Jay, Peter Shore and David Stoddart, while among MPs, Austin Mitchell has been a particularly loyal and helpful colleague, as have others, not in Parliament, particularly Brian Burkitt and his colleagues at Bradford University, and Charles Starkey and Edward Barber who have provided consistent support and encouragement over many years. Outside the political world, partly through the Economic Research Council, I need to thank Christopher Meakin and, very specially, Geoffrey Gardiner, who has taken a huge amount of trouble in providing detailed comments, acknowledged in the endnotes to this book, almost all of which I have adopted.

I also have the good fortune to belong to an exceptionally large and tolerant family, and to run a substantial enough business to provide the facilities of secretarial support and computer systems, which have been invaluable. My wife Barbara – no mean scholar – has read and reread endless drafts, insisting on clarity, short sentences and not many adverbs, aided and abetted in this respect by Charles Starkey. My sister Eleanor, and her husband Stephen, have let me use their house in the Luberon, near Avignon in the South of France, for research and writing, away from all the distractions of my life in London. My mother has also put up with writing weekends in her exceptionally welcoming home not far away, but sufficiently distant to avoid attention being diverted from the task in hand. In my office, Jan and Janet have complained remarkably moderately about the extra work they have been asked to do in connection with my writing.

In the end, however, it is always authors themselves who have to accept responsibility for what their writings say and, as with other books which I have written, I do so on this occasion with considerable trepidation. The subject that this book covers is a large one. The views expressed are not the conventional wisdom. I do not have a high opinion of much which passes as economic expertise. Indeed I share the view of Joseph A. Schumpeter who wrote almost half a century ago that 'At all times, including the present, in judging from the standpoint of the requirements of each period (not judging the state of the theory as it was at any time by standards of a later date) the performance of economic theory has been below reasonable expectation and open to valid criticism.'[22] Attacking generally accepted opinions is nevertheless a dangerous game, which readily invites either being ignored or dismissed. I do not believe, however, that the ideas in this book deserve such treatment, and I therefore ask you to read the chapters to come with an unusually open mind. Let me see whether I can persuade you that much in economics as currently taught and practised is still wrong, that there are important and intelligible reasons why this has happened, and that a better alternative view is available.

1
Introduction

Let us not go over old ground; let us rather prepare for what is to come.

Cicero (106BC–43BC)

Economics is a discipline against which this book argues that serious charges need to be laid. Of course, there has been progress over the last two and a quarter centuries since it is generally reckoned to have come of age with the publication of *The Wealth of Nations*, published by Adam Smith, in 1776. The indictment is a different and more subtle one. It is that not as much has been achieved as could and should have been, that avoidable mistakes have been made along the way, and that there is much unfinished business.

The biggest problem facing economics as a discipline can be simply stated. It has no generally accepted, comprehensive theory about how to achieve, in combination, the major economic policy objectives which the vast majority of people evidently want to see attained. These are a reasonably substantial rate of economic growth; full employment; inflation at an acceptably low level; the alleviation of at least extreme poverty; and a sustainable future. Some people, of course, would put more emphasis on one or more of these goals than others. A small minority might argue that some of them were not the right targets at all. It is not hard to believe, however, that a large majority of the world's population would settle for a combination of economic growth running at 3% or 4% per annum, and perhaps more; jobs at reasonable pay being available for everyone who wanted to work; inflation contained at no more than about 5%, and less if possible; a distribution of wealth and income which ensured the absence of conspicuous poverty and destitution, and an ecologically viable future.

Viewed from the perspective of most mature Western economies, whose performance in recent years has left a good deal to be desired, let alone others which have done much worse, the combination of objectives set out in the previous paragraph may seem utopian. It is therefore worth recalling

1

that these conditions are ones which a majority of people in the developed world remember well. They were the norm in nearly all of Western Europe for the quarter of a century after the Second World War, and in Japan to an even more marked extent until the early 1990s. Elsewhere, the record has been more patchy. Apart from the recent – and probably unsustainable – period, the US economy has on average grown more slowly than it did both during the 1920s – at an average of 4.8% a year between 1921 and 1929 – and during the Second World War, when between 1938 and 1944 the US economy expanded by an astonishing cumulative 13.6% per annum.[1] The British economy grew at an average of 4.6% a year between 1933 and 1937, but has never done so since for more than an isolated year or so at a time.[2] Indeed, the general picture in the Western world over the last quarter of a century has been one of slow growth – averaging little more than 2% per annum in national income, and considerably less than this in output per head, allowing for population expansion. Meanwhile unemployment, especially in the European Union, has become a major problem, as has underemployment, reflected in remarkably low productivity and low pay over swathes of the US economy. These developments have occurred despite the removal of significant numbers of people from the potential workforce by a variety of means ranging from a fourfold rise in the prison population in the USA to a large increase in, sometimes doubtfully valuable, higher education.[3] Inflation was very high by historical standards in the 1970s, lower in the 1980s but now appears to be much less of a problem as we move into the twenty-first century. Over the same period, the distribution of income and wealth has become hugely more uneven, and obviously and embarrassingly so to many people.

While these may be the conditions which, in varying degrees, almost all of the West has had to bear, it is not true that they exist everywhere else. In much of the world, the economic conditions to be found are much more like those achieved in Western Europe in the 1950s and 1960s. In particular, this is the case for many of the countries on the Pacific Rim. It is sometimes argued that the reason why many of these economies are doing so well – despite the disruptive problems which most of them sustained in 1997 – is that they are in a 'catch up' phase, and that before long they will fall into the same slow growth pattern as has overtaken much of the West. This argument is looking increasingly unconvincing, however, as Pacific Rim living standards approach, and, in some cases, now exceed those in the West, with little sign of the growth rate falling off. Income per head in Taiwan is now about to overtake that in the UK, while the Taiwanese growth rate, though currently less than it was, shows no sign of slackening to Western levels.[4] Furthermore, if the USA, with one of the highest living standards in the world, can achieve an increase in GDP averaging some 4% per annum in the late 1990s,[5] can it really be true that you have to be catching up to grow fast?

If the economic conditions to which a vast majority of humanity aspires have been attained over long periods of time in many parts of the world, why can they not be achieved all – or almost all – of the time, everywhere? This is the fundamental question which this book sets out to address. One possible answer is to assert that they can only be realised in special circumstances, which no combination of practical policies can reasonably expect to replicate, and that therefore the most sensible approach is to recognise that a less satisfactory outcome is the best that is realistically likely to be attainable. This indeed appears to be the view shared by a large majority of professional economists and the policymakers whom they advise. It also seems to be accepted by nearly all the public at large, at least in Western countries, who have given up hope of anticipating anything better, as their expectations have gradually been lowered in the light of a quarter of a century's relatively disappointing experience. There is, however, another possibility, which is that there are policies which will produce the desired conditions, but that economics as currently practised does not show how to achieve them.

Could this conceivably be the case? Is it possible that the enormous amount of intellectual effort which has gone into developing economics as a subject has, somehow or other, failed to find the keys to solving the central dilemmas which humanity faces in dealing with economic problems, even though these keys do in fact exist? This book argues that this is indeed not only possible, but what has actually happened. It maintains that it is possible to set out general solutions to the problems of combining adequate levels of growth, employment, inflation, poverty alleviation and sustainability, and these are laid out in Chapter 2 of this book. Why does mainstream economics not provide them? The remaining chapters set out to explain why it is that the way the subject has developed largely accounts for why it has failed to do so.

This is not to deny that great technical progress has been made in many branches of economic inquiry, the cumulative effect of which ought to have been to make economic problems of all sorts easier to solve. Nor, of course, does this imply that there are easy solutions to the very complex problems facing all modern societies, and that there is a magic wand to be waved which will produce a painless cure for all their economic ills. The claims to be made are much more modest than this. Certainly, no great success will be achieved anywhere without responsible government, hard work and discipline among the labour force, a tolerably fair and effective legal system, some restraint on special interest groups, adequate education and training, and all the other well-known requirements necessary for reasonable economic achievement. Given these desiderata, however, if they have made it possible to achieve for considerable periods of time in widely varying parts of the world the conditions which almost everyone seems to want – combining growth, full employment, moderate inflation, no very obvious poverty, and sustainability – why has it proved to be so extraordinarily difficult to replicate them? Why cannot economists spell out how to do it? This book also sets out to answer this question, and to put forward an explanation as to why economics has developed in a way which has meant that it has not produced convincing and generally accepted prescriptions, which evidently the world would very much like to have, on how to deal with the central issues described above. While much supporting detail – covered in the chapters which follow – needs to be added, to set the scene, it may help to describe at this stage the essentials of the thesis which this book aims to establish. It argues that the reasons why economics still has these major lacunae stem from three interacting sources.

First, economics, as a discipline, could have advanced differently from the way it did. Unfortunately the way in which ideas evolved led surprisingly often, and in a number of important areas, to dead ends. In short, a number of key ideas, which were influential over long periods, simply turned out to be wrong. Three of the most conspicuous examples, to be covered in detail later, were the Labour Theory of Value, associated particularly with Adam Smith and David Ricardo, the population theories championed by Thomas Malthus, and Say's Law which essentially states that supply creates its own demand, so that there can never be a depression which will not soon cure itself. The result was that much of the slant given to economics during the nineteenth century, some of which is still reflected in views expressed today, was built on very insecure foundations.

Second, economics has always had a tendency to produce theories, many of baffling complexity, with exceptionally little prescriptive content. Part of the explanation is that the work of many of those who made major contributions was more orientated to describing what was happening than providing proposals for achieving better economic performance, although economists generally have never been particularly reluctant to express views on how the world should be run. This may well have been due to the extent to which economics became an academic rather than practical discipline from the late nineteenth century onwards. Whatever the reason, the result was that the impact of the growth of economic theory on the way policy developed was remarkably small, particularly during the period from about 1875 to 1930. This explains why, when the slump hit the world from 1929 onwards, most economists had extraordinarily little of any use to say about how to deal with it.

These are the contingent parts of the argument. Major thinkers could have expressed other ideas, and the development of economic thought could have been more productive than it actually turned out to be. The third major strand of the thesis in this book is much more of a constant. It is that, throughout the period since economic thought began, there has been a relentless tendency, for entirely understandable reasons, for the prescriptions produced by many writers and thinkers – though obviously not all – to favour those to whom they were principally addressed, who were usually the rich, the powerful, and the established. The only way to stop this factor dominating the development of economics was for sufficiently powerful ideas to be put forward to gain general acceptance despite all the social and ideological pressures against them. Sometimes, ideas like this did materialise, but not very often, and generally later than they might have done. If more of them had appeared, and had done so earlier, not only would history have been very different, but the prospects for humanity in the future might have been much improved.

Because of the way in which economics has developed, therefore, although there has been a huge proliferation of ideas, theories, concepts and precepts, relatively few have challenged the status quo effectively. Their impact, in consequence, has not changed the policies which most people responsible for making economic choices would have made anyway. Of course, as circumstances altered, the policies and the arguments for them changed too, and this accounts for a substantial part of the development of economic thought. Much of this theorising was, however, deeply conservative in content and outcome, largely orientated to justifying the status quo, and therefore did not make a great deal of difference to what actually happened. Even when dissentient economic views did challenge established thought – as, pre-eminently, with Marx in the nineteenth century – their proponents generally did so with all too obvious axes to grind, allowing them to pick and choose elements from the prevailing economic theory to buttress ideological opinions which they had already formulated on other grounds. Most intellectual disciplines are quite unlike this. They do not have these heavy overtones of self-interest and self-preservation. There is no great ideological content in science proper, and much less in most of the social sciences than there is in economics. The difference is that economics is pre-eminently and uniquely about power, and in particular about producing justifications for the way in which huge tranches of resources are to be distributed among competing interests. This gives it a flavour which no other subject of inquiry shares, at least to anything like the same extent.

The consequence is that new ideas in economics which are sufficiently coherent, clear, powerful and appealing to shift the intellectual tide, and thus make a real difference to the way the world has been run, have been relatively few and far between. At the same time, there has always been a marked tendency for conventional economic opinion, even after it has been disturbed by new concepts too potent to ignore, to regress back to the cautious and conservative norm. The history of economic thought, therefore, exhibits a constant tension between attempts to explain what was happening in new and sometimes disruptive ways, and the reappearance of older ideas, sometimes in novel guises, to counteract the impact of radical new approaches.

There are other interesting features of the way in which economic thought has developed, which have an important bearing on why the subject now has some of its current characteristics. One of the more significant is the apparent reduction as time goes on in the number of people making any major difference to the ideas which shape the subject. With a comparatively small number of notable exceptions, there is a remarkable absence of major figures likely to leave a substantial and lasting impact on the whole sweep of economics during the twentieth century, although this is not to deny the importance of a number of people who have made significant but mostly technical contributions. In the light of history, the two real twentieth-century heavyweights, both of whom are widely perceived to have moved the ideological scenery a significant distance, are almost certain to be John Maynard Keynes and Milton Friedman. Bearing in mind, however, the huge increase in the number of professional economists now in existence, it seems odd, at first sight, that there should be so few figures of major significance on the economic scene now compared to the nineteenth century, particularly as most of those who reached prominence then were self-taught.

Perhaps this has something to do with specialisation, and the tendency for economic presentation to become both more mathematical and more abstruse. It may be the case that as the subject has been carved up into smaller and smaller parcels, it has become more difficult to achieve an overview. Probably much more important, however, has been the increasing difficulty which many economists – although with some notable exceptions such as John Kenneth Galbraith and Paul Krugman – have had in getting their views across to the public at all. Complex formulations and abstract mathematical notation have certainly not helped them, and it may be that some who have had worthwhile ideas have been unable to get a hearing because of communication problems. When Professor Galbraith says that 'there are no useful propositions in economics that cannot be stated accurately in clear, unembellished and generally agreeable English'[6] he might well be reinterpreted as saying that any proposition that cannot be expressed in this way will simply not get across to the public, and is therefore unlikely to have any significant impact, even if it is correct. It may also be the case that those best at expressing economic ideas have not always had the most profound understanding of how the subject needed to be moved on. They therefore failed to articulate adequate new insights and persuasive ideas needed to deal with unresolved problems.

This leads on to a key feature of all the ideas in economics which have made a lasting impression over the centuries. This is that – at least as they have been perceived – they are almost all clear, simple and understandable by any reasonably intelligent and interested person. The question of perception here may be as important as the way the ideas were expressed in the first place. The reality is that almost all those who have contributed to the development of economic thought worked and wrote over long periods, often several decades, during which their ideas matured and changed. When they wrote about them, they were generally well aware of their weaknesses as well as their strengths, the qualifications which needed to be attached to them, and the limitations to which they were subject. As these ideas seeped out into the public domain, however, they tended to be simplified. The qualifications, limitations and shadings, born of years of study, tended to disappear. Only strong and coherent ideas can stand this sort of treatment, and the history of economic ideas therefore tends to concentrate round a comparatively small number of concepts, put forward with exceptional force and clarity, by a relatively small number of key people.

These ideas, however, are the ones which made not only the history of economics but also – because of their impact on the way problems and policies were perceived – history in the widest sense develop in the way it has over the last two and a half centuries. This book is primarily concerned with the impact of these concepts. The objective is to state what these ideas were, to see how they changed the way in which history developed, and, above all, to assess the extent to which they helped or hindered economics to develop ways of achieving the major objectives associated with the central issues with which economics is, or ought to be, concerned: growth, employment, inflation, the alleviation of at least the extremes of poverty, and a path to a long-term future for humanity.

Lost opportunities

If economics as a discipline has failed to provide a reasonable guide to policymakers about how to achieve desired levels of growth, employment, inflation, poverty alleviation and sustainability, how important is this deficiency? In the great scheme of things, how much difference has it made to the way history has developed over the last two and a half centuries since the Industrial Revolution began, and economics came of age?

The answer is that it has made a truly enormous difference. Before the Industrial Revolution, there was no evident way in which even the most clear-sighted person could have seen that it was feasible to increase massively the standard of living of the whole of humanity. No doubt good government, the absence of war and freedom from plagues and other natural disasters all helped to improve prosperity, but the degree to which these conditions could improve the material welfare of the average citizen was strictly limited. Estimates of the extent to which the mean standard of living rose in countries where statistics have been compiled for the period before the beginning of the Industrial Revolution suggest that in a number of cases, especially in Europe, there was an incremental improvement, but of very modest proportions. While national incomes slowly increased, so did the population, so that the rise in income per head was small.

Furthermore, what increases there were depended largely on factors which were not in any meaningful sense economic at all. Competent government, peace and the absence of natural disasters are still needed to achieve a high level of prosperity, but their attainment is only tangentially the stuff of economic theory.

Once the existence of the Industrial Revolution became evident, however, at least in principle, Pandora's box – in the form of the way to achieve a generally rising level of prosperity – was open. Furthermore, at least some of the potential thus released was recognised for what it was remarkably early on, particularly by Adam Smith. Not for nothing was his major work on economics called *The Wealth of Nations*. Much of this book, particularly those sections dealing with the way industrial processes were undertaken, homed in accurately on the essential requirement for rising living standards, which is increased output per head among the working population. The fact that early stages of industrialisation were accompanied by exceptionally arduous working conditions may have obscured what was happening, and coloured the views of contemporary – and later – observers about the trends in material welfare among the population. At least by the early part of the nineteenth century, however, it was obvious to even the most casual observer that living standards in Britain were noticeably higher than they were in continental Europe. By 1850, GDP per head in Britain was 42% higher than in France and 60% more than in Germany.[7] Writing a few decades later, Karl Marx was in no doubt of the capacity of industrialisation to create additional wealth, whatever reservations he had about the way its fruits were distributed. While his views on the stability of capitalist accumulation were not shared by his more conventional contemporaries, his assessment of the power of industry to increase the national income, and thus at least the average income per head, was a good deal more optimistic and prescient than most of theirs.

Given that this was the case, it might have been thought that one of the primary aims of economic theorising, following Adam Smith, should have been to explain the way in which industrialisation made possible large increases in output, and then to put the benefits of this analysis to work to make the process work better and more expeditiously. Astonishingly, this never happened. Neither the nineteenth nor the twentieth century has produced a generally accepted and convincing explanation for what produces economic growth, let alone how to combine this with the other main goals of good economic management. The cost of this failure has been prodigious. A few relatively simple calculations, with all the usual sorts of qualifications which have to be attached to this kind of figurework, show how large this may be.

World gross domestic product (GDP) per head rose in constant dollars from about $650 in 1820 to $5,145 in 1992, a rise of 690% over the period, entailing an average cumulative increase of 1.2% per annum.[8] If the increase had been 1.5% per annum on average, other things being equal, the mean standard of living of the world's population would have been about two-thirds higher by the end of the twentieth century than it actually was. If the annual growth rate per head had been 2% – a ratio well below that achieved by a substantial number of the world's economies in recent decades – the output per person on average would now be far higher, at almost four times its current level. While 1820 might be regarded as a rather early starting date – though 44 years after the first publication of *The Wealth of Nations* – the point to be made does not alter greatly if a considerably later date for the beginning of a higher growth rate is used – say 1870 – by which time knowledge about industrialisation was much more widely diffused, and world average output per head was $895.[9] The world's average growth in output per head between then and now was 1.44% per annum. If it had been 1.7%, we would all now, on average, be 36% better off, and if it had been 2.0%, the world's mean standard of living would be about twice what it currently is.

If the application of better economic theory had made the world's economy grow more quickly, however, other things would not have been equal. In particular, it seems a safe bet that the world's population would now be considerably smaller, despite all the improvements in public health and medical care which increased incomes make possible. There is overwhelming evidence that rising living standards tend to lower the birth rate. The world's population is estimated to have been 1.07bn in 1820, and 2.51bn in 1950, implying a cumulative growth rate of just under 0.7% a year during this 130-year period. Since 1950, largely as a result of huge population increases in relatively poor countries, it has averaged nearly 1.9% per annum.[10] If the result of higher living standards had been to stabilise the world's population at about its 1950 levels, the total number of people with whom we all have to share the planet would be well under half the present number, and about a quarter of the total expected to be alive by the middle of the twenty-first century. The implications of having this far smaller number of people drawing on the world's supplies of water and other raw materials, creating rubbish and sewage, and generating greenhouse gases, hardly need be emphasised.

With a fair amount of good will, better management of the world's economy might well have achieved other desirable objectives. While inevitably this is a matter of speculation, it might have reduced a fair amount of the destructive warfare which has taken place over the last 250 years. In particular, it ought to have decreased substantially the chances of the Second World War taking place, since it was largely caused by the economic mistakes of the inter-war period, many of which could have been avoided, if there had been a secure base available for taking more appropriate policy decisions. Even more speculatively, it might also have produced a world with smaller gulfs in living standards between the rich and the poor, both within and between countries. As we shall see, higher growth rates depend heavily on employing the available labour force more intensively than would otherwise be the case, which certainly tends to even up wage and salary rates within economies. Perhaps diffusing more effective economic policies would have achieved the same results between different countries and regions of the world. Much less a matter of guesswork is that the contentment of humanity with its lot would have been greatly enhanced if living standards had risen more rapidly, and with them better housing conditions, medical care, educational prospects and leisure opportunities.

The cost to us all of the relatively stunted growth in economic theory, leading to its failure to produce an agreed core of teaching about how to optimise choices on growth, employment, inflation, the relief of poverty and sustainability, has thus been extremely heavy. Why have these problems not been solved over the whole of the last two centuries and more? This is the question which this book sets out to answer.

The method employed to do so is relatively straightforward. First, if there is a way of dealing more effectively with all the central problems which economics needs to address, we need to know what it might be. The next chapter sets out proposals about how all these objectives could be achieved, explaining the inter-relationships between them, and the limitations which can be expected to apply. The following chapters then turn to the history of economic ideas as they have actually unfolded, to see whether we can discover why, despite the talent and effort devoted to developing economic theory over a long period of time, the results have been so relatively unsuccessful at dealing with the central problems described above.

Chapter 3 looks at the foundations which were laid before the Industrial Revolution began, emphasising how much the subsequent development of economics was shaped by ideas which pre-dated the start of serious industrialisation. It may be no coincidence that the framework within which subsequent economic theorising developed had been established before the increases in productivity achievable by industrialisation had become apparent. A sufficiently substantial change in mindset to take account of this seminal change, and to harness the new potential thus made available, never really happened.

Chapter 4 is particularly concerned with why this transition never took place, notwithstanding the lead given in *The Wealth of Nations*. Why did Classical Economics, developed during the first half of the nineteenth century largely in Britain where the Industrial Revolution was initiated, ignore almost totally some of Adam Smith's key themes, for example around productivity growth, which might have made the subsequent development of economic theory so different? Instead, the most significant ideas, developed by Malthus, Say and Ricardo, were mostly attempts to deal with new problems within the framework of pre-industrial theorising.

Worse still, as subsequent history showed, several of their key ideas were not only inapposite, but were also not even correct, providing an exceptionally unhelpful basis for subsequent development.

Chapter 5 is about dissent, largely from the political left, with Karl Marx as the most important, although by no means the only figure. If the mainstream, established views on economics were regarded as unsatisfactory from their perspective, these critics might have been expected to generate alternative policies whose strengths would have carried them to fruition. To some extent they did. The development of the welfare state, with all that this achieved in knocking off some of the rough edges of economic progress, was to a significant extent their progeny. Having powerful and persuasive things to say about how to divide up the product of economic activity is, however, a different matter from putting forward convincing proposals for making the economy overall more productive. In this regard, their prescriptions were no better than those of the classical economists, on whom, in any event, Marx and others largely depended to explain how the economy functioned. Nor has history been kind to the practical implementation of socialist economic policies.

In fact, the major and successful challenge to some of the central ideas of the classical economic school did not come from outside mainstream sources but from within. Chapter 6 describes how the Marginal Revolution displaced the Labour Theory of Value, setting the scene for further development in economic theorising. Indeed, it became the major preoccupation of the economic profession, which largely came into being in the last quarter of the nineteenth century and the first quarter of the twentieth. Again, however, the focus was not on the central issues which this book argues should have attracted attention. Little of the work which was done was relevant to the practical economic problems the world faced, particularly after the disruption caused by the First World War. When the slump arrived around 1930, the mainstream economic profession was largely bereft of practical proposals about how to remedy the disastrous situation which presented itself.

Chapter 7, however, is about more positive developments, with the key figure being John Maynard Keynes. Confronted with the evident lack of purchasing power during the Great Depression, Keynes developed in detail a convincing explanation for unemployment, and produced remedies for dealing with it. The adoption of the policies which he advocated accounted for much of the world's excellent economic performance for the quarter of a century after the end of the Second World War, though Keynes never had much to say about achieving growth as opposed to reducing unemployment. Keynes died in 1946, but the prosperity which was to a remarkable extent his legacy lasted until the early 1970s. The exchange rate stability which underpinned it then broke up under the strain of the parity misalignments which by then had become overwhelmingly apparent.

Economic performance, at least in the developed world, thereafter declined sharply. The growth rate fell; unemployment rose; inflation shot up; and the distribution of income widened hugely.

Into the vacuum left by the discrediting of Keynesian policies moved a new intellectual fashion in economics, although one with strong links to the precepts which had underpinned much of the nineteenth-century classical tradition. Monetarism did not see slow growth and high unemployment as the major enemy. Inflation filled this role. Chapter 8 shows how the monetarists explained the way to combat it, and the results which were achieved as a result of the policies which were implemented under their banner. Yet again, the economics profession turned its back on growth and full employment as major goals. Indeed, it became fashionable to say that these were virtually unattainable, since, in the light of the then conventional views of the dominant economic ideology, almost everyone believed that there was no discernable way in which they could be achieved.

Chapter 9 then draws the threads from the previous chapters together. It reiterates that the pessimism about finding solutions to the major economic problems faced by the world are misplaced. It stresses the need for concentrating effort on agreeing a consensus on what needs to be done, and then getting more effective and focused policies implemented. It reviews where the main strands in economic thinking are now leading, and makes assessments of the significance of the contributions of those who appear to have been most influential in developing them during the last few decades, particularly since the Second World War. Finally, it looks ahead to the prospects for the century which has just started, to see where developments in economic thinking might lead us.

2
Economic Theory

Every man prefers belief to the exercise of judgement.

Seneca (4BC–65AD)

It is all very well to criticise the development of economic theory on the grounds that it has failed to provide satisfactory answers to important economic questions, but unconvincing unless the missing answers can in fact be found. An important legacy of the way in which economics has developed is the notion that even to suggest that there might be persuasive ways of explaining how to achieve desired levels of economic growth, employment, inflation and the elimination of gross poverty, combined with a sustainable future – and all at the same time – is utopian and thus absurd. The general view is that the variables involved are too unreliable to be sufficiently quantifiable, the vagaries of human nature too uncertain to provide a manageable degree of consistency, and the links between cause and effect too convoluted and tenuous to be successfully disentangled.

As has happened in many other subjects, however, when the unifying theory needed to make cause and effect comprehensible does not exist, or has not yet been recognised, there is an inevitable tendency to assume that no such theory is possible. Rule of thumb, hunch, experience and judgement then have to take the place of reason. Hardly surprisingly, the results are worse – often much worse – than could have been achieved if better theory had been available to provide a more secure background against which practical decisions could have been taken. There is no shortage of contemporary examples. The unemployment rate in the European Union (EU), even when measured by the claimant count, is still not far short of 10% – and much higher if all those who would be willing to work for a reasonable wage, but who are not claimants, were included.[1] A vast swathe of blue collar workers in the USA are earning less per hour in real terms now than they were in 1973.[2] The distribution of wealth and income in Britain has recently been calculated as being more unequal than it was during the heyday of nineteenth-century industrialisation, or perhaps even centuries previously when weak medieval kings allowed local robber barons to hold sway.[3] Much of the 1970s and 1980s, particularly in the developed Western world, exhibited economies suffering grievously from the pernicious combination of high inflation and low growth known as stagflation. The Japanese economy, fabled for its success for decades after the Second World War, hardly grew at all in the 1990s. Meanwhile, about one-fifth of the world population – 70% women – live in abject poverty, with incomes of less than $1 per day.[4] The current view is that most, if not all, these developments have been unavoidable – just one of those things, like bad weather or a sudden accident, which have to be accepted as part of the human condition. Their occurrence has to be accepted with whatever fortitude can be mustered. Stopping them happening is beyond human control.

This is, however, an extraordinarily pessimistic attitude, and one which is wholly at variance with the general success achieved by humanity in making a much better job of explaining and controlling events in other fields of inquiry. Why should the problems in economics be any more difficult to solve than they are in other disciplines? Why can't we find the answers to these basic questions about growth, employment, inflation and extreme poverty and sustainability?

Part of the thesis in this book is that economics has not found the right answers because generally economists have not asked the right questions. What might the answers be if they did? This chapter sets out to deal with this issue by synthesising a picture of how modern economies operate. Its objective is not to cover the whole of economic theory, which would be both an impossible and unnecessary task. On the contrary, its intention is to simplify down a complex subject to a number of key essentials, clarifying the extent to which conventional economics fails to deal with key issues, and indicating the remedies which need to be applied. To reiterate, the principal objectives are to explain what causes economic growth to happen, how to achieve and maintain a close approximation to full employment, and how to combine this, given reasonably competent government, with a moderate and stable level of inflation. At the same time, it needs to be shown how to contain the distribution of wealth and income within narrow enough boundaries to make extreme poverty a thing of the past, and to provide humanity with a sustainable path to the future. We start with economic growth.

Economic growth

Economic growth can come from a number of sources. It can occur as a consequence of rising population, as has been common throughout recorded history, although increasing output in this way does not necessarily result in any improvement in living standards. The kind of growth which is of much greater importance economically is the sort which leads to higher output per head, or increasing productivity. This is the only way in which rising standards of living can be achieved.

Making output per head increase, in turn, can be achieved in a number of different ways. It may result from better training and more efficient work practices. It can come about as a result of investment in machinery and other capital equipment which makes it possible for those working with it to turn out, with no more time and effort being expended, more goods or services than they did before. It can happen as a result of the discovery of new raw materials or new processes, which again means that more output can be achieved with the same labour inputs as were employed previously. The key feature, in all cases, is that the market value of the goods and services produced by the labour force rises, either as a result of greater output in relation to inputs, or because greater inputs make greater outputs possible. Better education and training are prime examples of the first, and increased capital equipment of the second.

The key questions on economic growth are to determine what kind of economic activities are most likely to lead to greater output per head, and what conditions are then required to enable them to flourish. Where are the best opportunities for productivity increases to be found, and how are they to be encouraged? It might be thought that the scope for securing more output per head would be fairly evenly spread throughout the average economy, but this is not the case. In fact, there is an extremely skewed distribution, as Table 2.1 shows. The figures in this table are drawn from statistics for the USA, an exceptionally large and broadly based economy, but they are representative of trends to be found all over the world.

The table shows that, over the 20-year period which they cover, changes in output per head on average each year fell broadly into three divisions. The highest increases were in Agriculture, Forestry and Fishing (5.7%), Wholesale Trade (3.2%), Mining (3.1%) and Manufacturing (3.0%). All these increases were far above those achieved for the economy as a whole, which averaged only 0.8%. The second category comprised parts of the US economy which did better than the average, but not by a wide margin. These include Transport and Utilities (1.6%) and Retail Trade (1.0%). All the rest of the economy did worse than the average – considerable sectors of it much worse. Finance, Insurance and Real Estate achieved only a 0.4% average annual increase, while output per head actually fell across the whole of the rest of the US economy, employing a fraction under half the labour force. It went down by 0.2% a year in Government, 0.7% in Construction and 0.9% in what is described in American statistics as Services – a broad category of employment covering 29% of all jobs in the USA not covered under the other headings.

These figures show beyond reasonable doubt that the way to get any economy to grow rapidly is to concentrate resources as far as possible on

Table 2.1   Changes in Output per Head of the Working Population between 1977 and 1997

	Output Value in Constant 1992 $bn	Labour Force '000s	Output per Head $
1977			
Manufacturing	796.5	19,682	40,468
Construction	213.8	3,851	55,518
Mining	82.4	813	101,353
Sub total	1,092.7	24,346	44,882
Agriculture, Forestry & Fishing	61.1	4,143	14,748
Transport & Utilites	346.8	4,713	73,584
Wholesale Trade	201.0	4,723	42,558
Retail Trade	364.5	13,792	26,428
Finance, Insurance & Real Estate	742.7	4,467	166,264
Services	712.5	15,302	46,563
Statistical Discrepancy	37.3		
Not Allocated	–2.4		
Government	717.4	15,127	47,425
1977 GDP	4,273.6	86,613	49,341

	Output Value in Constant 1992 $bn	Labour Force '000s	Output per Head $	Output per Head Percentage Change from 1977 to 1997	
				Total Change	Annual Average
1997					
Manufacturing	1,369.9	18,657	73,426	81.4%	3.0%
Construction	274.4	5,686	48,259	–13.1%	–0.7%
Mining	109.9	592	185,642	83.2%	3.1%
Sub total	1,754.2	24,935	70,351	56.7%	2.3%
Agriculture, Forestry & Fishing	127.6	2,867	44,506	201.8%	5.7%
Transport & Utilites	644.3	6,395	100,751	36.9%	1.6%
Wholesale Trade	532.0	6,648	80,024	88.0%	3.2%
Retail Trade	713.5	22,011	32,416	22.7%	1.0%
Finance, Insurance & Real Estate	1,286.0	7,091	181,357	9.1%	0.4%
Services	1,398.6	36,040	38,807	–16.7%	–0.9%
Statistical Discrepancy	–45.4				
Not Allocated	–25.0				
Government	884.0	19,570	45,171	–4.8%	–0.2%
1997 GDP	7,269.8	125,557	57,900	17.35%	0.80%

Source: Tables B.13, B.46 and B.100, *Economic Report of the President*, February 1999.

those sectors which have the greatest potential for productivity increases. Of the sectors which the US figures show are most likely to be able to achieve this, however, Agriculture, Forestry and Fishing employs only 2.1% of the labour force, and Wholesale Trade no more than 5.3%. In total terms, therefore, Manufacturing, employing 14.9%, was much the most significant. In this respect, however, the US economy is not typical of most of the rest of the world. The proportion of the labour force employed in manufacturing is much lower in the USA than it is in most other countries, particularly, and hardly surprisingly, those with the fastest growth records. In South Korea, where in 1997 31% of the labour force worked in manufacturing,[5] between 1980 and 1995 (roughly the same years as are covered in Table 2.1) the average annual growth rate in output per head across the whole economy was 7.4%.[6] In Singapore the corresponding figures were 30% and 5.6%, and in Malaysia they were 18.4% and 4.2%.[7]

How do policymakers ensure that their economies have a sufficiently large proportion of their activities concentrated in the high growth sectors? The answer is that they need to make certain that the macro-economic policies they adopt are designed to make their economies attractive locations for these types of activity, compared with the international average. For this to be done, the cost of producing goods and services – the cost base – has to be competitive. The cost base is made up of all the components which form the expense of operating in one place rather than another. These are land, labour and capital, which are then charged out to the rest of the world through the prism of the exchange rate. These costs have important linkages between them.

The crucial point about labour costs is not the average pay which those employed receive. It is the wage costs per unit of output. If the labour force is highly productive – because it is well trained, educated and managed, and because it is well endowed with good quality capital equipment – its remuneration, including oncosts such as social security payments may be high, but it can still be competitive. By contrast, if the average worker suffers from the reverse of these qualifications and conditions, low wages may still leave the output concerned unable to compete. The critical factor is how much is charged to the rest of the world in export prices after making full allowance for differences in productivity.

The cost of capital – and land to some extent too – is linked to the exchange rate. If interest rates are high and money is hard to borrow, the costs of capital and premises will tend to be high. So, also, will be the exchange rate, since the conditions which make capital and land expensive are exactly the same as those which drive up the parity. A higher exchange rate, however, also implies charging out labour costs at a higher price. The two critical factors in determining the cost base are therefore the productivity of the labour force and the exchange rate.

The significance of getting the cost base right is not, however, simply a matter of a once and for all static comparison with the world average. It has a highly dynamic component to it. This is because of the impact which varying competitive conditions, flowing from the cost base, have on almost every company operating within the economy. Put simply, those located in economies with lower than average cost bases have an enormous advantage over those who do not have this benefit, and consideration of the circumstances of the average company operating in the international market quickly shows why this is the case.

Take the relatively typical case, illustrated in Table 2.2, of three manufacturing companies, one operating in an economy where the cost base is average, one where it is 20% below the average and a third where it is 20% above. In all three cases, selling prices are determined by world markets. Let us assume that in the average cost base economy raw materials represent 20% of selling prices, capital depreciation 10%, and that of the remaining 70%, 10% represents net profit while the other 60% pays for all the labour, goods and services, and loan interest required to keep the company operating, the charges for which are directly proportional to the local cost base. How does the outlook now appear to the other two companies?

Table 2.2   Options Available to Companies Producing Internationally Tradable Goods in Economies with Parities at Varying Levels

	Countries with Average Parities	Countries Undervalued by 20%	Countries Overvalued by 20%
Costs fixed in World Prices			
Raw Materials	20	19	21
Capital Depreciation	10	8	12
Total Internationally determined Costs	30	27	33
Costs fixed in Domestic Prices			
Labour Costs)			
Local Supplies)			
Land & Premises)			
Interest Charges)	60	48	72
Total Costs	90	75	105
World Prices for the Company's Output	100	100	100
Trading Profit or Loss at World Prices	10	25	–5

Source: Derived from OECD National Accounts.

In the one where the cost base is 20% below the norm, prospects look excellent. All the locally determined costs are 20% lower than in the average case, making them 48% of world selling prices instead of 60%. This now means that, while selling at world prices, this company can make a 22% net profit instead of 10%. In fact, it can probably do much better than this. It will make more money by selling at cheaper prices and expanding output. If, therefore, it sold at 15% below world average prices, and used the increased output thus achieved both to drive down its buy-in costs and to employ its capital equipment more intensively, it should still be able to make a 10% net profit while at the same time securing a rapidly expanding share of the market.

This would not, however, be the end of the benefits to be found from these propitious circumstances. As wave after wave of investment takes place to keep up with demand, the latest technology is likely to be embodied in the company's capital equipment. Because of high profitability and expanding opportunities, it will be relatively easy to attract high calibre staff at every level. Employees who are already intelligent and well educated are likely to gain exceptional benefit from training opportunities. Research, development and product innovation are relatively easy to afford, as are expensive sales and marketing forays into new foreign markets. Furthermore, the prestige and rewards resulting from this kind of success tend to shape the view of the world not only within the companies concerned but in society as a whole in the countries in which they operate. Business leaders in world-beating export companies become role models. Political power accretes to them and their associates, enabling them to exert pressure on the country's leaders to maintain the conditions which led to its economic pre-eminence.

It is now not difficult to see that in the economy where the cost base is 20% above the world average, all these helpful effects are reversed. If locally determined costs are a fifth higher than the mean, so that they amount to 72% of selling prices instead of 60%, unless prices are raised the company will sell at a loss as all the net profit and more is wiped out. With higher prices – making any such company even more vulnerable to those located in low cost base countries – market share is almost bound to be lost, unless there are exceptional, and therefore inevitably fairly rare countervailing circumstances. The usual results of declining market shares and fierce cost pressures are below average wages and salaries, poor prospects, declining investment and trimmed marketing and sales budgets. The prestige of export-orientated businesses falls, talent and political power go elsewhere, exports falter, imports rise, and the economy stagnates.

This is only a brief summary of the basic processes at stake, but it nevertheless delineates sharply the basic factors involved in determining whether any country is to be in the fast or the slow lane in terms of economic growth. There are, however, two other factors which strongly reinforce the powerful underlying impact of competing costs and the pressures which they exert on performance and growth.

The first has to do with the reasons why international trade takes place on the huge scale which it now does. The traditional explanation for foreign trade being worthwhile, publicised by David Ricardo at the beginning of the nineteenth century (though the original formulation may have been by James Mill[8]), turned on the fact that the relative production costs of different goods and services varied between economies. This made it worthwhile for countries to trade with each other, exporting those goods which they could produce relatively cheaply, and importing those where the domestic costs were high. While no doubt this still partly explains the existence of foreign trade, nowadays a far more important reason for it is that the production of most goods and services which are bought and sold between countries is characterised by falling cost curves. This means that while the cost of the first unit of output may be expensive, all subsequent production is much cheaper, and therefore more profitable to sell in volume. This drives companies involved in this kind of production to sell wherever they can. Clearly, those companies operating in economies with the lowest cost bases have the greatest opportunities to exploit the prospects thus created.

Second, there is another characteristic of many internationally traded goods and services which also reinforces the advantages of concentrating the economy on producing them. This is the fact that, while their production generally involves significant investment in capital equipment and research, design and development, the lapse of time from when this activity starts to when saleable goods or services are produced is typically quite short, while the returns are high. Furthermore, the pay-offs do not just go to those who have invested financially in the projects involved. In addition there is also a substantial 'social rate of return', in the form of higher wages and salaries, larger tax base and better products. The social rate of return is often 50% or more, while the time for investment to come on stream may be no more than six months. A simple calculation then shows that this type of investment is capable of producing an astonishingly high cumulative return.

The way to achieve a high rate of economic growth, engineered by a sustainable and continuing rise in demand for all the goods and services which the economy can produce, thus turns out to be relatively simple. For any individual country, it is to keep the cost base comparatively low, which is largely a matter of doing nothing more complicated than adopting a macro-economic policy of low interest rates, an accommodating monetary stance and a competitive exchange rate. The result will be to promote the type of economic activities which generate high and sustainable rises in output per head. The economic history of the last two centuries across the world shows how universally effective this kind of policy stance has been at promoting growth. The key characteristic of almost all economies which have grown quickly has been a highly competitive export sector, generating exactly the sort of cumulative economic success attributed above to low cost base economies. Conversely, those with high cost bases have seen their economies stagnate.

Does the adoption of such a policy involve abandoning any attempt to tame market forces, and accepting that nothing can be done about all the negative features of globalisation? Not at all. The stronger any country's economic position, the better placed it is to control its destiny and to decide for itself how it wants its affairs to be run. Of course, there will still be trade-offs. Using the political process to take the rough edge off economic forces nearly always has its costs, but a growing and successful economy can afford them much more easily than one which is stagnant. Included among the weapons which might be employed are various forms of protection. Generally speaking, however, protection is not the best solution. Free trade is better, provided that the exchange rate is in the right position. Low or zero tariffs help to keep the cost base down, provide the spur of competition, help to optimise the use of scarce resources, assist in curbing inflationary pressures, and allow the domestic economy to benefit from the most cost effectively produced goods and services, whatever their provenance.

If the variation in growth rates between different economies is really – at least in principle – as simple as this, why is it not obvious that this is the case? There are at least three interlocking reasons, all of which are bound up with the thesis in this book about the way economics has developed, which provide an explanation.

First, for a variety of reasons, economics as taught and practised, is not orientated to looking at the causes of growth – or the lack of it – in the way set out above. Its approach and methodology are different. Much of it – micro-economics – is concerned with theories about matters such as prices and value, which have little bearing on anything to do with growth. Macro-economics, which is, of course, relevant to creating the appropriate conditions for growth to take place, is dominated by concerns about inflation. Economists who have been particularly interested in explaining why economies grow fast or slowly have tended to concentrate heavily on the 'supply side' reasons for different levels of prevailing performance. The 'supply side' concerns matters such as the size and quality of the labour force and the volume of capital investment. Because these are difficult factors to influence directly by policy changes, they have tended not to come up with any very revealing or policy-orientated remedies as a result. Concentration on these supply side factors, however, has tended to obscure the crucial way in which demand for increased output needs to be used to create the supply conditions best capable of responding to it.

Second, nearly everyone's views on economic matters are heavily coloured by self-interest, and the pressure from the well established has always tended to favour exactly the opposite to the conditions needed to promote fast growth. Especially in stable economic conditions, as the generations pass, wealth and power move away from the entrepreneurial classes to their descendants and legatees whose interests are guarded by bankers and salaried employees. These are people whose natural instincts tend to favour exactly the wrong conditions required for sustained fast rates of economic growth. Those with established riches always tend to favour high interest and exchange rates, which increase the scope for extracting the maximum return from existing accumulations of wealth. The stronger these interests are in any economy, the more the intellectual climate tends to be influenced in their favour. It is an interesting and revealing fact that economics as a subject has tended to flourish most strongly in countries which are growing relatively slowly. This may be an important reason why its precepts then tend to reflect the views and interests of those dominating the political and social pyramid in the societies they have produced.

Third, the layperson's opinions are understandably confused by much of the terminology which is used. For example, most people have problems disentangling the relationship between productivity and competitiveness. It is very easy to assume that there is a simple relationship between them, and that increasing the former must raise the latter. In fact, productivity has almost nothing to do with competitiveness. It is true that the only way to a higher growth rate is to raise the increase in output per head. It is also true that making the economy more competitive, by lowering the cost base, will achieve this objective. It is not true that raising productivity by better education and training or in any other way will, by itself, make the economy more competitive, though many people apparently think it will. If the total demand on the economy, set by its export prices to the rest of the world, remains the same, increased productivity and output from some people has to be offset by less output – and generally unemployment – for others. Inaccurate lay perceptions thus tend to reinforce the poor guidance provided by professional economists.

If the whole world is to prosper as a result of increased economic growth, however, it is not just individual countries which need to ensure that the demand for their output remains strong and that they have a reasonable proportion of their economies devoted to those activities where productivity increases are most easily secured. These conditions need to apply everywhere. International economic governance needs to shift its priorities to ensuring that this happens at a global level as much as governments of particular countries need to do so. Some fairly simple calculations show that, if the growth potential of the most productive economic activities were spread and encouraged in this way, it ought to be possible to increase output per head, or productivity, cumulatively by about 3% to 4% per annum, without compromising other economic objectives.[9] It may seem paradoxical, but this is the kind of growth target the world is going to need to adopt to provide it with the best chance of lifting humanity into an eco-logically viable future.

Full employment

If a key target is to achieve full employment, the world at the beginning of the twenty-first century shows how far short of achieving this goal we are. The scale of the problem, and the ways in which it manifests itself, vary greatly both between developed countries and those with lower living stan-dards. In Western Europe, the most conspicuous figures are those for the numbers registered out of work which, in the European Union, peaked in the middle 1990s at over 11%,[10] and where, at the end of 2001, the figure was still 7.7%.[11] These figures, however, only tell part of the story. The true number of currently unemployed people who would be willing to work, if reasonable jobs were available at sufficiently attractive levels of pay, is much larger that the number registered as out of work.[12] Years of high levels of unemployment have generated swathes of people who have given up hope of trying to find a job, or who are trapped in social security payment systems which make the extra income gained by getting a job not worthwhile, or who have worked their way round the system by getting themselves classified as unfit for work by a sympathetic doctor. Recent figures in the Netherlands show that over 20% of the potential workforce was registered as disabled, despite the quality of medical care now available being higher than ever before.[13] There is also a particularly acute problem in getting younger people into the labour force, resulting in exceptionally high unemployment rates for those under 25 – still averaging over 15.0% in the European Union at the end of 2001.[14]

In the USA, by contrast, there is a different problem. The US economy has been enormously successful at creating jobs. Between 1970 and 1999 the US Civilian Labour Force rose from 83m to 139m, while the proportion of those of working age who were in employment rose from 60.4% to 67.1%. The problem in the USA has been that the quality of large numbers of the jobs created has been very poor, reflected in the low productivity and stagnant real incomes of a large proportion of the labour force. In many parts of the Third World, and indeed in Russia and some of the Soviet Union's former satellites too, the problem is one of chronic under-employment, this time combined with far lower living standards than in the West, exacerbated in many cases by a total absence of any formal social security underpinning. By contrast, as in other aspects of the ways in which they have run their economies, many of the Pacific Rim countries have managed better, with lower levels of unemployment, and higher rates of productivity growth, spread throughout the labour force. Korea, which saw its output per head grow cumulatively by 7.4% per annum between

1980 and 1995, had average unemployment for these 15 years of only 2.6%, and similar figures were achieved by other fast growing economies in the same part of the world.[15]

Why is there such poor utilisation of the world's labour force, particularly when there is clearly a vast amount of pent-up demand for what it could produce if it had the chance to do so? The conventional answer is that the main problem is on the supply side. Too many of those potentially available for work are insufficiently well trained and thus not productive enough to be able to hold down a job in the competitive modern economy. If this is the root cause of the problem, the solution is obvious. It is to concentrate resources on education and training, to produce a potentially more skilled labour force capable of pricing itself into jobs. This is indeed where the thrust of a vast number of government and private sector initiatives are directed, often involving exceptionally large outlays. France, recently afflicted by unemployment rates of more than 12% of its labour force, peaked at spending almost 0.75% of its entire gross national product on training schemes. Sweden and Denmark spent even more – over 1% of their GNPs.[16]

Few people are in any doubt about the general benefit of education, especially if it is broad based, concentrating on providing the whole of the population with the reading, writing and mathematical skills which are not only the basic requirements for almost any job, but also the keys to full participation in society. There is evidently a strong case, too, for improving the quality of any economy's labour force both by widening the availability of higher education and vocational training, and by strengthening all the attributes which lead to greater productivity. These include encouraging greater motivation and initiative, stressing the need for team effort, and emphasising the importance of good attendance records. The issue, however, is whether the absence of these characteristics is the reason why so much of the world's labour force is so poorly used, or whether the real reason lies not in the quality of the labour supply being inadequate but in the demand for its services being insufficient.

History certainly suggests that high levels of unemployment have much more to do with lack of demand than inadequate supply. There is no doubt that the labour force is much better educated and trained in most countries now than it was a quarter of a century ago, but this has not stopped unemployment rising sharply in many of the same countries. Nor is it the case that the countries with the best educated and trained labour forces always have the lowest levels of unemployment, or even tend to do so. On the contrary, there are far more people who are either unemployed or underemployed in the high income West than there are in many of the Pacific Rim countries, which may be growing fast, but which still have a way to go before they catch up with Western standards of education and training. Furthermore, the history of individual countries shows in nearly all cases wide variations in the levels of unemployment, which seem impossible to correlate with any employability attributes of the labour force. The USA had 24.9% of its labour force out of work in 1933 and 1.2% in 1944.[17] By contrast, Western Germany had an unemployment rate averaging about 1% in the 1960s,[18] but 8.5% in 1997, this latter figure excluding the former East Germany, where 14.5% of the insured population was then out of work.[19] Similar contrasting figures can be produced for practically every country. How can it be that, within a short enough period of years for substantially the same people to be making up the labour force, such huge differences in the level of unemployment can be found?

The answer is that the proportion of the labour force in work has only a relatively small amount to do with education and training, and all the other attributes which make it more readily employable, other things being equal. A much more potent factor is in operation, and this is the extent to which the conditions in any economy lead to a greater or lesser demand for labour. If the demand is low enough, as it was in the trough of the American depression in 1932, and as it was in Germany in 1997, there simply is not enough work to go round. In these circumstances, those with any significant disadvantages are likely to find themselves out of a job, as others with more favourable attributes are chosen. If, however, there is enough work for everyone, then, hardly surprisingly, almost everybody will find employment, as indeed has happened for long periods in all parts of the developed world. Furthermore, in these circumstances, the need which employers have to get the best they can out of more marginal candidates for the positions they need to fill tends to lead to much more serious efforts to get them trained to a standard where they can hold down their jobs effectively. Hardly surprisingly, in these conditions, productivity rises fast. Between 1940 and 1944, US GDP grew by 84%,[20] and industrial output by 89%,[21] while those in civil employment rose by 13.7%,[22] implying a cumulative growth in output per head across the whole of the US economy of nearly 13% per annum. While this performance was exceptionally good, the growth and productivity records in the USA after the Second World War were not particularly impressive. There are, however, many other examples to be cited of high rates of growth in economic output and productivity which were sustained over long periods. Nearly all of Western Europe achieved results of this sort, combined with almost full employment, throughout the 1950s and 1960s, as did Japan from shortly after the end of the Second World War until about 1990, while the Tiger economies, Hong Kong, Singapore, South Korea and Taiwan, are still doing so. If they achieved these enviable standards of performance, why cannot everyone else produce the same results?

Why indeed? There is no reason, at least in principle, why they should not do so. The reason why their growth rates are in fact lower and their unemployment rates higher has little to do with the deficiencies in their labour forces. They result from macro-economic policies which under-stretch their economies and which therefore generate too little demand to keep everyone in work. The solution to unemployment therefore lies only marginally on the supply side, in policies to improve education, training, and so on. On the contrary, the way to provide work for everyone who wants a job is to reform macro-economic policy so that there is sufficient demand on the productive resources of the economy to provide employ-ment for almost anyone who wants to be an active part of the labour force. The most important requirement to secure the achievement of full employ-ment turns out to be the same condition which is needed to maximise the rate of economic growth, which is to keep up the level of effective demand, particularly on those parts of the economy most readily able to respond by increasing productivity. These two policy objectives therefore strongly interact and reinforce each other, while at the same time raising output per head also provides an important key to keeping inflation at bay.

Inflation

Keeping inflation down to 2% to 3% per annum – sometimes lower, as is the case in the European Union – is now the primary economic target in almost all developed countries, and in much of the rest of the world as well. It is argued that, if the rise in the price level can be kept this low, interest rates will fall, stimulating growth and investment and creating jobs. Thus, although achieving low inflation is the immediate goal to which other objectives may need from time to time to be subordinated, the result over any reasonable time span from this discipline will be better eco-nomic performance across the board than if higher immediate priority had been given to other objectives, such as growth or full employment.

An important second limb to this conventional view on inflation is that any depreciation in the exchange rate will add significantly and almost immediately to rises in the price level. Furthermore, it is argued that there has to be a cost borne as a result of the exchange rate falling in that more will have to be paid for imports in relation to the income from exports, imposing a real cost on the economy which is likely further to exacerbate inflationary pressures. This contention reinforces the case for raising inter-est rates, and tightening the money supply, as soon as there is any sign of price increases moving away from the target band, both to damp down demand and to hold up the exchange rate.

There are, however, a number of important flaws in these arguments. In the first place, is it the case that inflation has always been a severe threat to economic stability, or even that there is a natural tendency for it to increase unless a constant battle is fought to contain it? Economic history does not suggest that either of these questions justifies a positive answer. The evidence suggests that once annual price rises get into double figures, the distortions involved by this rate of inflation start to have a real cost, but that up to a level somewhat below 10%, the negative implications on real growth are negligible. The most authoritative study on this important topic was carried out by the International Monetary Fund in 1995. It concluded that there was no systematic evidence that inflation rates of anything less than about 8% per annum caused enough disruption to slow down growth or to increase unemployment;[23] 8% is a long way from the 2% to 3% target now considered mandatory by most monetary authorities.

Furthermore, the notion that inflation is a constant threat, liable to spiral out of control unless vigorously combated all the time, is controverted by a wealth of historical evidence. For almost all the long period in history for which reasonably reliable statistics are available, the price level either oscillated up and down, or rose slowly. During the Middle Ages in Europe, there was almost no significant net increase in prices. In England, for example, the price level rose between the 1260s and the 1510s by only 30%, implying average price changes over the whole of this 250-year period of about one-tenth of a percentage point per year. From the 1510s until the 1660s, prices rose more quickly, by a total of 480%, though the annual average increase, at just under 1.2%, was still quite small.[24] From around 1660 through to the early 1930s average prices were by no means completely stable, but they rose and fell by about the same amount. In Britain, while there were substantial fluctuations in the costs of goods and services throughout the economy, the price of gold, fixed by Isaac Newton, the Master of the Mint at £3 17s 9d per ounce in 1711, remained intact until 1931, except for two short suspensions during the nineteenth century, and during the Napoleonic Wars and the First World War. During the 1930s, prices barely rose at all in the developed world. Since the end of the Second World War and its immediate aftermath, excluding the years from 1973 to 1983, the average increase in prices in Britain has been just over 4.0% per annum, about 2.5% in Germany and 3.0% in the United States.[25] Leaving aside wartime years, therefore, the only period in the whole of recorded history, at least since the Middle Ages, when annual price rises got anywhere near the 8% level was during a short period of exceptional world economic instability about three-quarters of the way through the twentieth century.

If this brief excursion into economic history fails to suggest that there is a chronic tendency for inflation to take over, the evidence also shows that devaluations do not cause the price level to rise, despite all the folklore to the contrary, although the faster growth which they generally induce may do so if the depreciation is very substantial. There have been plenty of large exchange rate changes over recent years against which this proposition can be tested, and the relevant statistics for the years surrounding a number of them are shown in Table 2.3. The figures also indicate what happened in each case to the real wage and to the Gross Domestic Product. The table shows beyond all reasonable doubt that depreciating the currency, even on

Table 2.3   The Effects of Exchange Rate Changes on Consumer Prices, the Real
Wage, GDP, Industrial Output and Employment
All figures are year on year percentage changes

	Year	Con-sumer Prices	Wage Rates	Real Wage	GDP Change	Industrial Output Change	Unem-ployment Per cent
Britain – 31%	1930	–6.0	–0.7	5.3	–0.7	–1.4	11.2
Devaluation	1931	–5.7	–2.1	3.6	–5.1	–3.6	15.1
against the US	1932	–3.3	–1.7	1.6	0.8	0.3	15.6
dollar in 1931	1933	0.0	–0.1	–0.1	2.9	4.0	14.1
	1934	0.0	1.5	1.5	6.6	5.5	11.9
France – 27%	1956	2.0	9.7	7.7	5.1	9.4	1.1
Devaluation	1957	3.5	8.2	4.7	6.0	8.3	0.8
against all	1958	15.1	12.3	–2.8	2.5	4.5	0.9
currencies in	1959	6.2	6.8	0.6	2.9	3.3	1.3
1957/58	1960	3.5	6.3	2.8	7.0	10.1	1.2
	1961	3.3	9.6	6.3	5.5	4.8	1.1
USA – 28%	1984	4.3	4.0	–0.3	6.2	11.3	7.4
Devaluation	1985	3.6	3.9	0.3	3.2	2.0	7.1
against all	1986	1.9	2.0	0.1	2.9	1.0	6.9
currencies over	1987	3.7	1.8	–1.9	3.1	3.7	6.1
1985/87	1988	4.0	2.8	–1.2	3.9	5.3	5.4
	1989	5.0	2.9	–2.1	2.5	2.6	5.2
Japan – 47%	1989	2.3	3.1	0.8	4.8	5.8	2.3
Revaluation	1990	3.1	3.8	0.7	4.8	4.1	2.1
against all	1991	3.3	3.4	0.1	4.3	1.8	2.1
currencies over	1992	1.7	2.1	0.4	1.4	–6.1	2.2
1990/94	1993	1.3	2.1	0.8	0.1	–4.6	2.5
	1994	0.7	2.3	1.6	0.6	0.7	2.9
Italy – 20%	1990	6.4	7.3	–0.9	2.1	–0.6	9.1
Devaluation	1991	6.3	9.8	3.5	1.3	–2.2	8.6
against all	1992	5.2	5.4	0.2	0.9	–0.6	9.0
currencies over	1993	4.5	3.8	–0.7	–1.2	–2.9	10.3
1990/93	1994	4.0	3.5	–0.5	2.2	5.6	11.4
	1995	5.4	3.1	–2.3	2.9	5.4	11.9
Finland – 24%	1990	6.1	9.4	3.3	0.0	–0.1	3.5
Devaluation	1991	4.1	6.4	2.3	–7.1	–9.7	7.6
against all	1992	2.6	3.8	1.2	–3.6	2.2	13.0
currencies over	1993	2.1	3.7	1.6	–1.6	5.5	17.5
1991/93	1994	1.1	7.4	6.3	4.5	10.5	17.4
	1995	1.0	4.7	3.7	5.1	7.8	16.2
Spain – 18%	1991	5.9	8.2	2.3	2.3	–0.7	16.3
Devaluation	1992	5.9	7.7	1.8	0.7	–3.2	18.5
against all	1993	4.6	6.8	2.2	–1.2	–4.4	22.8
currencies over	1994	4.7	4.5	–0.2	2.1	7.5	24.1
1992/94	1995	4.7	4.8	0.1	2.8	4.7	22.9
	1996	3.6	4.8	1.2	2.2	–0.7%	22.2

Sources: IMF International Financial Statistics Yearbook, Eurostatistics and British statistics.

a large scale, normally neither pushes up the price level significantly, except perhaps very temporarily as in the case of France at the end of the 1950s, nor does it cause a reduction in the real wage or the GDP. On the contrary, exactly the opposite occurs.

How can this be? There are perhaps surprisingly straightforward explanations. It is true that a devaluation necessarily pushes up the cost of imports, as the buying power of the domestic currency falls in the world economy. This is the inflationary impact on which attention always tends to be focused. Devaluations also reduce costs, however, in the domestic economy in a number of significant but often overlooked ways. Production runs are increased, lowering average costs. Sources of supply are switched away from foreign to now cheaper domestic sources. Interest rates come down thus reducing borrowing costs. The fiscal balance improves with greater activity, providing opportunities for net tax reductions. Some fairly straightforward calculations show that these offsetting factors are likely just about exactly to offset the increased costs of imports.[26] This is why devaluations, of themselves, seldom increase inflation, though if they lead to much faster growth, the price level may start to rise a little faster.

Nor do they involve any net cost to the economy as a whole. The usual effect of a devaluation is to increase the prices of both imports and exports but, even if import prices rise faster than export prices, the stimulus to the economy as a whole from a lower exchange rate easily generates the resources to offset any cost involved. This is reflected in the fact that GDP invariably rises more quickly after a devaluation than it did before, as the whole economy becomes more competitive *vis à vis* the rest of the world, necessarily implying a rise in GDP per head, which is a close proxy for living standards. The implication from this assessment of the evidence, and explanation of what it shows, is extremely significant. It means that depreciating the currency to improve economic performance – if accompanied by the otherwise reasonably competent government which is always required in any circumstances – carries no penalty either in terms of increased inflation or in reduction in living standards.

Does this mean, therefore, that the risks and problems associated with inflation can be safely ignored? Certainly not. Reckless economic management has a long history of debasing currencies. It does mean, however, that, with competent management, the risks which can reasonably be taken are much less dangerous than is often supposed, and that the upside benefits are both larger and more easily accessible than they are generally believed to be. Far from inflation being a major threat, history shows that there are strong tendencies for the price level to be remarkably stable, perhaps surprisingly so, and for inflation to subside, usually quite rapidly, when it does occur. It is absorbed, especially in modern conditions, by a combination of productivity increases and competitive pressures, much more than by institutional arrangements geared to keeping inflation under control. Some downside factors still remain as threats, nevertheless, and it is important to recognise these for what they are. The main ones are: leading sector inflation; the sorts of shocks to the system which triggered the steep rise in prices during the 1970s; and subjecting the economy to too much of the wrong kind of stimulation, leading to excess demand.

Leading sector inflation is relatively benign, and difficult to avoid. It is a shortcut description of the outcome of an averaging process which is particularly evident in economies which are growing very fast as was the case, for example, in Japan during the 1950s and 1960s, when the growth rate averaged 9.6% per annum.[27] Productivity rose much faster than the average in the economy's industrial sectors, especially those concerned with international trading, generating the capacity to pay high wages and salaries. The result of wave after wave of investment in Japan's world-beating exporting sectors was that Japanese export prices rose by only just over 1% per annum during the whole of the 1950s and 1960s.[28] Domestic inflation during these two decades, however, was much higher, averaging 5.2% for the 20-year period.[29] This happened because the rises in wages and salaries which were so marked in manufacturing triggered comparable increases in other parts of the economy, where higher productivity was much more difficult to secure. These included nearly all the service industries, which were then, and still are, generally poorly run by world standards, and which were unable to generate productivity rises to pay for higher incomes. This was the cause of the relatively rapid rate of domestic inflation in Japan during the post-Second World War decades, even though Japanese export competitiveness increased substantially at the same time.

Much the same phenomenon was seen, albeit on a more modest scale, in much of Western Europe during the 1950s and 1960s, where inflation averaged just over 4%[30] while labour productivity grew at an annual 4.7%,[31] and average economic growth was 4.6% a year.[32] The same pattern emerges in Pacific Rim economies, especially in the period since 1973 when growth in output has accelerated there, in contrast to the marked slow-down in the West. Even including some large but poorly managed economies such as Indonesia, between 1973 and 1992, and excluding Japan whose performance by then was worse than the average, mean GDP increases per annum were 5.7%, while inflation averaged 10.6% per annum.[33] There may well be problems with prices increasing at this rate, though it is not necessary that they should do so. The key lesson to be learnt, however, is that it is very difficult to combine high rates of growth with rates of inflation as low as 2.5% – the British target – or 2.0%, the objective set by the European Central Bank.

Much less benign has been the impact of shocks to the world economic system, of which the fourfold oil price increases, from $2.50 to $10 a barrel,[34] in the early 1970s were the symptom, although by no means the only cause. The immediate trigger for the OPEC price increase was the alienation of the Arab world caused by Western, and particularly American, support for Israel during the Yom Kippur war. The background, however, was an explosion in credit which had taken place as a result of the removal of the constraints set by the Bretton Woods exchange rate system, as a result of the devaluation of the US dollar in 1971. Unrestrained credit creation led to an unsustainable world boom, as output climbed steeply, commodities doubled and trebled in price, and property prices soared, leading to a proliferation of risky loans, many of which materialised as bad debts when the boom broke. The resulting inflation during the 1970s, occurring at a time when the world was largely at peace, was unprecedented. Year on year price increases peaked in Britain at 24%, in France at 14%, in the USA at 11%, and in Germany at a much more modest 7%.[35]

The most important result of the inflationary experience in the 1970s was a major change in intellectual fashion away from Keynesian policies to those advocated by the newly ascendant monetarists. It is far from clear, however, why the policy mistakes which caused much higher price rises than had been experienced previously could not relatively easily have been avoided. The world did not have to pay the heavy deflationary price which harder line monetary policies brought in train. There was nothing inevitable about the credit explosion which was the underlying cause of the shock to which the world was exposed. Nor was it the case that the economies which adopted monetarist policies most wholeheartedly saw their inflation rates falling back most rapidly. Inflation receded everywhere, and often as quickly in countries such as Norway, which never adopted monetarist policies, as in those which implemented drastic reductions in their money supply along the lines of the new orthodoxy.[36] The most critical lessons to be learnt from the 1970s were to avoid creating the conditions which allowed excessive credit generation to occur in the first place, but then to avoid an equally excessive reduction to compound the unnecessary problem which had been created.

The experience of overheating in the 1970s also has a more general application, evident in many of the economies in the world which have had the worst experiences of rapid and often long-lasting price rises. A consistent theme throughout this book is that sound economic policies are only a part of good government, and not a substitute for the need to get other components right. Maintaining a high and steady rate of growth can only be achieved if a number of essentially non-economic factors are present. These include the absence of war, tolerably restrained behaviour by special interest groups, a reasonably effective legal system for the enforcement of contracts, education and training to provide an adequately qualified labour force, and a sufficient lack of corruption and pork barrel politics to enable the market to work effectively. Given these desiderata and appropriate economic policies, there is no reason why any economy cannot expand at 4% or 5% per annum, perhaps faster, without paying anything like an excessive inflationary cost. With fast growth rates, the annual increase in prices may not be as low as 2.0% or 2.5% per annum, but it is likely to stabilise at well below the danger level. Historical experience suggests that average yearly price rises of about 4% are the probable outcome in an otherwise well-run economy of a sustained growth rate of about 5% or even 6% per annum, with the cost of most goods remaining almost stable, and with nearly all the increases concentrated in the service sector. Nor does experience tell us that there will be any chronic tendency for prices to rise faster each year, provided that excess demand is avoided. For those whose future income depends heavily on prices being as close as possible to stability, such as pensioners, this may not be an ideal immediate outcome, but for everyone else – the vast majority of the population in all developed countries – the benefits to be won from much more rapid growth easily offset the minimal downside effects from the risk of slightly higher inflation. In the end, too, even those who are the losers from falling interest rates often tend to gain as the economy as a whole becomes richer.

The relief of poverty

Providing all humanity with an equal income may be the favoured distant goal of a few idealists, but this objective has never been practical politics. It is very unlikely that it ever will be, however much the standard of living advances. It seems much more likely that some countries will always be more prosperous than others, and certain that, within each economy, some individuals will continue to accumulate more wealth and income than the average, while others will do worse. Dealing with the details of redistribution of income and wealth is therefore a political rather than an economic matter, where reasonable and defensible choices can be made, designed to achieve or, at least, to tolerate greater or lesser measures of inequality.

Where the relief of poverty ceases to be purely a political issue and becomes a matter of general economic policy, this book argues, is when the distribution of wealth and income gets well outside the pale of reasonable choice, and becomes both an affront and a serious danger to everyone. Both within and between countries, this is the situation which it is becoming increasingly clear we are approaching, if, in the judgement of many people, we have not already reached it. Both anecdotal evidence and the statistics speak for themselves, not least the attacks on New York and Washington on 11 September 2001. The motivation for these appalling events were evidently by no means entirely economic, but it is hard to avoid the conclusion that the disparity in living standards and hence power and influence between the USA and much of the Arab world had a good deal to do with the underlying resentment which led to them taking place.

For across almost the whole of the developed world, during the last quarter of a century, there has been a regression away from the relatively low dispersions of income and wealth achieved by about three-quarters of the way through the twentieth century. In the United States in 1980, the top 5% of income earners received 14.6% of the total, and the bottom 20% 5.3%. By 1998, the figures were 20.7% and 4.2%.[37] As a result, the incomes of the bottom 20% of families remained almost exactly static in real terms between 1980 and 1998, while those of the top 5% grew by 33%. The richest 5% of US families now have incomes 6.7 times as high as the bottom 20%, whereas in 1980 the ratio was 5.3.[38] Interestingly, while most of the widening took place during the Reagan and Bush presidencies, the dispersion actually increased under President Clinton, no doubt mainly as a result of the huge stock market boom which took place in the 1990s. Much the same tendencies have been documented in Britain, particularly in a report from the Rowntree Foundation[39] published in 1999, and in academic studies covering the whole of Western Europe.[40] Taking the world as a whole, between 1960 and 1995, the ratio of income between the richest and poorest 20% of the world's population rose from 30:1 to more than 80:1.[41]

The consequences of increasingly unequal distributions of income and wealth are not only to be found in greater or lesser ability to buy goods and services, but also in every other aspect of life chances. With increasing levels of poverty go rising chances of ill health, higher deaths in child birth and shortened life expectancy, greater exposure to crime, inferior housing conditions, poorer educational attainment and worse job prospects. While most people realise that this is the case, and appear to be willing to tolerate the consequences, at least while no realistic way to avoid these conditions is available, at some point the cost to society as a whole of increasingly unequal life opportunities seems likely to become unacceptably high. The inconvenience to the rich of rising crime may become intolerable. The destitution of the poorest members of society tends to be hidden away from those who are better off most of the time. Nevertheless, developments such as the proliferation of young homeless rough sleepers in the West End of London may have brought home to some people, who would not otherwise be aware of it, the plight of a significant number of the disadvantaged young. At the very least, if the climate of opinion does change, and a greater determination to reduce these inequalities than we have seen recently manifests itself, economics needs to have on hand realistic and workable policies to implement the changes which will need to be made. It may also be the case that both the existence and availability of such policies will help to trigger a change of heart.

If the increasing inequalities of income and wealth within nations in the developed world ought to be a matter of concern, there is an even stronger case for believing that the disparities between countries are an even greater issue, partly because the variations across the world are so huge. At one extreme are the richest countries, with – in 1995 – average GDP per head of $26,721 in Switzerland, $25,390 in Norway, $22,247 in Denmark and $20,716 in the USA. At the other end of the spectrum were Tanzania with $155, Ethiopia with $154 and Cambodia with $133.[42] These figures show the average citizen in Switzerland to be almost exactly 200 times as well off as his or her Cambodian equivalent. The difference in income levels between the large groups of people living in rich and poor countries is thus much wider than between major groups within most countries.

These figures are disturbing enough, but might not be so discouraging if the gap between the richest and the poorest countries was showing signs of closing. Unfortunately, this is not the position. The richer countries are continuing to grow and, because they nearly all now have low population growth rates, the standard of living per head is still rising too. In the poorest countries, however, the reverse conditions tend to apply. Even if there is some growth in the economy, this tends to be swamped by an even faster rate of increase in the population, leaving the average income per head static at best, but – worse than this – still tending to drift downwards in many cases. Indeed, of all the 33 countries in Africa with statistics reliable enough to be included in a recent report covering the period 1980–95,[43] 21 showed a declining figure for GDP per head and only 12 an increase during these 15 years. Among the latter countries, however, were some which were doing well, particularly Botswana, with a cumulative GDP per head increase per annum of 4.9%, and Guinea-Bissau and Lesotho with 2.7% each. This is an encouraging sign that overall trends can be bucked, though, as always, there were some special circumstances to be taken into account in each of these cases.

Some of the reasons why the poorest countries are doing so badly has nothing to do directly with economic policy. Warfare, corruption, nepotism and arbitrary or anarchic government are conditions for which economic policy can have no remedy. The fact that these conditions tend all too frequently to exist among the nations with the lowest living standards does not, however, absolve the developed nations from a fair measure of responsibility for the state in which the poorest countries find themselves. Many of them were former colonies, leaving the ex-colonial powers with at least a residual accountability. Apart from any obligations of this sort, however, looking ahead, there is clearly both a moral and a practical obligation for the richer world to assist in bridging the widening gap between the First and the Third World.

Part of the solution to the problem lies in aid programmes, and the transfer of skills from First World to Third World countries. The record in this regard, though considerable, is not as great as it might be, with few developed countries achieving the UN target of aid comprising 0.7% of donor countries' GDP.[44] Of much greater importance to Third World countries than aid, however, are adequate opportunities to trade with the developed nations. It is in this respect that the richer countries have failed the poorest most comprehensively. Although world trade has expanded much more rapidly than world GDP over recent decades,[45] partly as a result of a succession of trade liberalisation measures, these have mostly benefited trade in manufactured goods between developed countries. The poorest countries have largely been left out. Africa, for example, where many of the poorest countries are to be found, saw its total world trade fall from just over 4% in 1984 to just over 2% ten years later.[46]

Part of the reason for the disappointing trade performance of the poorest countries in the world may be attributable to internal political and economic conditions, but a good deal of it rests with the attitude which the developed world has taken to the exports which poorer countries are best placed to produce. As with everywhere else in the world, the only long-term solution to low living standards in Third World countries is to raise the productivity and output per head of their labour forces. The best route to doing this is to improve agricultural efficiency so that exportable surpluses can be created, and especially to industrialise, because productivity increases are so much easier to achieve in manufacturing than they are elsewhere. The way to get this done follows a familiar pattern. It starts with relatively simple, low tech production, where the capital equipment required is comparatively cheap, the technology well within the state of published knowledge, and where the benefits of low labour and other overhead costs can be easily translated into competitive pricing for the home and the export markets. The classic industries which are then likely to be established are those involved in textiles, shoes and other comparatively simple products to manufacture. Unfortunately, however, these have often been industries which have been badly hit in the developed world, and where resistance to cheap imports has been particularly acute, generating just the kind of import restrictions, such as the Multi Fibre Agreement, which the Third World least needs. In the meantime agricultural protectionism in countries with high living standards, combined with dumping their surpluses on world markets, has done much too much to undermine opportunities for raising productivity on the land in poor countries.

The key economic policy issue raised by the disparities in wealth and income both within and between countries, therefore, is how to create an environment in which the gaps can at least be stabilised, and where the opportunity for narrowing them will exist, if the will to allow this to happen is there. The problem is that, for this to occur, the incomes of the poor are going to have to rise significantly more quickly than the rich both between and within countries. Furthermore, to narrow significantly the gap where it is greatest, which is between the poorest and the richest nations, there will have to be a long and sustained period when this is going to have to happen. Even if Cambodia, with an average income per head of $133, were to achieve consistently the 4.9% growth in GDP per head achieved by Botswana, it would take about 110 years for the Cambodian standard of living to equal that of the USA today. If, in the meantime, the GDP per head in the USA continued to rise at its recent trend rate of 1.6% per annum,[47] the catch-up time would stretch out to about 160 years.

These are daunting figures, but at least for the next few decades, the sacrifices which the rich world would have to make to enable this catching-up process to start are not so difficult, mainly because the aggregate incomes of all of the poor people in the world are so relatively small. The result is that the impact of a substantial improvement in the prospects of the poorer countries on the already rich would be almost insignificant. The disruption of their trade patterns would be barely noticeable. Furthermore, there is no reason why the rich nations should not benefit from increased trading opportunities with the poorer countries in the world. They would gain by receiving from low wage economies those goods and services which they were especially well placed to produce economically, particularly if those who were adversely affected by new competition in the richer countries were somehow compensated.

In the end, the problem of dealing with wealth disparities, both within and between countries, comes back to the same economic policy issue which unites the others discussed in this chapter. It is a question of effective demand. If poverty within countries is to be alleviated, far the best way of doing it is to ensure that there is sufficient demand for conditions to be created where almost anyone who wants to work can find a job. Similarly, if the poorest countries in the world are to be lifted out of poverty, and are to be given the opportunity to catch up with those who are much better off, then conditions have to be created which will increase disproportionately the demand for the output which they are capable of producing. This will entail the world allowing these countries to develop exceptionally competitive cost bases, and then permitting them to export their production to the developed world.

This is exactly what most of the Pacific Rim countries have managed to achieve over the decades since the Second World War, largely, it has to be said, by accident rather than design. For a variety of reasons, they established themselves in the world economy with highly competitive exports from which their subsequent high growth rates were able to be achieved. The issue is whether the world will show the wisdom required to allow the same conditions to be created for the poorer countries which have not, up to now, had the opportunity to emulate them.

Sustainability

The final, but by no means the least important goal of economic policy has to be to ensure that the outcome of the growth, full employment, tolerable levels of inflation and the alleviation of extreme poverty, also leaves the world in a condition where it can sustain all the extra demands which will be put upon it. There are four key issues. The first relates to population growth, the second to the environment, the third to resources, and the fourth to catastrophic warfare.

The world's population is now about 6bn. It was just over 1bn in 1820, and a little more than 2bn in 1929. By 1950 it was 2.5bn, and 4bn in 1975.[48] The increase between 1820 and 1929 was just under 0.6% per annum. During the last 25 years it has been 1.6% a year, through the rate of increase is now slowly falling. The reason it is still so high is that the countries whose populations have grown fast, and whose total number of citizens is now much higher than it used to be, are the countries which still have the highest birth rates. The population of India, now approaching 1.1bn, has been growing recently at 2.2% per annum. Across the whole of Africa, whose inhabitants have more than trebled since 1950, the population, now about 850m, is growing at 3% a year. In South America the number of people has recently been rising at 2.2% a year. It is true that the rate of population increase is much lower in some other parts of the world – about 0.3% in most of Europe, and only about 0.7% in Japan, but the higher rates elsewhere pull up the average.[49]

Why is the number of people inhabiting the earth rising so rapidly, particularly in the countries with the fastest growth in population? Part of the reason is that life expectancy has risen dramatically as a result of the application of Western technology to basic hygiene, waste disposal and medical care. The result is that the high birth rates, which were always the characteristic of most underdeveloped societies, are no longer offset by corresponding death rates. Meanwhile, the main social reason for large families, which is that they have always been the best protection against hard times, particularly in old age, remain in place. This happens because nearly all the countries with the highest birth rates cannot afford the social underpinning which is taken for granted in richer countries.

A pressingly urgent requirement, however, is to reduce the birth rate, and to stabilise the world's population. Even on the most optimistic assumptions, this is now unlikely to happen for another 50 years or so, by which time humanity may well number 10bn or more. By far the most promising overall way to achieve this goal is to raise the standard of living in the countries with the highest birth rates. All the evidence suggests that, when GDP per head reaches the levels achieved in Europe at the beginning of the twentieth century, the birth rate slows up, whatever the cultural or religious background of the population concerned. Specific policies such as the empowerment and education of women are also crucially important,[50] but are often easier to achieve against a background of rising prosperity. The previous section has suggested how higher growth rates might be achieved, but there is still going to be a difficult race against time.

Furthermore, the more that is done in the short term to raise living standards in populous poor countries, while the developed world also goes on growing, the more acute the problems are going to be for world's environment and ecology. The threat of global warming and the depletion of the ozone layer are now taken seriously by almost everyone. The extent to which climate change is likely to present humanity with costs which it is going to be unable or unwilling to bear is clouded by disagreements among those expert in the subject, largely because of difficulties about interpreting accurately all the data which is now available. Nevertheless, the size of the threat appears to be thought to be increasing rather than diminishing, and with it the urgency to secure international agreements, through the Kyoto process or in some other way.

Other problems may be going to be even more difficult to deal with, their impact being even more imminent. Some of these are already becoming pressing, even in advanced countries. One is the availability of sufficient fresh water. Another is going to be the world's capacity to generate enough energy. Both of these shortages now seriously affect the United States, particularly in the west of the country, though misguided pricing and regulatory policies have been as much responsible as real resource shortages for the problems there. There are also increasing problems about disposing of used materials of all kinds, including sewage, household rubbish and industrial waste. As the water table falls, so farming gets more difficult to manage successfully, and with it the problems of feeding the world's rising population. As pressure mounts to contain the emission of greenhouse gases, so does the difficulty of finding ways of generating sufficient electricity to provide the world with all the power it needs without resorting to atomic energy, which brings different environmental problems in train. The reason for the recent brown outs in California has been partly caused by opposition to the construction of additional power stations using any of the available technologies. As societies get richer, their capacity for generating waste of all kinds rises almost exponentially, producing levels of pollution which become increasingly hard to contain. There is an added problem which is that the technologies based round atomic power, which might look best suited to deal with energy shortages, are themselves prone to very high costs[51] and some of the most difficult environmental hazards, waste disposal being high on the list.

Some of the problems caused by increasing living standards can also be solved by the increasing wealth which is created. In any event, as GDP per head rises, there is comforting evidence that the strain on the world's environment does not increase proportionately. More demand is directed either to complex products whose cost is more a function of their intricacy than their raw material content, or to services whose impact on the ecology is relatively small. There is also reasonable reassurance that food supplies are unlikely to be a limiting factor, despite the potential shortage of fresh water. Certainly, during the last few decades, when the world population has been rising very rapidly, food output has risen much faster – by some 14% more rapidly than the rise in the number of mouths to feed during the last quarter of a century.[52] Nevertheless, if an essential element in containing the rise in the number of people inhabiting the world is to increase living standards, especially in those countries with the fastest growing populations, this is not going to be achieved without further strains on the environment. The only way of squaring this circle is by combining expenditure to contain the ecological impact of further growth in output with population control policies which need to be sufficiently effective to contain the total environmental impact of the number of people living in the world, when, and if, it stabilises at a level which is still sustainable. This looks like a daunting task, but one to which appropriate economic policies have a pre-eminent contribution to make.

While this process is taking place, or subsequently, will the world run out of the resources of raw materials needed to keep up with the economic growth necessary to solve the other problems involved with sustainability? Probably not, given reasonably competent management, and the continuing ability of human ingenuity to provide solutions to the problems of shortage which have been the lot of humanity ever since civilisation began. All the prognostications of those who have predicted that the world would run out of resources within a finite period of time have certainly proved wrong so far. The predictions of the Club of Rome, made in 1972[53] are a salutary example. Every single one of them proved to be false.[54] In the longer term, it may well be that the world will run short of particular raw materials, not least of those which cannot be recycled, such as fossil fuels. The challenge will then be to find substitutes which are sufficiently safe and cost effective to fill the gap. Again, however, these problems look as though they are probably soluble, given sufficient investment and appropriate technology. There can be no certainty, but these look like being easier problems to resolve than the others.

The key sustainability issues therefore look like being the interacting factors associated with population growth, economic growth and their combined impact on the environment. These are likely to be the central problems faced by humanity over the next century and beyond. Whether they can be contained in acceptable ways also bears heavily on perhaps the biggest uncertainty of all, which is whether it is going to be possible to avoid the spread of catastrophic warfare, as resources run short. There is little doubt that local conflicts will continue to exist. The danger is that these become much wider spread. There can be little doubt that the more acute the shortage of resources of all kinds becomes, the greater the danger will be that desperation will lead to armed conflict developing between the haves and the have-nots. Again, the events of 11 September 2001 give little cause for comfort.

The question is whether economics, as it now exists, is capable of providing a framework of answers to deal with these issues, central as they are to the future of humanity, as well as all the others which this chapter has covered. We turn now to seeing how economic thought has developed, to see how well and relevantly it has responded so far.

3
The Pre-Industrial World

The Study of History is the beginning of political wisdom.

Jean Bodin (1530–1596)

The kinds of interactions between human beings which are the stuff of economics go back to the dawn of civilisation, but the systematic study of these relationships is heavily skewed towards recent times. From the time when language developed some 100,000 years ago,[1] there must have been buyers and sellers, borrowers and lenders. The need for credit must have been critical from the beginning of settled agriculture about 11,000 years ago.[2] Indeed, the reason why some 5,000 years elapsed between the time of the first permanent settlements in Mesopotamia in the Middle East and the rise of the first city states of significance in the same area may well have had to do with the lack of any way of recording more debts than could be remembered by the village headman. It was finding ways of keeping track of increasingly complex webs of obligations which, as much as anything else, made the growth of larger-scale polities possible. There is ample evidence, however, in the form of clay tablets, that sophisticated methods of recording obligations were in operation when the earliest cities were established about 3,700 BC.[3]

The invention of money came much later. Barter tokens were minted by the Chinese in the second millennium BC. True coinage, however, was first used in the kingdom of Lydia in about 700 BC. Originally made of electrum, a local natural amalgam of gold and silver, the first coins were produced by the fabled king Croesus (died 546 BC).[4] The development of coinage led directly to the vast increase in trade and colonisation which took place in the Mediterranean basin over the subsequent centuries, as the Greeks and others spread their culture and customs throughout the ancient world, creating the civilisation which the Romans subsequently made their own.[5]

While the Greeks developed a trading system, and the Romans a structure of administration, which between them managed to support a huge empire for hundreds of years, the economic achievements of the Ancient World were otherwise surprisingly modest. Manufacturing never proceeded significantly beyond the output of small groups of individual artisans. There was little technical advance. Almost none of the scientific speculations of the Greeks were orientated to practical purposes. The economy of the Roman Empire stagnated under the weight of increasing taxation, disruption occasioned by plagues, and the uncertainties caused by periodic severe inflations. Probably the most important contribution made by the Romans to the subsequent development of the world economy was their system of law, particularly their law of contract. This, on its own, however, was insufficient to generate anything remotely equivalent to the start of the Industrial Revolution, which took another millennium and a half to materialise.

An additional underlying reason why nothing approaching sustained economic advance took place in the Ancient World was the lack of as effective a method of performing and recording complicated calculations as was provided by the spread of Arabic numerals, particularly the concept of zero. The ability of previous systems of calculation, based on the abacus, can easily be underestimated by those not familiar with their capacity to deal with multiplication and division, but they provided no satisfactory basis for modern mathematics. Although the latest view among some scholars is that it may have originated in Babylonia,[6] the idea of zero is generally credited to Indian thinkers in the fourth century AD. This notation, however, took eight hundred years to reach Europe, via the Islamic Arab states. Its use was first successfully publicised in the West by Leonardo Fibonnacci (c1170 to c1250) in his *Book of the Calculator*, published in 1202,[7] although a book on Arab arithmetic had been translated into French in about 990 AD.[8] The inadequacy of ancient mathematical systems may have contributed not only to the lack of scientific and technical advance which might otherwise have been possible, but also inhibited the development of the sophisticated banking systems, depending, as they did, on records as well as calculations, which were an important precursor to the Industrial Revolution. It is no coincidence that double entry book keeping and the much wider availability of credit which better systems of recording and managing liabilities made possible provided important underpinning to the creation of the new wealth which led to the Renaissance.

Nevertheless, the Ancient World left powerful and influential legacies to subsequent generations, and did much to shape the perceptions of those who wrote about economic subjects hundreds of years later. We turn now to what these were, and who were the people who left the deepest impressions on subsequent thought.

The Ancient World

There may have been thinkers who made significant contributions to the economic thought of their time in India, China or in the Islamic states which were established after Islam began to spread in the seventh century AD.[9] If so, few of their writings have survived, and their influence on subsequent thinking on economic matters, at least in the West, has therefore been negligible. The same certainly cannot be said about the Ancient World, where much of the thought which set the framework for subsequent theorising on economic issues was established. There were two key sources. One was the ancient Greeks, particularly Plato and Aristotle, and the other was the Christian tradition handed down by the Church. The Romans made little intellectual contribution, although, as has already been mentioned, Roman law was one of the foundations for subsequent commercial development. In particular, the sanctity and enforceability of contracts was of pivotal importance, and in sharp contrast to the more capricious arrangements found in other parts of the world.

The intellectual legacy of the ancient Greeks was immense. The fifth century BC saw the first true emancipation of humanity from astrology and magic, and the beginning of an immense effort to use logical thought as a way of understanding how the world operated. The framework of ideas within which Plato and Aristotle worked was established by a long series of thinkers, some of whom contributed ideas which still resonate today. Heraclitus (c535 BC–475 BC) articulated concepts about strife and balance which find modern echoes in the notion of competition.[10] Democritus (c460 BC–c370 BC) wrote a treatise on economic matters, although only some three hundred quotations have been preserved. Those that remain, however, show a remarkably acute understanding of the motivation for economic activity, including concepts such as the decreasing utility of additional units of goods and services. Democritus's opinion that private property is likely to be better cared for than if it is owned communally has rung down the ages.[11] More practical observations, noting in particular the damaging economic consequences of war – a matter arguably not given due attention for the next two thousand years[12] – and anticipating some of the most important tenets about the division of labour in Adam Smith's *Wealth of Nations*, are to be found in the writings of Xenophon (c430 BC–c355 BC).[13]

There was, therefore, a considerable legacy upon which to draw when the first major attempt to synthesise the theorising which had accumulated up to that point was undertaken by Plato (c427 BC–c347 BC). Plato's main interest was in politics rather than economics. His major work *The Republic* is much more concerned with defining justice, and establishing the best form of governance, than it is with strictly economic matters. Nevertheless, his conclusion that the best form of state was one run by a philosopher king entailed a form of organisation which had significant economic implications. Plato believed that human beings were unequal, and that, in consequence, specialisation was required. He therefore favoured the creation of a form of economic hierarchy which would encourage and facilitate the establishment of different groups of people, each concentrating on particular political and economic activities. At the apex were philosophers. The next tier down was occupied by soldiers, and below this were those engaged in farming and trade, reflecting the relatively low esteem in which the more productive parts of the economy was held.[14]

This contempt for commercial activity, which Plato regarded as being much inferior to the functions of rulers or soldiers, was an aspect of his thought and teaching which had a major impact. Echoes of his view that those activities most closely orientated to increasing the standard of living were of the least significance and importance are still to be found. So too was his disdain for wealth, which he viewed as being corrupting. Indeed, a constant theme running through *The Republic* is the virtue of austerity, which was to be a key hallmark of the rulers he favoured, untainted by the temptation to go into moneymaking commerce. A third was his authoritarianism and lack of respect for the private sphere of individuals, which shaded into his toleration of slavery as an institution, perhaps made easier to understand by the fact that about one-third of the population of Greek city states of his time consisted of slaves.[15] Despite the celebration of ancient Athens as the progenitor of democracy, there is little enthusiasm for this form of political organisation in Plato's works. Generally, his influence has been to reinforce a conservative, quietist approach to economic policy.

The next major synthesis of Greek ideas was undertaken by Aristotle (384 BC–322 BC), whose father had been physician to King Philip II of Macedon (382 BC–336 BC), the father of Alexander the Great (356 BC–323 BC), whom Aristotle in turn tutored.[16] While Aristotle was concerned with a wide range of matters other than economics, his works contain a variety of references to economic issues. His main contributions to the subsequent development of economic thinking lay first in what he had to say about the economic organisation of society, second on his views on the merits of private versus communal property, and third on value and exchange. Because his stature as a thinker was so huge, the influence of his opinions on economic issues was disproportionately large, although not all subsequent thinkers have been kind to him. Joseph A. Schumpeter who, it has to be said, had a high opinion of his own abilities, described Aristotle's contributions as 'decorous, pedestrian, slightly mediocre, and more than slightly pompous common sense'.[17]

The word *economics* is of Greek origin, and literally means 'management of the household',[18] and Aristotle's thinking reflected this small-scale view of most economic activity. Like Plato, he condoned slavery, observing that 'from the hour of their birth, some are marked out for subjection, others for rule',[19] and elsewhere that 'It is clear, then, that some men are by nature free, and others slaves, and that for these latter slavery is both expedient and right.'[20] Aristotle also shared most of Plato's reservations about trade, condemning the accumulation of wealth as 'unnatural'.[21] This led him to censure the use of money as a store of wealth, as opposed to a means of exchange, again reflecting Plato's yearning for austerity. Aristotle, in particular, condemned the lending of money for interest, a concept which, as we shall see, became a major plank in the Church's teaching. 'The most hated sort [of moneymaking], and with the greatest reason, is usury ... For money was intended to be used in exchange, but not to increase at interest.'[22] Money, in Aristotle's view, was only justified as a way of making bartering more efficient, though he recognised that it did this very effectively, not least in foreign trade. Despite his reservations about wealth accumulation, he offered a spirited defence of private as opposed to communal property, following a by then well established Greek tradition. Aristotle was also concerned about the relationship between value and price, and the important medieval concept of the 'just price' owes much to him. This was based essentially on what later came to be known as the Labour Theory of Value, implying that the value and hence the fair price for anything was its labour content.[23]

Aristotle's over-riding aim, emphasised particularly in his *Ethics*, was to promote the concept of moderation as the principle guide to human behaviour. Whether this was the best foundation for formulating a framework of ideas about how most efficiently to run either the relatively simple economies of his time or the increasingly more complex ones which were to follow, is, however, very doubtful. Aristotle's influence was, nevertheless, immense, though other ideas from ancient Greece also had their place. The Cynics, whose moving spirit, Diogenes (c412 BC–323 BC), made his home in a barrel, advocated extreme austerity. The Stoics, following Zeno (c336 BC–c264 BC), favoured a life free of emotion and passion, while the Epicureans preferred and advocated a simple but undemanding lifestyle.[24] All these reactions to life in Ancient Greece had their counterparts later on. All were essentially ways of coming to terms with scarcity rather than finding ways of overcoming it. Of course, they reflected conditions at a time when there was no feasible way of increasing economic output, other than by allowing existing trade and production techniques to flourish as best they could in the absence of war. In these circumstances, ways of thought which brought everyone to terms with the shortages and privations of life had their merit. Once economic growth began to get under way, however, and the Industrial Revolution began to make possible a huge improvement in human welfare, the resigned nature of much Greek thinking, which still dominated the education of most of the governing classes in the countries where a sustained rise in living standards was taking place, became considerably less apposite.

The contribution made by the Romans to the development of economics was both smaller and differently focused from that of the Greeks. It was more practical, orientated, as the Romans pre-eminently were, to running a very large area for many centuries, in which substantial trade took place. While the history of the Roman Empire was one of almost continual warfare at one or more of its boundaries, within most of the Empire itself peace prevailed for hundreds of years. Roman rule was not, however, without its downsides. The maintenance of substantial armies and a large administrative machine required heavy taxation. Stagnant technology meant that there was no way in which output per head could be significantly increased. Bouts of inflation weakened the economy. By 265 AD the silver content of the coin representing the chief unit of money, which had been solid silver since 212 BC, but which had been gradually diluted from Nero's time (54–68 AD), had fallen almost to nil. This development was only partially excused by the declining supplies of silver as mines in Spain were exhausted.[25] As the Empire became slowly less able to withstand attacks from outside, partly because of plagues – probably measles and smallpox – which appear to have halved the population after it peaked in about 200 AD,[26] the depredations of the tax collectors became sufficiently onerous for the economy largely to cease functioning as a whole. Increasingly, it fractured into self-contained and self-supporting units, setting the scene for the manorial system which characterised much of Europe after the collapse of the western Roman Empire.

The economic stagnation of the Empire, or at least its lack of technical advance, was partly a reflection of the practical rather than intellectual orientation of Roman society. Certainly, the Romans made little contribution to the economic ideas which formed the backdrop to medieval thinking, other than those to do with the legal system. Pliny the Elder (23–79 AD) reflected the Roman agricultural ideal, and also expressed reservations about slavery, noting that 'it is the very worst plan of all to have land tilled by slaves let loose from the house of correction, as indeed is the case with all work entrusted to men who live without hope'.[27] He also expressed views about gold being a particularly suitable means of exchange,[28] though as he died in 79 AD, when Pompeii was engulfed in a volcanic eruption by Vesuvius,[29] his views long antedated the worst of the Roman Empire's inflationary problems which occurred some two centuries later in the time of the Emperor Diocletian (245–313). The Roman legal system, however, in economic terms was the key contribution to the future. This was so partly because of the foundation it provided for the enforcement of contracts, thus divorcing the establishment of their merits from the ethical footing which had been favoured by Aristotle.[30] It was also important because it embodied the notion of citizenship, inherited from the Greeks, which implied that the state existed for the benefit of the citizen and not the other way round.[31] This was a very different view of this key relationship from that applied in most other parts of the world, and may have been one of the more significant reasons why economic advance eventually took place in Europe, which inherited this Greek and Roman concept, rather than elsewhere.

The importance of the individual *vis à vis* the state was also a key concept in the other major influence on subsequent attitudes to economic questions, which was the body of teaching passed down through the Christian Church. Heavily affected by the tradition of the Old Testament prophets, a clear vision of a new social structure for the future was never a major part of its view, which was primarily directed to the next world.[32] In the sayings of Jesus, no weight is attached to economic considerations, because there is no need to care for production and material welfare in the Kingdom of God, whose coming is imminent.[33] Whereas the Greeks looked backwards, Jesus's teaching looked forwards to the Kingdom to come, though the messages in the Gospels still reflected much of the legacy of Greek thinking. Indeed, it was an amalgam of Jesus's teaching and the Greek tradition which formed the basis of Church doctrine in the Middle Ages.[34] Jesus exhibited the same contempt for trading and moneymaking, and denounced usury – although allowed for Jews[35] – in terms which Aristotle would have found entirely acceptable, in contrast to the Christian attitude to slavery, where souls to be saved were to be found as readily among slaves as anywhere else.

As the Church slowly gained strength, finally becoming the official religion of the Empire in 313 at the instigation of the Roman Emperor Constantine (285–337),[36] the Gospel teachings were codified and expanded. The Christian view of the relative unimportance of this world compared to the one to come, nevertheless, was seldom far away, and became increasingly significant as the Roman Empire declined. This other-worldliness reached its peak in the writings of Augustine of Hippo (354–430), whose seminal book *The City of God*[37] emphasised perhaps more than any other writing the insignificance of earthly life compared to what was to come thereafter. Nevertheless, as the Church became richer and more powerful, it could not fail to become more involved in worldly matters. The result was the development of a view of how life should be conducted which became more and more important as the Empire disintegrated and the Church became the main repository of knowledge and civilisation during the Dark Ages. Its teachings gradually became more tolerant and supportive of trading and commerce, although usury and large accumulations of wealth and private property were still condemned.[38]

The legacy of the Ancient World was, therefore, a powerful one. Through the Church and the Canon Law, it shaped most of the way in which men and women thought about economic issues until the end of the medieval period. Its frame of reference was inevitably, however, one in which economic progress was regarded as strictly limited to, at best, exploiting the opportunities provided by peaceful conditions and the absence of unduly oppressive government. Nevertheless, some components of this legacy were critically important in enabling medieval society to evolve into the increasingly rapidly changing and economically advancing polities of the Renaissance and beyond. These included the significance of the individual, the Roman tradition of contract law and the evolving notion that the state existed for the citizen and not the other way round, as well as the legacy of the power of knowledge and organised thinking encapsulated in all that was recovered from the Greeks and Romans during the Renaissance. The Ancient World provided Europe with a far better springboard for later progress than did any of the intellectual traditions established elsewhere.

The medieval Church

Little economic progress was made in Europe during the thousand years which followed the fall of the western Roman Empire. The collapse of organised civil authority, and its replacement by warlord government, meant that contracts could no longer be enforced. What little manufacturing there was declined. Even pottery ceased to be produced in England after about 400 AD.[39] In these circumstances, economic relations, based mostly round subsistence agriculture, were largely non-market orientated.[40] The form of organisation established by the late Roman latifundia – large self-sufficient economic units – became the pattern for manorial medieval feudalism.[41] Relationships between landlord and tenant and the Church revolved round obligations such as tithes rather than money payments. Outside agriculture, artisans were organised in guilds, modelled on Roman *collegia*.[42] Average standards of living, having peaked in the Roman Empire at about 180 AD,[43] sank to much lower levels. With the decline of both Europe and China from about 400 AD onwards, India became the main centre of civilisation, developing, among other ideas, the crucial key to the advancement of mathematics, the concept of zero. Three hundred years later, the remarkable spread of Islam produced a new focus for civilised living. The Islamic states were also the first to base their economies on global commercial leadership, although their prowess in agriculture, especially between 700 and 1000 AD, provided the world with a precursor to the Green Revolution which occurred a thousand years later.[44]

Slowly, however, Europe's fortunes began to revive. With a very high proportion of the population dependant directly on agriculture, much turned on how efficiently this activity was organised. The substitution of horses for oxen at the end of the first millennium, and the development of the heavy plough, allowing three- rather than two-year cycles, greatly increased productivity, as did the spread of water mills.[45] A series of other inventions also made a radical difference to the efficiency with which economic life could be carried on. The discovery of the escapement mechanism allowed reliable clocks to be produced, and by 1300 virtually all cities had at least one.[46] During the thirteenth century, Europeans began to use the magnetic compass, having acquired it from the Arabs, who may have learnt of its possibilities from China, or who may have discovered its use independently.[47] By the mid-fifteenth century, thousands of pairs of spectacles were being produced in Italian cities for both long and short sightedness[48] – doubling the working life of the average craftsman. In 1421, Florence issued the first known patent, which was for a canal boat equipped with cranes.[49] Europe also had its disasters during this period, however, not least the Black Death which, between 1346 and 1351, wiped out a third of the population. Although a terrible catastrophe at the time, this event helped economic prospects forward in some respects by weakening feudal bonds. At the same time, the slowly reviving economy, and perhaps the increased requirement for manpower in the armies fighting the wars of the time, triggered the need for more productive uses for the remaining labour force.[50] It was not, however, until the middle of the sixteenth century, two hundred years later, that Europe regained its pre-Plague population.[51]

As economic life quickened, so interest revived in how it should be regulated. During the Dark Ages, the absence of much beyond subsistence activity had rendered such thinking largely redundant, and little had been done to progress beyond the Church teachings on how economic relationships should be regulated, summarised most effectively by St Augustine of Hippo during the closing years of the western Roman Empire. While the Church was never really interested in social reform, its eyes being on the afterlife,[52] by the thirteenth century, new developments in the Canon Law, the Church's partly legal and partly moral regulatory system, were under way. These were led by St Thomas Aquinas (1225–1274), an Italian citizen born in France, who became the first of the Schoolmen, the Church scholars who took it upon themselves to reinterpret and reformulate Canon Law.[53] To St Thomas and the Canonists, economics meant a body of laws, not in the scientific sense, but as moral precepts designed to ensure appropriate conduct in the economic world. Avarice and covetousness were condemned, and the material advancement of the individual was to be subordinated to the needs of salvation in the next world.[54] Within this context, some of the themes which were then revisited were old ones, which were given new life. St Thomas shared St Augustine's fear that trade would turn men from the search for God, and the doctrine that *nullus christianus debet esse mercator* – no Christian should engage in trade – was common in the early Middle Ages. As both the Church and society became richer, however, and across Europe subsistence agriculture slowly gave ground to more sophisticated trade-related activity, this precept gradually fell into disuse.[55] By the mid-thirteenth century, when St Thomas was writing, it was clear that the Church's original purist stance was no longer realistic, prompting him to observe that 'Profit in itself is neither reprehensible nor praise-worthy – morally neutral – provided the trader pursues an honourable purpose.' The slow rehabilitation of the businessman was thus joined with the gradual recognition that there was also merit in the ownership of property.[56]

The Church also continued to condemn usury, which was banned at the Council of Tours in 1163,[57] and even more emphatically at the great Lateran Council of 1179, although not all Schoolmen, particularly Duns Scotus (c1265–1308), took such a censorious view.[58] Perhaps partly for this reason, usury was another doctrine, shared by Islam[59] although not applicable to the Jews, which, increasingly widely came to be ignored as its impracticality became apparent, exemplified by the rise of the great Christian moneylenders in the late Middle Ages, the Fuggers, Imhofs and Welsers.[60] Nevertheless, opposition to lending money with interest had important practical consequences, particularly on the way in which business risks were financed. Equity partnerships became a preferred form of investment, because they were not tainted with usury.[61] Lending at rates of interest of up to 10% was not made legal in England until 1545, following decades of inflation, although the interest rate allowed was cut to 8% in 1624 and further to 6% in 1651. Recovery of interest through the courts was not, however, permitted, although it was legal to sue for the repayment of the principal debt.[62] It was not until the nineteenth century that the taking of interest up to the maximum rate established by the law of the land was given implicit approval by the Roman Catholic Church.[63] Usury was also denounced by Martin Luther (1483–1546), while John Calvin (1509–1564) took a more conciliatory view, although both condemned lending at interest to the impecunious.[64] Not everyone, however, was convinced that the canonical view on lending with interest was right. Peter Ramus (1515–1572), who later became the century's most famous logician, earned his master's degree in Paris in 1536 by defending the thesis that 'Everything which Aristotle had said is false'![65]

The third major area of interest for St Thomas and the Schoolmen was in determining what constituted a 'just price' – another issue central to the Aristotelian tradition. In the fragmented and inchoate state of most markets in the Middle Ages, where there was little opportunity for prices to be set in any objective way by large numbers of buyers and sellers, some idea of what constituted a reasonable and acceptable price had its advantages.[66] St Thomas denounced those who tried to charge what the market would bear, when taking advantage of buyers in a weak position, in forthright terms. 'I answer that it is wholly sinful to practise fraud for the express purpose of selling a thing for more than its just price ... To sell dearer or to buy cheaper than a thing is worth is in itself unjust and unlawful.'[67] Determining what a just price should be, however, if this was something different and more wholly acceptable than whatever the conventional price happened to be, proved to be no easy task. The same kind of problems were involved as were later to be encountered when more highly developed versions of the Labour Theory of Value were put forward. Even St Thomas had to recognise that prices fluctuated, and that too many exceptions had to be made for the 'just price' concept to have the rigour he would have liked. Gradually, more and more flexibility had to be introduced, leading eventually to recognition of the impersonal forces of the market.[68] All the same, the appeal of prices which are 'fair' is still with us in modern legacies such as controlled rents, guaranteed prices to farmers and minimum wages.[69]

The story of the medieval Canonists is therefore one of tactical retreat in the face of the major changes which were taking place in society. While the Church was powerful enough during the early Middle Ages to control the relatively limited level of economic activity which was then taking place, as Europe began to burgeon, the constraints which the Church tried to impose became increasingly out of touch with the times. An important result was that economic thought became more and more independent of religion, which in turn became one of the reasons for the decline in the Church's once all-embracing hegemony.[70] This outcome, however, opened up new opportunities for thinkers with an independent cast of mind, of whom Nicole Oresme (c1320–1382), Bishop of Lisieux, was perhaps the most important during the late medieval period. He was the first to attempt to write a history of money, and to recognise some of the factors which led to its either holding or losing its value. Indeed, he has been described as the world's first monetarist.[71] He took the existence of trade for granted, and was much more concerned about the impact of the state, and particularly kings and princes who wanted to finance warfare, than the activities of traders on the state of the currency.[72] He was the first to link clearly the responsibility for maintaining the value of the currency with the government of the day, and he railed against the debasement of the coinage which too many rulers, in his view, had allowed to occur. 'Who, then,' he asked 'would trust a prince who should diminish the weight or fineness of money bearing his own stamp?'[73]

Questions about maintaining the value of money were also the major concern of the last major figure in economics prior to the completion of the shift in intellectual fashion away from the Canon Law to the new Mercantilism. By the time of Jean Bodin (c1530–1596), a French jurist whose fame also lies in the field of political science to which he contributed the theory of sovereignty,[74] Europe was experiencing the increase in the price level which had started in the second decade of the sixteenth century. Although others, such as Navarrus (1493–1586), who had shared a spell at the University of Toulouse with him, had also done work in the same area, Bodin was the first to articulate clearly the Quantity Theory of Money. He attributed the rise in prices in Europe at the time to the abundance of gold and especially silver which was flowing in from the New World, following the discovery of America in 1492. Bodin saw in the abundance of gold and silver the 'principal and almost only reason'[75] for the inflation which concerned him, but he was not much impressed by the accumulation of treasure as a major national objective. In this he differed sharply from the Mercantilists who were soon to follow him.

Mercantilism

Mercantilism, or Merchant Capitalism, provided the dominant framework for thinking about economic issues for roughly the 300 years from towards the end of the fifteenth century to the closing years of the eighteenth century.[76] It had no acknowledged spokesperson. It was a system rather than a theory, developed mostly by people in business and the professions, although some, particularly on the continent, were government officials. The appeal of its tenets waxed as Europe prospered in the shadow of the Renaissance and the development of the nation state. It waned as the intellectual climate moved in a different and more sophisticated direction, prompted by the advent of the Industrial Revolution, and exemplified by the publication of Adam Smith's *Wealth of Nations* and the American Declaration of Independence, both of which occurred in 1776.[77]

Mercantilism was strongly associated with the rise of commercially dominant cities. Venice, Florence and Bruges were in an earlier wave, giving way later to Antwerp, Amsterdam, London and the Hansa cities.[78] Its development as a system was heavily influenced by the changes in perception of what it was possible to achieve, occasioned particularly both by the discovery of America and the route to India, and the impact on government revenues of vast quantities of silver from the New World.[79] The new sea routes opened up much greater trade possibilities than had existed previously, generating in turn the need for colonies to protect the territorial interests of the big trading monopolies which became established, such as the British and Dutch East India Companies, founded respectively in 1600 and 1602.[80]

Medieval support for monopolies made this form of organisation seem the natural way to support trading activities,[81] while the need to protect extended commercial ventures strongly increased the bonds between the state and merchant interests all over Europe.[82] The abundance of money plus the inflation which came with it were a major incentive to economic expansion,[83] while the increased revenues received by state treasuries provided the finance for larger-scale warfare. Max Weber (1864–1920) estimated that military expenditures accounted for about 70% of all Spanish revenues during this period, and about two-thirds of those of other European countries.[84] Prices increased particularly fast in those regions most affected by the advent of New World treasure. They rose fivefold in

Andalusia in Southern Spain between 1500 and 1600, and increased every-where else too, even if generally not so sharply.[85] It was not clear, however, that this inflation was entirely caused by bullion from the New World. The rise in prices throughout Europe had started in the 1510s, well before major shipments of gold and silver began. Potosi, the main silver mine, was not discovered until 1545, and gold shipments did not average 1,000kg a year until the 1530s.[86]

The thinkers and writers who shaped the Mercantilist consensus came from many countries: Antoine de Montchrétian (1576–1621) in France; Antonio Serra (precise dates unknown) in Italy; Philipp W. von Hornick (1838–1712) in Austria; Johann Joachim Becher (1635–1682) in Germany; and Thomas Mun (1571–1641), an employee of the British East India Company and perhaps the best known of all, in England.[87] All of them shared the leading features in the Mercantilist outlook. Gold bullion and treasure of every kind was the essence of wealth. Foreign trade should be regulated to produce an inflow of gold and silver, by ensuring that more goods and services were exported than imported. Industry should be encouraged to buy cheap raw-material from abroad, matched by protective duties on imported manufactured goods. Exporting, particularly the sale overseas of finished goods, should be fostered wherever possible. Population growth was favoured, both to strengthen the state and to keep wages down. The core of the Mercantilist doctrine was that a favourable balance of trade was desirable because it was seen as the key to national prosperity.[88]

Powerfully underpinning these ideas, across Europe strong unitary states were emerging and consolidating themselves. To what extent were these new states created for, rather than used by, the new merchant interests? The answer is that it is difficult to explain the evolution of state policies during the long period during which Mercantilism held centre stage without acknowledging the extent to which the state was the creature of commercial interests, one of whose main objectives was to make sure that they could manipulate it to their best advantage.[89] Mercantilism had firm roots in national defence and aggression,[90] and was pre-eminently an ideology suited to the powerful merchant classes which had emerged. Serra took it for granted that everyone understood 'how important it is, both for peoples and for princes, that a kingdom should abound in gold and silver'.[91] Becher had no doubt that 'it is always better to sell goods to others than to buy goods from others, for the former brings a certain advantage and the latter inevitable damage'.[92]

How effective was Mercantilism as a doctrine? Adam Smith began his well-known critique of it with an accurately targeted attack on the popular notion that 'wealth consists in money, in gold and silver' rather than in the value of goods and services.[93] There were soon few people who doubted that he was right. Smith not only produced a highly convincing theoretical case against some of the central tenets of Mercantilism, but was also in tune with the changing climate of opinion among key parts of the now increasingly rapidly evolving economy. By the eighteenth century, the Mercantilist support for monopolies was starting to fall foul of the rising number of industrialists who saw them as obstacles to the advancement of their interests, and wanted to get rid of them.[94] As industry began to develop, there was also increasing opposition to Mercantilist-inspired protectionism. This including prohibitions on the exports of tools and skilled craftsmen, and the Navigation Acts – with their equivalents in other countries – which confined the carrying of British goods to British ships.[95]

It does not follow, however, that all the elements of the Mercantilist approach were wrong or worthless, or that some of the concepts which it spawned did not have lasting value. Mercantilism was defended at least in part by Keynes in *The General Theory*: 'As a contribution to statecraft, which is concerned with economic systems as a whole and securing the optimum employment of the system's entire resources, the methods of the early pioneers of economic thinking in the sixteenth and seventeenth centuries may have attained to fragments of practical wisdom which the unrealistic abstractions of Ricardo first forgot and then obliterated.'[96] The Mercantilist view that trade depended on sufficient quantities of money being available to finance it was surely correct, and at a time when banking was relatively undeveloped and paper money barely existed, this meant adequate coinage. Where money was scarce, trade was sluggish; where it was abundant trade boomed.[97]

The notion that bullionism – the accumulation of gold and silver as a prime policy objective – was necessarily wrong was therefore wide of the mark. European prosperity had been held back by a severe shortage of coinage during the early Middle Ages until, towards the end of the twelfth century, silver finds in Germany and elsewhere greatly increased the money supply.[98] Everyone could see how the fresh bullion supplies from the New World were stimulating trading conditions. At a time when adequate coinage was the only way of ensuring a sufficient money supply, running a balance of payments surplus to make sure that coins were accumulated, and did not drain out of the country, made sense. Furthermore, careful thought about the conditions required to achieve this objective led to other advances. Thomas Mun was one of the earlier writers to realise that it was the overall balance of trade which mattered, not bilateral trade balances.[99] To Mun, money was primarily valuable, not for itself, but as a medium of international exchange to 'drive trade'.[100] Such sophistication was not, however, always evident. Confusion between bullion accumulation for its own sake and the more sophisticated concept of a trade surplus remained. Regulations to stop the export of bullion failed to work, but were not formally abolished in Britain until 1663.[101]

The Mercantilists were also right to regard high interest rates as being a deterrent to good trading conditions. The fact that, during the seventeenth century, interest rates in Holland, averaging about 6%, were well below the 10% or so prevailing in Britain, undoubtedly was a factor in keeping the effectiveness of the merchant capitalism of the Dutch well ahead of the British.[102] Concern on this score was eloquently expressed by Sir Josiah Child, at the time the richest merchant in Britain, in his book *A New Discourse on Trade* which went through many printings.[103] Child was the first person to propose the idea of general economic progress, setting an English trend towards an empirical and undogmatic attitude to economic statecraft.[104] His arguments echoed those of Sir Thomas Culpeper (1568–1662) who in 1621 published his *Tract Against the High Rate of Usury*, a publication which was reprinted in an expanded version in 1668 by his son of the same name.[105] The Culpepers argued, quite rightly, that interest was a cost and that those countries with the lowest interest rates would be more competitive. The idea that high interest rates lowered prices first surfaced in 1832,[106] and had as little evidential support then as it has now.

No account of Mercantilist views should conclude without describing a new approach to the creation of wealth, which did not depend on gold and silver, but on paper money.[107] This was pioneered by John Law (1671–1729), a Scotsman who found his opportunity in Paris in 1716, the year after the death of Louis XIV whose many wars and other extravagances had left the French Treasury empty. State receipts were only half the expenditure which needed to be financed, and Law's proposal to establish a bank, whose primary function was to lend money to the state, received a ready hearing, although Law's previous efforts to establish such ventures in Paris, Edinburgh and Savoy had all been turned down. Law was a man of considerable intellect and experience, whose *Money and Trade Considered: With a Proposal for Supplying the Nation with Money*, published in 1705, shared the view, current among other writers of the time, that increasing the money supply would not cause inflation provided that the volume of business transactions expanded *pari passu* with the extra money that was made available.[108]

Initially the notes issued by the bank were eminently acceptable not only for the payment of taxes, but for all other purposes. This was because Law's bank promised to redeem the notes with the same weight of metal as at the time of their issue, in contrast to the coinage generally, which had long continually been debased by clipping and by reducing its bullion content. For several months the increased liquidity significantly improved not only the condition of the state's finances, but also business conditions generally, leading the Regent to propose a second issue. Law not only acquiesced in this request, but also found a way of augmenting what was now called the Bank Royale's reserves by promoting a new venture, the Mississippi Company, to bring to France the large quantities of gold believed to lie

ready to be mined in Louisiana. Three years after its foundation, a speculative boom was under way, as the public flocked to buy shares in the Banque
Royale and its associated ventures, with the finance for the share purchases
largely being provided, directly or indirectly, by the bank itself.

As always, however, the solvency of the bank depended on its ability to
redeem for hard cash any notes which were presented to it. As confidence
began to ebb, so did the number of people increase who wanted to cash in
their notes. By 1720 the Banque Royale was bankrupt, leaving lost fortunes,
depressed business conditions, an abiding French distrust of banks, and the
condition of the French Treasury no better than it had been four years previously. Only land kept its value,[109] a matter which was not lost on the
Physiocrats, whose views on economics were shortly to enjoy considerable
influence in France and elsewhere. John Law left France for Venice, where
he spent the remainder of his life supporting himself by gambling.

Where does this leave Mercantilism in the long journey towards modern
economics? There are perhaps three key points to be made. First, the sheer
volume of writings on the economic policy issues which Mercantilist concepts generated did much to establish economics as a separate branch of
study, and to provide a sophisticated structure of ideas on which others
could later build. Second, the writings of the Mercantilist period, partly
because of the occupations of those who produced most of them, were
heavily coloured by the interests of the rising merchant classes.
Mercantilism was mostly concerned with establishing how to run unitary
states as successfully as possible in the interests of those engaged in trade,
rather than how to achieve wider objectives. In serving primarily the interests of the rich and powerful, however, the economic thinking of the
Mercantilists merely reinforced a trend which was to be much in evidence
in the future. Third, the thrust of Mercantilist thinking was largely orientated to dealing as well as possible with practical problems. It had a down
to earth quality which much which was to follow lacked. It is easy to
criticise, in the light of subsequent developments, what Mercantilism got
wrong. It is not always so easy to recognise the extent to which many of its
tenets were basically valid, at least in the circumstances of the time.

The Physiocrats

The Physiocrats were a group of thinkers and writers in France during the
years leading up to the 1789 French Revolution. Whereas the Mercantilists
had generally been concerned with particular aspects of policy, the
Physiocrats were the first to develop a general description of the whole economic process, employing the scientific methods of isolation and abstrac-
tion.[110] They worked, however, in a strange environment. Pre-Revolutionary
France was teetering towards bankruptcy and collapse, and the Physiocrats
were aware of many of the deficiencies in the way the state was run.[111]

Their primary objective was not radically to change the structure of French society, as happened when the Revolution took place, but to reform it to a point where it could survive. Their system was therefore necessarily designed not to promote liberal capitalism but to perpetuate absolute monarchy.[112] They failed in this endeavour, but made a substantial mark on the progress of economics in the process.

In eighteenth-century France, agriculture was pre-eminent not only economically but socially too. The landed interest was at the apex of social hierarchy, and trade and commerce were generally despised. This backdrop provided the Physiocrats with the notion that all wealth derives from agriculture and the land, which was therefore responsible for producing all the *produit net* – what we would now call the value added – in the economy. Commerce and industry, referred to disparagingly by the Physiocrats as the 'Sterile Class', merely recycled *produit net* which had already been created by agriculture, adding no new value in the process. This view of the world naturally provided a justification for a class structure with landowners at the top, workers on the soil in the next layer down, with all those involved in other forms of commerce at the bottom. With this formulation, it was a short step to take to see the primary role of the state as supporting agriculture.[113] It also, however, had some odd by-products, not least being the problem of whom to tax. If the so-called Sterile Classes produced no *produit net*, it did not appear to be realistic to treat their activities as an appropriate source of revenue for the state. The logical conclusion was that all tax, ultimately at least, needed to be on land. This was an idea which was to find echoes in the land tax proposals advocated by Henry George a hundred years later,[114] when they encountered as little enthusiasm among landowners then as they did in pre-Revolutionary France. Indeed, land taxes had a long history of generating unmanageable opposition, as, among others, King James I of England and VI of Scotland (1566–1625) had discovered when, as part of his 'Contract with the People', he introduced proposals for one on his arrival from Edinburgh to take up the throne in London.[115]

To ensure that the economy worked as efficiently as possible, the Physiocrats advocated that what they called Natural Law should prevail as widely as possible. Natural Law was held to be self-evident, and was not therefore alterable by the positive action of statecraft.[116] It provided the justification for reforming many of the abuses of pre-Revolutionary France, whose economy was by then a tissue of tax farming, monopolies, tax exemptions for favoured groups and restrictions on trading. Natural Law promoted the interest of private property but otherwise lent in the direction of minimal interference in economic relationships by the state – generating the celebrated Physiocratic concept of *laissez faire, laissez passer*, which included free trade. This was a major break with the Mercantilist tradition, which had always tended to favour regulation.[117] Another major difference in the approaches of the two schools of thought was over the merits of exporting – especially manufactured goods – and the achievement of a balance of payments surplus. Instead of regarding this as a prime objective, the Physiocrats believed that high exports could only be achieved if prices were held down, which would damage agriculture. On the contrary, the Physiocrats believed that a *bon prix* – a high price – for agricultural output was in the national interest, and that exporting should concentrate on the sale of agricultural output abroad rather than manufactures. 'Happy the land which has no exports of manufactures because agricultural exports maintain farm prices at too high a level to permit the sterile class to sell its products abroad.'[118]

This quotation came from the writings of the most important figure among the Physiocrats, François Quesnay (1694–1774), who came to economics aged 62, after a varied career which included having been physician to both Madame de Pompadour and Louis XV.[119] He was responsible for all the main aspects of Physiocratic thought, and, in particular, for its economic analysis.[120] Not least of his contributions was his *Tableau Economique*, which was an early pictorial model of the circular flow of the national income, and of its annual reproduction.[121] The significance of this innovation was not only in introducing an idea which was subsequently to be developed into input–output tables, but to emphasise the concept and importance of equilibrium.[122] Quesnay also developed a variation of the Labour Theory of Value, associated with his notions of the *bon prix*, which added to the tradition inherited by his successors, not least the British classical economists.[123] The other major Physiocratic figure was Anne Robert Jacques Turgot (1727–1781) whose influence was augmented by his rise to become Comptroller General and Minister of Finance. Unfortunately, however, his attempts to push through reforms along Physiocratic lines led to his downfall in 1776, at the behest of the many vested interests whom he threatened, only two years after he had taken up his position.[124] Turgot's main contribution was in developing a theory of capital, reinforcing the view later enunciated as 'Say's Law', and not challenged by Adam Smith, that any saving is always 'immediately' converted into capital, thus making it impossible for it to lead to less demand for goods and services.[125] This was one of the less happy legacies of the Physiocrats.

While they produced some interesting and lasting ideas, it has to be said that the coherence and practical viability of the Physiocratic programme was extremely limited. Their concentration on the exclusive merits of agricultural output, while a reflection of the times and circumstances in which they lived, was more than anachronistic, coinciding, as it did, with the start of the Industrial Revolution. Their proposals for ridding the economy of the *Ancien Régime* of many of the restrictions and distortions from which it suffered no doubt had merit, and the case for taking the necessary action may have been buttressed by philosophical arguments based on Natural Law. Ultimately, however, the case for reform depended much more directly on appeals to common sense than philosophy, and, where they were successful, the practical effect of their taxation and *laissez faire* policies was to encourage trade and industry, however much the Physiocrats may have despised them.[126]

The more important legacy left by the Physiocrats was not so much in their practical policy recommendations, or the reasons they gave for advocating them, but in the way in which they approached the problems they set out to solve. They were the first to realise the significance of production as opposed to trading and exchange as the primary source of wealth, and in this respect they were well ahead of the Mercantilists. The central point of their analysis was the search for the *produit net* – not a bad proxy for the concept of value added, now central to all modern economic analysis – and how it should be distributed. The *Tableau* not only illustrated the extent to which all sectors of the economy were independent, but highlighted for the first time how crucial equilibrium between them was.[127] Adam Smith, who visited Paris and met some of the Physiocrats judged that 'This system ... with all its imperfections, is, perhaps the nearest approximation to the truth that has yet been published upon the subject of political economy.'[128] When he wrote these words, however, his own *Wealth of Nations* had not yet seen the light of day.

4
Classical Economics

> The experience of being disastrously wrong is salutary; no economist should be denied it, and not many are.

John Kenneth Galbraith (born 1908)

Classical Economics, developed largely, although not exclusively, in Britain, which led the way in the Industrial Revolution, had three main underpinnings. One was the philosophic liberalism, developed from its canonical origins, with the emphasis in the writings of Thomas Hobbes (1588–1679) and John Locke (1632–1704) on the individual and the state as the protector of property rights. The second was the foundation laid by the later writers on Mercantilism, and in particular its critics. The third was the French Physiocratic system and, in this case, not so much its particular recommendations, but more the overall approach taken by its leading writers to the way economic issues should be tackled.[1]

The background was the unfolding growth in output per head which was becoming increasingly apparent to acute observers in Britain during the eighteenth century, as both agriculture and manufacturing began to transform themselves. At the beginning of the eighteenth century, the Dutch had a better-developed economy, and a higher standard of living on average than the British, but over the next hundred years Britain moved well ahead. Whereas the Dutch depended on trade, reflecting the preoccupations of Mercantilist thought, the newly developing economy in Britain had different roots. In addition to the advantages shared with the Dutch of a stable political background, a developed system of contract law, and a reasonably well-developed banking system, Britain also had an entrepreneurial class which was attracted to agriculture and industry, as well as to trading. Coupled with the benefit of early developments in science, and a long tradition of able artisanship, British industry began to move ahead in textiles, pottery and metal work, as well as mining, canals and agriculture.

The first practical steam engine was developed as early as 1712 by Thomas Newcomen, and greatly improved by James Watt from 1769 onwards. John Kay's flying shuttle was invented in 1733, and Richard Arkwright's water frame in 1769. The first major British canal, for which James Brindley (1716–1772) was the consulting engineer, was completed in 1761, for the Third Duke of Bridgewater (1736–1803), to carry coal from his collieries to Manchester.[2] The resulting establishment of large commercial operations, often in areas such as much of the Midlands, where previously few large towns had existed, led to the continuing decline of wage regulation, the traditional apprentice system and the guilds. The outwork system, where entrepreneurs delivered work to the homes of those who carried it out before it was collected again, became more common. Monopolies gradually disappeared or became undermined, although the East India Company lasted until the second half of the nineteenth century.[3] The major change which took place as the Industrial Revolution started was away from the merchant, whose orientation was to the purchase and sale of goods, to the industrialist who concentrated on their production.[4]

The ideas making up Classical Economics were not, therefore, just occasioned by the coming together of English liberalism, late Mercantilism and the legacy of the French Physiocrats. The changes in perception which were taking place were also very much a consequence of the new conditions and prospects opened up by the Industrial Revolution. The key issue is the extent to which the scope for exponential increases in output and productivity which industrialisation presented for the advancement of humanity was adequately grasped and exploited by the economic theories which came to the fore at the end of the eighteenth and the beginning of the nineteenth centuries. A major part of the thesis in this book is that, after an excellent start with Adam Smith's *Wealth of Nations*, a great opportunity was wasted by the next generation of writers who took centre stage, as they failed to take adequate advantage of the foundation which Smith had laid. On the contrary, they tended to home in on and develop those parts of Smith's legacy where he was in error, while failing to carry forward his vision of the state's role in promoting economic advance by providing appropriate structures and incentives to enable the full potential of the Industrial Revolution to be realised.

The reaction against Mercantilism

Much of the reducing influence of Mercantilist thought on both policy-makers and among thinkers and writers during the eighteenth century came not so much from the deficiencies of Mercantilist policies – although these became increasingly attacked – but from a widening out in perspective generally about the scope and range of intellectual thought. The development of the scientific method, pioneered by Francis Bacon (1561–1626) at the beginning of the seventeenth century in a series of highly influential works, had provided the world with a much more effective way than had been available previously to sift out the most viable working hypotheses. Thomas Hobbes, who had for some time been Bacon's secretary as well as tutor to Charles II,[5] and John Locke, some 40 years his junior, had provided a coherent defence of individual rights, particularly to the private owner-ship of property, though there was some difference in their formulations. Locke viewed property as being a natural right, and its protection to be the principal purpose of government, whereas Hobbes had regarded it as being a creation of the sovereign state.[6] Either way, their emphasis on individual rights helped to shift the style of policymaking away from the collectivist approach, which broadly characterised both canonical and Mercantilist thinking, towards looking for solutions which might better harness private initiative, not least towards the *laissez faire* attitude advocated by the Physiocrats.

Rapid advances in mathematics, medicine and the physical sciences opened up new horizons, indicating how much further it might be possible to push human knowledge and control over events, given sufficient deter-mination and application to do so. Some of those involved in making new discoveries also played a major role in public life, such as Sir Isaac Newton (1642–1727), who not only had an important part in the early eighteenth century controversy over the respective valuations of gold and silver coins, and the recoinage of the latter, but who also became Warden of the Mint.[7] It was in this capacity that he was responsible for fixing in 1711 the value of the pound in terms of an ounce of gold at £3 17s 9d, which was still its value at the beginning of 1931.

John Locke, who, incidentally was on the other side of the recoinage con-troversy to Newton, himself made a significant contribution to economics as well as to philosophy. He wrote extensively on monetary matters and the implications of the quantity of money on changes in the price level, though he drew the wrong conclusions about the impact of liquidity on economic performance, denying that low domestic prices, caused by a shortage of money, would increase exports and thus restore the trade balance.[8] This was an issue which was not to be satisfactorily resolved until, as we shall see shortly, David Hume provided a clear explanation of the process at work.[9] Locke's writings also provided a basis for the Labour Theory of Value. This cornerstone of the highly influential writings of David Ricardo was to be one of the banes of economic theory until the 1870s.[10]

Other significant critics of Mercantilist thought included Sir William Petty (1623–1687), who had a varied and distinguished career in several different academic and practical fields. Although he followed Locke on the Labour Theory of Value, he made major contributions in other respects. He was very much an empiricist, and one of the first to empha-sise the need for reliable data and statistics.[11] He also conceived the idea of the national income – the aggregate of all output in the economy over a given period – and he made the first calculations as to what it might be, which was an outstanding achievement in taking economic thinking forward.[12] He was also the first to grapple with the concept of the velocity of circulation of money – i.e. the ratio between the amount of money in circulation and the total value of all transactions in a given period – a matter of critical importance to the control of the economy by monetary methods, and an outstanding example of how Petty hammered out concepts from, and in connection with, his statistical investigations.[13]

Another important work – his *Discourses* – was written by Sir Dudley North (1641–1691), published at almost the same time as he died. While the general tenor of Mercantilist thinking was opposed to free trade, North was strongly in favour of it, especially with France.[14] He was also the first to see the whole world as an economic unit, rather than just the individual nation state. He had little patience with the accumulation of wealth for its own sake, although he understood its importance for financing trade.[15] North also opposed proposals current at the time for restricting the maximum rate of interest on the grounds that it was better to let the market find its own level – another step towards the liberalisation of finance and commerce from detailed state control.[16]

Even more significant was the work of David Hume (1711–1776). As well as contributing significantly to philosophy, Hume also has an important place as an exponent of the new political economy. He viewed landowners as prone to extravagance and disinclined to save, and took a much more favourable view of the contribution to the prosperity of the economy of those engaged in commerce and industry. He recognised self-interest and the desire for accumulation as driving forces in economic activity, helping to reinforce the attitudes among business people which were then coming to the fore.[17] His most substantial contribution, however, was to explain clearly, and for the first time, how the flow of specie – gold and silver – was the controlling factor in promoting equilibrium between different economies trading with each other – the factor which had eluded Locke. A balance of payments surplus produced an inflow of gold and silver, which led to a rise in economic activity and upward pressure on the price level. This would work its way through to reducing export competitiveness, thus eventually diminishing the export surplus, and restoring equilibrium.[18] Hume also thought that there was a tendency for economic opportunity to migrate to areas with the lowest cost base – on account of 'the low price of labour in every nation which has not an extensive commerce, and does not much abound in gold and silver',[19] a concept to which this book argues that modern economics has paid far too little attention. He also viewed commerce as being a civilising influence, a point commented on by Smith.[20]

Finally, in this brief survey of the major figures prior to Adam Smith, mention needs to be made of Richard Cantillon (1697–1734), who was probably the clearest exponent of all the current economic issues prior to Smith.[21] Cantillon is a strange figure, who amassed a large fortune at a young age, much of it by speculating successfully in Law's banking activities in Paris, before he died in a mysterious fire when he was only 37.[22] His major work, *Essay on the Nature of Trade in General* was not published until 1755, nearly 20 years after his death, and then in a French translation. This, however, meant that his work became well known to the Physiocrats, as well as to English readers. Cantillon's main role was to synthesise and explain the concepts with which economics was becoming increasingly familiar. It was in this capacity that he played an important role in laying the foundations for the work which was to be carried forward by subsequent writers. He also realised the key role of the entrepreneur, and the fact that his work was published in France may have been an important reason why French economists never lost sight of this function and its central importance.[23]

By three-quarters of the way through the eighteenth century, therefore, economics had come a considerable distance. It has been argued that, although only a few writers prior to Adam Smith were free traders, all the basic elements of the classical approach to economic activity are embedded in Mercantilist literature, or its critics.[24] It now needed Smith to pull all the threads together into the clear and elegant exposition which he so effectively produced.

Adam Smith

Adam Smith, the first truly academic economist,[25] was born in 1723 in Kirkcaldy, a small port on the other side of the Firth of Forth from Edinburgh, where his father was the customs collector. After school, Smith went to university, first in Glasgow and then at Oxford. He then returned to Glasgow where he became Professor first of Logic and then of Moral Philosophy. He published his first book, *The Theory of Modern Sentiments*, in 1759. Four years later he resigned from the university to become tutor to the young Duke of Buccleuch. This appointment provided Smith with the opportunity to tour Europe with his aristocratic charge. They visited Voltaire in Geneva and Quesnay and Turgot in Paris. There is little doubt that the cosmopolitan tone of Smith's writing reflected the breadth of experience he had while travelling outside Britain. He began to write the *Wealth of Nations* while in France, and he continued to work on it for a further ten years after returning to Britain. It was published in 1776, the same year as the American Declaration of Independence. A consequence of the fame Smith thus acquired was that he was offered a sinecure – in the best Mercantilist tradition – as a commissioner of customs in Edinburgh, where he died in 1790.[26]

An Inquiry into the Nature and Causes of the Wealth of Nations,[27] to give it its full title, was an immediate success, and the first two-volume edition sold out almost at once. The reception it received was extremely favourable from the beginning, and of course the fact that it was so widely read was a major reason why its influence was as great as it was. Part of the reason why his book was so popular was that Smith's writing style, in contrast with far too many books on economics, is full of anecdote and side comments, and is highly readable. When Adam Smith's friend Edward Gibbon wrote to a mutual colleague saying 'What an excellent work is that with which our common friend Mr. Adam Smith has enriched the public ... [offering] ... the most profound ideas expressed in the most perspicuous language'[28] he echoed an opinion of the *Wealth of Nations* which is widely held and richly deserved.

Smith's book had three major themes: what, broadly, motivates economic activity? What determines prices and the distribution of income and wealth? What are the policies by which the state supports and encourages economic progress and prosperity?[29] In providing answers to these questions, Smith no doubt drew on all the previous literature dealing with economic issues, but by power of his expression and clarity of exposition, combined with his own common sense and intelligence, he succeeded in threading together an altogether different way of looking at most of the key economic issues of his day.

On economic motivation, Smith firmly gave self-interest pride of place. 'It is not from the benevolence of the butcher, the brewer, or the baker, that we expect our dinner, but from their regard to their own interest. We address ourselves, not to their humanity, but to their self love.' The individual 'is in this, as in many other cases, led by an invisible hand to promote an end which was no part of his intention ... I have never known much good done by those who affected to trade for the public good. It is an affectation, indeed, not very common among merchants, and very few words need be employed in dissuading them from it.'[30] Self-interest is the great unifying principle of the *Wealth of Nations*, harking back to Smith's earlier writing in *The Theory of Moral Sentiments*.[31] Though foreshadowed by writers such as Hume, this was a major change in perception from nearly all that had preceded it. Previously, the notion of self-enrichment as a motive had been regarded with mistrust and suspicion, a sentiment that could be easily traced back to the teachings of the Church. Now, the invisible hand was made the centrepiece of economic motivation – a position from which it has never since been moved.[32]

On the issues of value, distribution and prices, Smith was much influenced by the new conditions thrown up by the Industrial Revolution. As paid employment became much more prevalent compared to the self-employment of subsistence farming and small-scale commercial activity, so the issue of who should get what share of the value of whatever was being produced became more critical. Similarly, when the ownership of land became separated from the person who farmed it, the rent payable by the tenant farmer to the landlord became an increasingly important matter. How was each determined and justified?

Whereas on the issue of economic motivation, Smith carried all before him, his analysis of value and prices, and why they were distributed the way they were, is less satisfying and convincing. There had long been a baffling problem, going back to Aristotle, as to why the prices attributed to some commodities which were so important, such as water, were so low, while the prices of others, such as diamonds – described by Smith as 'the greatest of all superfluities',[33] should be very much higher. The solution to this problem was not to be found until the Marginal Revolution a hundred years later. In the meantime, Smith fell back on his own version of the Labour Theory of Value, which also had a long history. This is the concept that the worth of any goods or services is to be measured by the amount of labour required to produce them. As Smith said, 'The value of any commodity ... to the person who possesses it ... is equal to the quantity of labour which it enables him to purchase or command. Labour, therefore, is the real measure of the exchangeable value of all commodities.'[34] In another passage he says that 'The real price of everything, what everything really costs to the man who wants to acquire it, is the toil and trouble of acquiring it.'[35] In yet another section of the *Wealth of Nations*, where he compares the time taken to catch a beaver and a deer, there is much heavier emphasis on measuring solely the quantity of labour involved rather than allowing also for its quality, as is implied in his main exposition.[36]

Smith was aware, however, that all these formulations were less than fully satisfactory. Clearly, costs other than labour were involved in producing goods and services, not least rent. Furthermore, as capitalist production got under way, it was evident that costs were also bound up with the provision of capital equipment and a return to those who had invested in it. Additional difficulties were caused by introducing the concept of 'toil and trouble', implying that there were other reasons for costs being incurred than simply the application of a uniform unit of labour, whether or not it was graded for quality. There were also problems about the subjective perceptions of value, which sometimes cut across the work put into their production. On the whole, however, Smith inclined to the view that it was labour production costs which were most significant. The value of a unit of labour was essentially the cost of bringing a worker into being, and then sustaining him – references to female workers are virtually non-existent in nineteenth-century writings on economics – in a job. This was the subsistence theory of wages, which was later transformed by Ricardo and Malthus into the Iron Law of Wages, implying that the wages paid to the labouring classes would never be more than what was necessary for their survival.

Smith also struggled with the return on capital and to the entrepreneur, whether in the form of interest or profits, to which the Labour Theory of Value, in any of its varying forms, provided no satisfactory explanation. If it was only the labour content of production which determined rightful costs, it appeared that the capitalist's profit was an unjustifiable exaction – a view which underpinned much of Marx's work in the middle of the nineteenth century.[37] In the end, however, Smith himself recognised that this part of his work was less than satisfactory. In a characteristically honest comment, he explained that it was 'a subject extremely abstracted' and 'it may perhaps, after the fullest explication which I am capable of giving it, appear still in some degree obscure', a comment which has been described, perhaps justifiably, as 'the greatest understatement in the history of economic thought'.[38] Partly because of this confusion, the legacy left by Smith's Labour Theory of Value helped to establish two very different traditions. One, broadly adopted by the Classical Economists, was of harmony between the factors of production, while those who became radical critics inclined to accept that exploitation was the key characteristic upon which to seize.[39]

Rent was another topic on which Smith did not produce particularly satisfactory formulations. Sometimes it appears that he thought that rent was a separate cost from other components making up total prices. At others, however, he took it to be a residual, after other costs had been deducted. 'Rent ... enters into the composition of the price of commodities in different ways from wages and profit. High or low wages and profit are the causes of high or low price; high or low rent is the effect of it.'[40] He then explained that this was to do with the quality of the land. 'The rent increases in proportion to the goodness of the pasture.'[41]

On public policy, however, Smith was on much firmer ground. He drew on the work of his predecessors such as Sir William Petty and David Hume, but took his analysis well beyond theirs. His greatest emphasis was on the benefit of free internal and international trade, which would allow what he believed to be the key benefit of the Industrial Revolution – specialisation and the division of labour – to be exploited to a much greater extent than would be feasible without the largest possible market. Smith was fascinated by the pin factory with which he was well acquainted, and he describes in accurate detail all the different processes used to produce pins, and the far higher total output made possible by each worker concentrating on a particular part of the process. Interestingly, Smith did not really appreciate the extent to which the application of machinery and power was the engine of increased output rather than the division of labour.[42] In this respect, his pin factory, which was evidently not very highly mechanised, may have been a misleading example of where the Industrial Revolution was leading, weakening his argument for unrestricted free trade. Had Smith seen the much bigger factories which were to be commissioned shortly after the publication of his book, he might have taken a different view.[43]

Smith's attack on the accumulation of bullion as the talisman of the wealth of the nation, rather than the totality of output it was capable of producing has never been seriously challenged since he made it. The opening words of the *Wealth of Nations* proclaim that it is not its gold or silver which measures a nation's wealth but that 'the annual labour of every nation ... is the fund which originally supplies it with all the necessaries and conveniences of life'. The nation's wealth is produced by 'the skill, dexterity, and judgement with which its labour is generally applied; and, secondly, by the proportion between the number of those who are employed in useful labour, and those who are not so employed',[44] although Smith had some difficulties with those who were not 'usefully employed'. Among those he listed as being in this category were princes, churchmen, armies and opera singers,[45] a distinction eventually successfully attacked as being untenable.[46]

As to monetary policy, Smith thought that exports would attract sufficient money in circulation to keep the economy prosperous, with prices held down and an abundance of products available as a result of the increased competition made possible by free trade.[47] He did not envisage the likelihood of shortage of demand. He did not, therefore, challenge the critical assumption, carried through to Classical Economics, and not toppled, at least among mainstream economists, until Keynes, that savings would automatically create the same volume of spending on investment. Instead, following previous writers such as Turgot, he held that the portion of income which was saved 'is immediately employed as capital',[48] a mistake for which humanity was to pay a high price for the next 150 years. As regards foreign trade, Smith was not dogmatic about the benefit of unfettered markets. He was willing to accept that there could be cases where they were inappropriate, such as for essential defence industries, and in retaliation for foreign tariffs. He thought there might be occasions when even if tariffs needed to be removed, they should be reduced gradually to allow for adjustment.[49]

Just as Smith was generally against all forms of internal and external tariffs, he also opposed other forms of restrictions on trading. He denounced restrictive preferences, privileges and state grants of monopoly. He was also against combinations of both employers and workers in restraint of trade, though he characteristically noted that there were more laws against trades unions than there were against employers' organisations.[50] He was not, however, convinced that, even if they were outlawed, they would not re-emerge informally. In another often quoted passage Smith observes that 'people of the same trade seldom meet together, even for merriment and diversion, but the conversation ends in a conspiracy against the public, or in some contrivance to raise prices'.[51] From Smith comes the now almost universally held view that competition is to be preferred to monopoly, although Smith had in mind much more the owner-managed businesses characteristic of his time than the large corporations typical of the modern world. Some recent corporate boardroom behaviour nevertheless lends credence to Smith's view that 'Being the managers rather of other people's money than of their own, it cannot well be expected, that they should watch over it with the same anxious vigilance with which the partners in a private copartnery frequently watch over their own.'[52] Not that Smith had a rosy-eyed view of owner-managers. He constantly berated both merchants and manufacturers for wanting to 'widen the market and to narrow the competition'.[53]

As to the role of the state, Smith was strongly in favour of both a minimalist function, and parsimony in its execution. On countless occasions in the *Wealth of Nations*, he used the lessons of history and his contemporary experience to depict government as generally inefficient, corrupt, frivolous, wasteful and subject to the pressure of vested interests.[54] He therefore believed that the state ought to confine its activities to no more than the provision of defence, public works, and the administration of justice. Taxation should be certain, as convenient as possible, economical to assess and to raise, kept to a minimum, and levied proportionately to income. 'The subjects of every state ought to contribute towards the support of the government, as nearly as possible, in proportion to their respective abilities; that is, in proportion to the revenue which they respectively enjoy under the protection of the state.'[55]

The legacy thus left by Smith was a massive one. He did much to map out the field of economic inquiry in such a way that subsequent thinkers were guided by the landmarks which he established: production, value, distribution and the role of the state.[56] The *laissez faire* principle, competition and Smith's version of the Labour Theory of Value all became outstanding features of the Classical Economics.[57] The thought of most economists, including Ricardo, started from Smith, and it is widely recognised that most them never got much beyond him. At least until J.S. Mill's *Principles*, published in 1848, Smith supplied the bulk of the ideas for the average economist.[58] More than this, the *Wealth of Nations* set a standard for clarity of exposition and forward thinking which has perhaps never been equalled. There was much that Smith had to say about the new world which was opening up all round him. Perhaps even more important, however, was all that he did to undermine and demolish the legacy of previous thinking which was no longer apposite.[59]

Smith was not right about everything, and both his ideas about the Labour Theory of Value and saving automatically creating its own demand involved errors which were carried forward into the economic mainstream, with serious consequences. His achievements, however, surely outweigh these deficiencies. The clarity and precision with which he introduced new ideas such as self-interest, the importance of competition, and the significance of the division of labour, and the fervour with which he advocated older ones such as the benefits from freer trade and the removal of restrictions and monopolies, were huge achievements. It is true that it took time for his writing to have practical effects. With the exception of some import duty reductions introduced by Pitt the Younger in the 1780s, Britain's tariff wall was not lowered to any serious extent until the 1820s. The Law of Settlement, which restricted the mobility of labour, was only repealed in 1834, and the East India Company survived until the 1850s, only finally to be wound up after the Indian Mutiny.[60] It is also true, nevertheless, that the *Wealth of Nations* became close, in the end, to being the bible of the Industrial Revolution, and that its intellectual influence was massive, shaping the views of all economists who followed him.

Most important of all was Smith's breadth of vision. He was interested in the power of economics to address the whole spectrum of the human condition. It was a long time before anyone else was to tackle the canvas on this scale again.

Say, Malthus and Ricardo

The three most important economists to follow Adam Smith were all close contemporaries. One, Jean Baptiste Say (1767–1832), was French, and two, Thomas Malthus (1766–1834) and David Ricardo (1772–1823) were British.[61]

Jean Baptiste Say spent the early part of his career as a businessman helping to pioneer life insurance. He then joined the academic world, ending his working life at the Collège de France[62] where he was appointed France's first Professor of Political Economy in 1815.[63] He corresponded regularly with the other major economists of his day, including Malthus and Ricardo, as well as Sismondi, of whom more will be heard later. Say was a policy-orientated economist rather than a theoretical model builder like Ricardo, whom he described as one who 'pushes his reasonings to their remotest consequences, without comparing their results with those of actual experience'.[64] Say much preferred systematic analysis and empirical research to the abstract deductive method favoured by Ricardo and his followers.

Say's first claim to fame was as a translator of Adam Smith's work into French. This was not a literal translation, but a much more orderly work in the French tradition covering all Smith's major contributions. Although a great admirer of Smith, Say's book, *Traité d'economie politique* included a number of important concepts of his own. It was very successful both in France, where it did much to publicise Smith's ideas, and also in other languages, including English, into which it was in turn translated.[65]

One was the idea, subsequently validated by later more precise formulations, that the Labour Theory of Value was flawed, and that the reason for any good having a certain value or price depended not on the amount of labour which had gone into producing it, but to its utility. This was an important departure from the traditional view, and one which Say failed to persuade Ricardo to adopt despite correspondence between them culminating in a key letter written in 1822, shortly before Ricardo died. Say urged him to accept that it was 'the last quantity of useful things' which was crucial, this being the critically important element of the utility theory as it became accepted 50 years later. As we shall see, Ricardo never departed from his adherence to the fully fledged Labour Theory of Value, with baleful consequences for the development of economics in nineteenth-century Britain.

Say also carried on the tradition, established by Cantillon, and re-emphasised much later by Schumpeter, of ascribing a pivotal position in economic affairs to the role of the entrepreneur, this being another concept which was largely ignored by British Classical Economics. Say's interest in this aspect of economic development may well have stemmed from his own experience in commerce, and his background in a mercantile family with its own direct knowledge of entrepreneurial activity.[66] Interestingly, no major British economist from the eighteenth century onwards was a businessman, though Ricardo made a fortune as a stockbroker.

By far the most important contribution to economic thinking made by Say, however, concerned the vexed question of whether the reduction in current demand for goods and services caused by saving was automatically compensated for by increased spending on investment. On this issue, Say was in no doubt that it was, though there was some tension – which remained an outstanding issue – as to whether this happened as a matter of logic or as a matter of fact. Say's Law held that the proceeds from the sale of all the goods and services produced in the economy generated incomes which must exactly equal the value of all this output, although it has to be said that this is not exactly the way Say himself framed the proposition which is so closely connected with his name.[67] As so often happened with powerful ideas, Say's formulation was a good deal more subtle than the simplified version which became the common currency. As shaped by the tenets of Classical Economics, however, the concept gelled that there could, as a result of Say's Law, be no such thing as general overproduction and a shortage of demand for everything which was on the market. It was acknowledged that some part of all incomes was saved, but this was held to generate an exactly similar volume of investment, so that the balance between supply and demand was still there. In a rather more sophisticated version of Say's Law, it was recognised that not all the savings might be spent at the same time as they took place but, in these circumstances, prices were expected to adjust themselves downwards to cater for the temporary lower flow of income. There could still be no general excess of production in relation to the available purchasing power.[68]

This was an exceedingly simple and powerful idea and, although it was challenged from time to time, it remained the conventional wisdom until the 1930s. Malthus had early reservations about whether its tenets held good, as did Marx. Furthermore, the recurrent booms, followed by recessions and rising unemployment, which afflicted the developing economies of the nineteenth century, provided increasingly clear evidence that supply and demand were not always in balance. Such disturbances were not allowed, however, to undermine the sanctity of Say's Law. They were put down to temporary periods of adjustment and frictional problems in the labour market rather than to any general flaw in Say's argument.[69] It was not until Keynes and the Great Depression that the fundamental error in Say's Law was admitted. This was a major defect in Classical Economics, and it had very substantial practical ramifications.

For Say's Law imposed enormous limitations on the capacity of the state to remedy economic conditions which showed signs of under-demand. If no such state of affairs could exist, there was no reason for trying to counteract it. This then became a compelling argument for government non-intervention, ruling out the possibility of an activist approach to economic policy in a critical area where other perceptions might well have made it possible. The results were both to increase the attractiveness of radical alternatives to capitalism, and to reinforce the quietist approach to government favoured by the increasingly conservative financial and commercial interests in Britain and, to a lesser, but growing, extent elsewhere.

Thomas Malthus began his career as a clergyman and, from 1804 onwards, was Professor of History and Political Economy at Haileybury College,[70] the academic establishment at which young men were trained for service in the British East India Company. This organisation, which had employed several significant contributors to economics in the past, not least Thomas Mun, was also to have two other important British nineteenth-century economists on its strength, James and John Stuart Mill, although neither of the Mills, nor Malthus, nor, apparently, Mun ever visited India.[71] Malthus wrote two books, *An Essay on the Principle of Population*, first published in 1798, and *Principles of Political Economy*, first published in 1820,[72] although both books went through subsequent additions. In the second book he attacked Say's Law, and much of his current reputation stems from the fact that he was one of the few people, and a very early one at that, to have been on the right side of this particular controversy, although his reasoning does not have a modern ring to it. His case did not depend on there being a Keynesian imbalance between saving and investment intentions but on the general proposition that the numerous but necessarily indigent labouring classes would never be able to afford to buy all that capitalist production could produce. Nor was the shortage of demand likely to be filled by the capitalists themselves, who were, in Malthus's view, likely to be too fully occupied by business affairs. The gap might be filled by what Malthus described as a non-productive class of consumers, consisting of servants, statesmen, soldiers, judges, lawyers, physicians, surgeons and clergymen, but this could not be guaranteed.[73] Interestingly, this list of supposedly unproductive occupations has parallels with the one produced by Smith, who took a much less favourable view of their contribution to the general welfare. Another issue on which Malthus and Smith differed was on the overall merits of free trade, where Malthus expressed considerable scepticism.[74]

The arguments which Malthus produced on these topics were not strong enough to carry the day, but the same could certainly not be said of the propositions in his earlier book, which were enormously influential. These concerned the relationship between the size of the population and its level of income. Malthus began with two postulates, the first being that food is necessary to man's existence, and the second that the passion between the sexes is necessary and will remain in its present state. He then concluded that 'the power of population is indefinitely greater than the power in the earth to produce subsistence for man'.[75] This is so, he claimed, because population, when unchecked, tends to increase in a geometrical ratio, whereas subsistence, at best, increases only in an arithmetical ratio. Nature makes the two forces equal by checking the growth of population whenever it presses against the food supply. The two checks are vice and misery, 'these two bitter ingredients in the cup of human life', although subsequent editions of the *Essay* included 'moral restraint' as a third possibility.[76] If the population increases before the food supplies have expanded, food prices will rise and real wages will fall. In the ensuing distress, population growth will come at least temporarily to a halt.[77]

This was a compellingly simple idea, with many practical implications. One was that there could be no long-term hope of increasing the living standards of the labouring poor, since the rising population would always erode away any temporary gains in income per head. This was a concept onto which Ricardo latched, with his Iron Law of Wages. Another was that public relief to the poor can only defeat its own purpose in anything but the short term. Both these ideas rang down the nineteenth century. On the one hand, they fuelled dissatisfaction with the status quo among radical thinkers. On the other, they reinforced the existing tendencies towards a minimalist role for the state among the more established classes, who were only too willing to shift the blame for poverty to the poor and away from the upper echelons of society and the government.[78] Malthusian views about population and poverty became another part of the almost unchallenged conventional wisdom, accepted as a fact of life both by Classical Economics and by most of the public at large.

Yet the evidence that Malthus's views were incorrect was there from the beginning, both from practical experience and in the internal consistency

of his writings. Although Malthus produced a substantial amount of anecdotal evidence to support his views – even including references to 'the
wretched inhabitants of Tierra del Fuego'[79] – and while the squalor of the
early stages of industrialisation reinforced them, in fact standards of living
for working people were already rising when the *Essay* was first produced.
They certainly went up substantially over the next 30 years, when Malthus
was still writing.[80] By the 1830s, knowledge of increasing agricultural productivity, population and living standards was widespread, and readily
available from censuses and elsewhere.[81] There seems to be nothing to
suggest, however, that Malthus was interested in this kind of empirical
evidence. Even where he did attempt to quantify the issues at stake in the
Essay, it is far from clear that he did this fairly. In particular, it is not self-
evident that food production will only increase in an arithmetic ratio compared to the geometric ratio posited for population growth, and indeed this
is not what happened. Whatever his merits in other respects, Malthus's
views on population, colouring as they did both the opinions of the nineteenth-century economic establishment and the public, provided the world
with another direly wrong-headed legacy.

David Ricardo was the third child of a stockbroker of Dutch descent, who
had at least 17 children. Ricardo left the Sephardic Jewish faith and became
a Christian when he married his Quaker wife but, in doing so, cut himself
off from his own relations. He nevertheless continued the family tradition
and became a stockbroker himself, amassing a large fortune in about five
years. He then bought a country estate at Gatcombe Park, the same property as was to be purchased in the 1970s by Queen Elizabeth II for Princess
Anne and her family.[82] Shortly afterwards, when he was 27 years old, he
was by chance lent a copy of the *Wealth of Nations*. This sparked Ricardo's
interest in economics, although he did not start publishing until 1809, ten
years later. He was a close friend of Malthus', and was well known to all the
other economists active at the time. He was widely involved in all the
major economic controversies of his age, especially those to do with monetary policy, where he sided with Say against Malthus on the issue of possible deficiencies in demand.[83] In 1819 he became MP for the Irish rotten
borough of Portarlington, which had 12 voters, and which he never
visited.[84] He died four years later, in 1823.

Ricardo's influence as a theoretical economist derives as much as anything else from the forcefulness and vigour with which he expressed his
views. His cast of mind was analytical and abstract, and his conclusions
correspondingly firm and rigid, although in his later writings he tended to
modify and soften his position on many of the key issues with which he
was concerned.[85] As so often happened, however, it was not so much the
nuances which carried the greatest influence either with his fellow economists or with the public, but the raw conclusions. These covered much

the same ground as had been dealt with by Smith – on prices, rent, wages, and profits – but Ricardo tackled these issues in a different way. Whereas Smith was inclined to draw common-sense conclusions from wide empirical observations, Ricardo tended to use induction, the danger being that the validity of the conclusions then depended heavily on his premises being, and remaining, realistic and relevant. This is an approach which, it has to be said, is still just as hazardous now when used by modern economists as it was in Ricardo's day. A revealing insight into Ricardo's lack of interest in empirical information is that, despite all that he had to say about the evolving economy of his time, it appears that he never visited a factory throughout his career.[86]

On prices, Ricardo moved some distance from Smith's views by introducing the concept of utility as an important influence on cost, in addition to the labour content. 'If a commodity were in no way useful – in other words, if it could in no way contribute to our gratification – it would be destitute of exchangeable value.'[87] This was a move, shared by Say, towards the modern view in which prices are determined by the interplay of supply and demand, incidentally opening up the way to leaving a much more positive role for the entrepreneur.[88] This did not stop Ricardo from falling back on the Labour Theory of Value as the main determinant of prices, however, although he excluded products with special scarcity value, which could not be reproduced, 'such as rare statues and pictures, scarce books and coins, wines of a peculiar quality, which can be made only from grapes grown on a particular soil'.[89] Apart from these exceptions, in Ricardo's view 'It is natural that what is usually the produce of two days' or two hours' labour, should be worth double of what is usually the produce of one day's or one hour's labour.'[90] This was largely the hard line formulation to which Ricardo adhered.

Rent, for Ricardo as with Smith, was largely concerned with agriculture, for Britain was still at the turn of the nineteenth century a predominantly agricultural country, and landlords, as Ricardo observed, despite the fact that by this time he was one of them, 'love to reap where they have never sowed'.[91] Ricardo defined rent as 'that portion of the produce of the earth, which is paid to the landlord for the use of the original and indestructible powers of the soil'.[92] At the margin, with land only just capable of supporting those working it, the rent would be zero. Better land would produce a surplus, however, which would accrue to the landlord, and the greater the population, and the intensity with which it was therefore tended, the larger the surplus would be. 'The rise of rent is always the effect of the increasing wealth of the country, and of the difficulty of providing food for its augmented population.'[93]

Turning to wages, Ricardo defined them as 'that price which is necessary to enable the labourers, one with another, to subsist and to perpetuate their race, without either increase or diminution'.[94] This was the Iron Law of

Wages – another of the simplifications which for a long time carried almost all before it – implying that the standard of living of working people would never rise above subsistence level, whatever was done by beneficent governments, charity or trades union action. In fact Ricardo substantially qualified his views on the Iron Law, allowing for the equilibrium price of labour to include 'conveniences [which had] become essential to him from habit'.[95] He also allowed for the subsistence level to rise as a result of improved technology and rising investment 'for no sooner may the impulse, which an increased capital gives to a new demand for labour be obeyed, than another increase of capital may produce the same effect'.[96] He also believed, however, that the opinion prevailing 'in the labouring class, that the employment of machinery is frequently detrimental to their interests, is not founded on prejudice and error, but is confirmable to the correct principles of political economy.'[97] Perhaps partly for this reason, Ricardo's conclusion was still a pessimistic one: 'When, however, by the encouragement which high wages give to the increase of population, the number of labourers is increased, wages again fall to their natural price, and indeed from a re-action sometimes fall below it.'[98] This was the message which the public received, amplified by Ricardo's comment that 'Like all other contracts, wages should be left to the fair and free competition of the market, and should never be controlled by interference of the legislature'.[99]

As with others who had based their views on prices on the Labour Theory of Value, Ricardo had considerable difficulty in explaining how profits arose, and thus how they could be justified. If prices were determined wholly by the amount of labour expended on production, and if any surplus that might occur as a result of favourable conditions was entitled to go to the landlord as rent, where did the money to pay for profits come from? Ricardo's explanation that it arose from the contribution to production made by the entrepreneur in providing capital equipment was not difficult to attack, for this must reflect no more than the past labour costs entailed in its production. Furthermore, profits were much larger than could be accounted for in this way,[100] Ricardo's own fortune being a highly specific case in point.[101] The conclusion, which was all too easy to draw, and which Ricardo never successfully fended off, was that capitalists made no contribution to the production of goods and services warranting the profits they earned, but merely appropriated to themselves a surplus to which they were not entitled.[102]

The contribution towards the development of nineteenth-century economics of the main figures who followed Smith was therefore a depressingly misguided legacy, well justifying the description by Thomas Carlyle (1795–1881) of them as the 'Respectable Professors of the Dismal Science'.[103] The combination of Say's Law, Malthus's views on population and Ricardo's interpretation of the Labour Theory of Value, was to make it impossible for the central doctrines in Classical Economics, other than the ideas already formulated by Smith, to contribute anything of much use to practical policies for decades to come. It made it look impractical for the bourgeois state to ameliorate conditions among those benefiting least from the evolving economy, or for other reasons falling on hard times, leaving only a minimal economic role for the public action. At the same time, the same crucial concepts which underpinned Classical Economics also provided large amounts of ammunition to its critics. In doing so, however, the conceptual errors they took over also proved to be faulty enough heavily to undermine the theoretical case they put up against nineteenth-century capitalism. Economic and social progress were certainly made in Britain during the nineteenth century, and elsewhere, but hardly – despite their fame and influence – as a result of Say, Malthus or Ricardo. The impact of the major errors of judgement which their work contributed to Classical Economics – at least as these were interpreted by the world at large – outweighed the value of everything else they had to say.

Classical economics in transition

The Classical System, established by the time of Ricardo's *Principles*, saw a period of consolidation during the following 50 years as it slowly changed to what has come to be called Neo-Classicism. Much of it has remained intact, as micro-economics, ever since. Its major policy-orientated strength continued to be, however, the case for *laissez faire* and free trade.[104] The doctrine of maximum competition, partly going back to Quesnay, stayed as the pre-eminent practical economic prescription, at least outside socialist circles, throughout the nineteenth century.[105] Much of the rest of mainstream economic theory had little or no practical application – a problem which was to continue to dog economics for many decades to come.

This did not, however, stop important contributions being made to the less mainstream parts of economic and social thought during the nineteenth century. Jeremy Bentham (1748–1832), though primarily a lawyer rather than an economist, was thought by Marshall to be 'on the whole the most influential of the immediate successors to Adam Smith'.[106] His major aim was to develop a complete and rational code of law,[107] and in this capacity he was the original advocate of the utilitarian proposition that the aim of public policy should be to seek 'the greatest happiness of the greatest number'. This concept set out to provide an important new guide to public policy, but proved to be something of a two-edged sword in practice. It could be used both to warrant state action to ameliorate social conditions, but also as a justification for exploitation on the grounds that this was for the overall benefit of society, and was criticised accordingly.

The utilitarian banner was nevertheless forcefully carried forward by James Mill (1773–1836), who also may have contributed the theory of comparative cost to economics, although this is usually attributed to Ricardo.[108] This elegant theory explained how any two countries could benefit by trading with each other even if one was less efficient at producing everything than the other. It was still worth trading if one country was relatively good, compared to the others, at producing one product rather than another. James Mill, a strong supporter of Ricardo and the Labour Theory of Value, published the first economic text book in 1821, entitled the *Elements of Political Economy*. James Mill shared Malthus's concerns about population growth, which he described as 'the grand practical problem',[109] although this did not stop him having nine children of his own, one of whom was John Stuart Mill.

Much of the practical economic controversy during the early part of the nineteenth century related to monetary policy, and in particular what to do about the gold value of the currency. Britain had suspended payments in gold in 1797 because the provincial banks of the time could not meet the demand for cash caused by the threat of a Napoleonic invasion. Since then, prices had risen steeply, triggering the establishment of a Select Committee on the High Price of Gold Bullion, to whose report, published in 1810, most of the main economists of the day made contributions, including Ricardo who had been co-opted as a member. The main controversy then, and subsequently, was over what had caused the inflation, and therefore what policy to pursue to ensure that, as far as possible, price stability was maintained. The Currency School, led by Lord Overstone, George Warde Norman and Robert Torrens (1780–1864),[110] believed that the inflation had been caused by the lack of discipline triggered by the abandonment of the Gold Standard. The Banking School, led by Thomas Tooke (1774–1858), on the contrary, denied that a purely gold-based currency would operate in the manner claimed for it by the Currency School. They believed that banks would be sufficiently cautious and prudent in their lending for the risk of inflation to be no greater than it would be with a metallic standard, and that price changes were primarily to do with supply and demand rather than monetary factors.[111] The Currency School won the day, however, leading to sterling returning in 1821, after a severe deflation, to the pre-Napoleonic War gold valuation, originally set by Isaac Newton in 1711. Their final victory came with the 1844 Bank Charter Act, which locked the banking system still further to the same gold price, while effectively emasculating whatever scope there might have been for a more active monetary and exchange rate policy for Britain during the nineteenth century. There were protests from some industrialists, particularly Matthias Attwood (1779–1851) and his brother Thomas (1783–1856).[112] By this time, however, Britain was too dominated by powerful financial interests for complaints about the impact of a relatively high sterling gold value on industry to carry much weight, a situation which has changed little during the last 150 years.

The justification for capitalists receiving the return they did, nevertheless, remained unresolved, providing a continuing weakness to Classical Economics which Marx and others exploited with eventually highly significant consequences. An attempt was made to deal with this problem by Nassau William Senior (1790–1864) with his Abstinence Theory of Interest. This attributed the return to capitalists as being compensation for their austerity in deferring the use of resources to a later date, for which they needed to be rewarded. 'To abstain from the enjoyment which is in our power, or to seek distant rather than immediate results, are among the most painful exertions of the human will.'[113] Neither the scale of the rewards which capitalists managed to award themselves, nor the scale on which many of them spent them lent much credibility to this theory, though it lasted for some half a century before being overtaken by the Marginal Revolution, of which more in Chapter 6. While the Abstinence Theory never commended itself to the critics of the British economic system, Senior further alienated them by opposing the 1837 Factory Act with the notorious argument – bitterly attacked by Marx – that the last two hours of the day's labour alone constituted the capitalist's profit.[114]

During the nineteenth century, Britain, largely as a result of its economic pre-eminence at the time, established a substantial empire. Opinion about it was divided. Adam Smith had derided the empire as a project 'extremely fit for a nation whose government is influence by shopkeepers', and favoured its disbandment.[115] This was a view substantially shared by his early followers such as Ricardo and James Mill, but opinion gradually became more supportive, led by Edward Gibbon Wakefield (1796–1862), who argued that the empire might serve a variety of purposes: 'The objects of an old society in promoting colonisation seem to be three: first, the extension of the market for disposing of their own surplus produce; secondly, relief from excessive numbers; thirdly, an enlargement of the field for employing capital.'[116] As the nineteenth century wore on, however, the relatively poor performance of countries such as Britain, with the largest empire, gave little credence to the overall benefits to be secured from the control of overseas territories.

A more significant domestic issue related to free trade, not least in food products. The agricultural interest in Britain had always been strong enough to keep the price of corn relatively high, and legislation to prohibit or discourage the importation of cereals went back to the fifteenth century.[117] A new Corn Law was passed in 1815, which prohibited imports unless prices reached high trigger levels – 80 shillings a bushel in the case of wheat. This was strongly opposed especially by the rising manufacturing interest, which wanted to see the cost of living kept down. The result was a major campaign, led by Richard Cobden (1804–1865) and John Bright (1811–1889), to have the Corn Laws repealed, an objective which was achieved in 1846, following the outcry over the potato famine in Ireland, which had started the previous year. The success of this campaign led to the almost total dismantling of British tariffs. By 1860, the total number of dutiable items coming into Britain had been reduced to 48. By 1882, only 12 imported articles were taxed, and these purely for revenue purposes.[118]

The next major synthesis of the economic thought of the time was undertaken by John Stuart Mill (1805–1873), whose *Principles of Political Economy* was published in 1848. Mill took a reasonably optimistic view of industrialisation, believing – rightly – that conditions would improve as the economy grew, although he still took a Malthusian view, particularly of agriculture: 'It is the law of production from the land that in any given state of agricultural skill and knowledge, by increasing the labour, the produce is not increased in the same degree.'[119] He was also sceptical about how far economic growth could go, opining that 'It is only in the backward countries of the world that increased production is still an important object: in those most advanced, what is economically needed is a better distribution.'[120] In general, however, Mill followed the same line as Ricardo, although somewhat softened, not least because of the mounting attacks on Classical Economics at the time from the socialist left. Although he never lost faith in Utilitarianism or a general belief in the superiority of competitive capitalism over other economic systems, he was considerably more willing than his predecessors to advocate reform of existing institutions, even if these involved government interference with private interests.[121] Nevertheless, Mill still largely accepted Ricardo's view on the Labour Theory of Value, and he forcefully re-formulated, but did not essentially alter, Say's Law.[122]

As the role of the City of London as Britain's – and the world's – financial centre became more pronounced, so the way in which the banking system operated became more sophisticated, and, in particular, the function of the central bank, the Bank of England, in reacting to crises. An additional reason for the stability of the British economy – militating against radical change – was the mechanism developed by the Bank of England for acting as the lender of resort, providing the banking system with sufficient liquidity to ward off disaster, even though this involved risks with convertibility. Walter Bagehot (1826–1877), for many years Editor of *The Economist*, did much to develop and clarify the issues which were involved, further securing the leading role of sterling, although the Gold Standard, on which it depended, did not become the basis for Western Europe's international trade and finance until the 1870s, and the rest of the world's until the end of the nineteenth century.[123] The Gold Standard may have benefited the City, but it did little to advance the performance of the British economy, which did significantly worse than most of its continental competitors, especially from about 1870 onwards.

The classical economic tradition

What, then, is a fair assessment of the contribution of the whole sweep of the development of Classical Economics from the thinking which proceeded it? In its early phases, the new ideas formulated particularly by Adam Smith unquestionably produced a more appropriate intellectual environment than had existed previously for allowing the benefits of the Industrial Revolution to work through to improving the lot of humanity by generating better economic performance. The medievalists had been inclined to rely on charity as the best solution to the chronic problems of economic scarcity. The Mercantilists were essentially involved in a zero sum game, where one country's gain was another's loss. The Physiocrats saw the benefits of getting rid of the web of self-interested regulation which was the bane everywhere of pre-industrial societies. Their obsession with agriculture, however, and their contempt for trade and industry, combined with their concern for maintaining France's absolute monarchy and thus opposing democracy, left them ill prepared for the Industrial Revolution which was coming. On the contrary, it was British liberalism, and the enlightened self-interest which flowed from it, which turned out to provide the best framework for using the new economic power which had been unleashed.

Smith stands out, because he was interested in growth in output, and much of what he had to say was designed to facilitate this occurring by getting the state to pursue appropriate policies. By Ricardo's time, however, the emphasis had shifted to how and why the fruits of production were divided up the way they were, and Classical Economics never really overcame this bias. Part of the reason was that, at the heart of the Ricardian system, was the notion that economic growth must sooner or later peter out owing to scarcity of natural resources.[124] This was a theme which ran right through the classical tradition to J.S. Mill.[125] An important implication of the essentially static conditions it entailed was an inevitable antagonism between landlords, capitalists and workers. If there was no growth in overall output, and the rewards to one group went up, the returns to others must come down. Although there were inevitably conflicts of interest between different classes during the nineteenth century in Britain – as is always the case – it was clear to anyone who looked hard that the economy was far from static. Living standards were rising for almost everyone. This typifies the extent to which Classical Economics drifted away from the real world. The implications of its main concerns, especially those emphasised by the most influential contributors were not, therefore, seen much, if at all, in practical economic prescriptions, although elements of them, such as the Iron Law of Wages, had significant implications for social policy. The reality is surely that the major components of nineteenth-century Classical

Economic thinking provided remarkably little guidance to those in government and elsewhere who had to decide how to deal with practical issues.

The same cannot be said about a number of the more peripheral economic issues to which thinkers at the time addressed their minds. Policies on foreign trade, monetary matters, the Empire, the Gold Standard, banking regulation, let alone the many issues on which Utilitarianism or population policies impinged, were all undoubtedly affected by the background thinking of those who determined what the outcomes were to be. Making sure that day to day, or even year to year, matters are dealt with sensibly, however important they may be, is nevertheless altogether a different matter from considering the wider issues to which economists in the early nineteenth century might have turned their minds. Nowhere in nineteenth-century Classical Economics is there the development of any theory about the process by which economic growth is achieved, and therefore the policies which need to be pursued to make sure that it takes place to whatever may be deemed to be the optimum degree. At the same time, the almost universal belief in Say's Law precluded any serious study of unemployment and how it might be avoided. Both these weaknesses left the British and other economies doing less well than they might have done in terms of growth and stability, while leaving their performance open to radical challenges based largely on the same defective theory.

The great achievement of Classical Economics, taken as a whole, was to provide a compelling justification for sweeping away the multifarious barriers to trade inherited from the Mercantilist period, and to consolidate the rule of the market. By doing this, the Classical Economists helped to establish firmly the whole complex of political, social, legal, economic and indeed cultural conditions which form the framework within which, at least in the advanced countries of the world, life was thereafter to be lived.[126] Their great failure was never to capture the scale of the real possibilities which were opening up although, certainly by the first half of the nineteenth century, vast potential was maturing into reality in front of the eyes of anyone interested in seeing what was happening. The writers who lived at the threshold of the most spectacular industrial developments ever witnessed up to that time, with the notable exception of Adam Smith, mainly saw cramped economies, with most of the population struggling with diminishing success for their daily bread. They were convinced that technological improvement and increase in capital would, in the end, fail to counteract the fateful law of decreasing returns. James Mill, in his *Elements* even offered a 'proof' of this.[127] In other words, they generally saw nothing better in the fairly near future than the arrival of the stationary state. Their views were coloured by pressure of population, nature's decreasing response to human efforts to increase the supply of food, and hence falling net returns to industry, more or less constant real wages, and ever-rising rents.[128] This was a huge underestimation of the potential which the Industrial Revolution had opened up for the future of both Britain and the rest of the world. It needs to weigh heavily in the balance against the significant achievements which Classical Economics secured in other respects.

5
Dissent

People are usually more convinced by reasons they discovered themselves than those found by others.

Blaise Pascal (1623–1662)

While the tenets of Classical Economics were largely accepted as a matter of course by the established classes in Britain, then in its heyday, they were by no means universally welcomed. During the nineteenth century, they received three serious challenges. One, mostly from Germany, but also from the United States, came from a group of writers and thinkers led by the German historicist school. The second came from the radical left. The third, towards the end of the century, came from the new marginalist school, of whom more in the next chapter. This chapter is concerned with the first two, and especially with the writings of Karl Marx and his many associates. We need to begin with the earlier challenges from German and American thinkers, however, whose views were generally less opposed to liberal capitalism as such than those of the socialist school, and more concerned with how to allow industrialisation and economic expansion to take place successfully in countries which did not, at the time, have the dominance which Britain possessed.

Germany, during the first half of the nineteenth century, was far behind Britain in terms of economic development. The country was divided into a large number of small states, each responsible for multifarious tariffs and other restrictions on trade.[1] It also had a very different dominant intellectual tradition, with subservience to the needs of the state given pride of place compared to the British emphasis on individual liberalism,[2] and with romanticism, some of it shading into irrationalism,[3] much to the fore compared to British empiricism. There were two main roots to German historicism and the economic thinking which developed from it, and the reaction to developments in English economics which it entailed. One was a search for ways to enable Germany to start obtaining the benefits of industrialisation. The other, which partly overlapped, was to do so in a way which accorded with the German political and social *Zeitgeist*.

Much of the German tradition came from the influence of Georg Wilhelm Friedrich Hegel (1770–1831), who considered the study of history the proper approach to the science of society.[4] Most of the German historical economists who followed his lead exalted in the nation and the work of the government,[5] a view exemplified by Adam Müller (1779–1829), a conservative defender of the landed and feudal interest, whose view was that the state 'is not merely a fundamental human need; it is the supreme human need'.[6] Müller was familiar with the *Wealth of Nations* but claimed that Adam Smith's ideas were unsuitable to German conditions, a view not wholly different from the attitude taken by British critics such as Edmund Burke (1729–1797), who also romanticised the past and opposed individual liberalism.[7] Fundamentally against industrialisation, the factors of production for Müller were not land, labour and capital, but nature, man and the past.[8] It was a relatively short step from this kind of thinking to complete autarky, allowing no contaminating foreign influences to undermine the state, favoured by writers such as Johann Gottlieb Fichte (1762–1814).[9]

It was against this background that Friedrich List (1789–1846), an altogether more substantial figure in economic history, lived and worked. List was an early advocate of liberal trading policies between the German states, which led to the Zollverein – a tariff-free zone within Germany – eventually established under Prussian auspices in 1828.[10] For advocating this proposal as early as he did, however, List fell foul of the authorities, and spent some time in gaol. When he was released he eventually found his way to the USA, where the policies to encourage economic development were very different from those advocated by British Classical Economics. In particular, partly under the influence of writers such as Alexander Hamilton (1757–1804), who had done much to formulate US economic policy after the Declaration of Independence, the USA had always had a high external tariff. Armed with this experience, when List returned to Germany in 1831 he advocated in his *Das nationale System der politischen Oekonomie* an external tariff for the Zollverein, although with qualifications. He favoured free trade in agriculture, and believed that, while tariffs might be desirable to protect industries which were establishing themselves against world competition, they should be removed once such enterprises had matured. He regarded untrammelled free trade as a doctrine suitable only for countries already in the lead rather than those in the process of catching up.[11] Unlike Müller, List was therefore in favour of industrialisation, which he saw as the culmination of a series of stages through which all economies had to proceed.[12] Indeed, one of List's important original contributions, in contrast to the British tradition, was to see economic development as a dynamic rather than a static process, and one in which the state needed to play a key role.[13]

List's writings made a significant practical difference to the way that German and US economic policy developed, on the whole with beneficent results in both cases. Thereafter, however, the work of German historical economists became much less interested in the real world, and much more concerned with academic method. Wilhelm Roscher (1817–1894) aimed to reconstruct economics 'based on the historical method'. This meant the establishment of the laws of economic development, which were to be derived from the investigation of national histories. Attention was to be given not only to their economic development but also to their legal, political, and cultural conditions, all forming a whole made up of interdependent parts.[14] He succeeded in establishing an academic tradition with a considerable longevity, leading through Bruno Hidebrand (1812–1878) and Karl Knies (1821–1898) to Gustav von Schmoller (1838–1917) a particularly powerful figure in German academic life, but their work had little practical consequence.[15] Though sceptical about 'economic man', they were not generally against capitalism, and they favoured the development of trade and industry.[16] Their detailed study of history, however, failed to throw up any useful guidance about how to use economic policy more effectively in the future than had been done in the past.

List's views on the use of tariffs to protect infant industries – while actually not so different from those of Smith, who was never a doctrinaire free trader – were well received in the USA. Indeed they were used to help to justify still higher tariffs than had been there before with the introduction of the Morrill Tariff in 1861, designed to make the importation of most mass produced goods into the USA completely uneconomic.[17] German economic thinking also had other influences on the USA, not least because there was always a steady interchange between American and German universities. These included greater scepticism about laissez faire than was prevalent in Britain at the time, provoking more positive attitudes to social policy and other forms of interventionism, mirroring what was to happen in Germany. There are also links between the German historical approach to economics, and the early establishment in the USA of the collection of statistics and historical fact finding.[18]

The USA produced far fewer economic thinkers during the nineteenth century than did Britain, but one who managed successfully to make his mark was Henry Charles Carey (1793–1879). To begin with, he was much attracted to the work of British Classical Economics, but as time went on he became increasingly doubtful about its teachings. He agreed with List that external tariffs were a more appropriate policy for the USA than free trade, and wondered, too, whether it could make sense for Americans to buy goods made thousands of miles away in Britain rather than those produced much closer to the consumer.[19] Carey also began to realise that the

Ricardian notions of continual land scarcity and static real wages had no congruence at all with what he could see happening all round him in the USA. He accepted that sooner or later population pressures might become critical – he even referred to a position being eventually reached where there was 'standing room only'[20] – but this time was clearly a long way away. In the meantime, Carey could see that there were significant advantages to a growing population, a view on which he claimed biblical support. 'God had said "Be fruitful and multiply." Better God's words than Malthus's "Be not fruitful; do not multiply"'.[21]

The work of the German historical economists also had some followers in Britain, particularly Richard Jones (1790–1855), who succeeded Thomas Malthus as professor at Haileybury. Jones, like his equivalents in Germany, proposed to use inductive historical methods to elucidate the way economies worked, criticising Ricardo and other Classical Economists for their failure to pay sufficient attention to the real world. While this was a charge with considerable merit to it, as with German historicism, it was not clear that simple amassing of facts by itself was a sufficient substitute for analytical deliberation, although Jones succeeded in producing a clearer exposition on rents than Ricardo's, influencing Marx in the process.[22] More significant was the impact that the writings of economists such as List and Carey had on the views of British thinkers and politicians on free trade, which gradually lost some of its lustre as the nineteenth century drew to a close, and the Tariff Reform movement gathered strength.[23] In the meantime, however, a much more effective attack on Classical Economics came not from this direction but from those who wanted to throw over the system altogether – the radical left.

Early socialist thought

Those who opposed the capitalist system, at least as it manifested itself in nineteenth-century Britain, fell broadly speaking into two camps, as indeed tended to be the case in all countries. On the one hand were those who put the main emphasis on practical steps to ameliorate conditions, which was where the strongest tradition in Britain lay, despite the limitations on political action which could be undertaken when working people were excluded from the suffrage.[24] On the other hand were others, more strongly represented in France and Germany, who believed that the only way of achieving radical change for the better was to get rid of the capitalist system altogether.[25] Discontent with the conditions of exploitation and degradation found in Britain, and everywhere else during the early stages of industrialisation, in turn sprang from three main sources. One was the unfulfilled promises of the liberal utilitarian tradition. The second was religious and moral conviction, which had a major revival in nineteenth-century Britain, and, to some extent, elsewhere. The third was the ammunition provided by the defects in Classical Economics.[26]

Early support in France and Germany for the fruits of the Industrial Revolution, whose impact was then becoming increasingly obvious in Britain, began to wane in some quarters as the squalor and degradation of early industrialisation started to spread to the continent. Jean Charles Léonard de Sismondi (1773–1842) was an early follower of Adam Smith, but later became much more critical as the less attractive social consequences of the Industrial Revolution appeared in France.[27] Sismondi became increasingly aware of the differing interests of capitalist and workers, and it was he who introduced the concept of social classes, with particular emphasis on the inevitable antagonism, as he saw it, between the capitalists and the workers.[28] This was a new and important concept 'to prevent men being sacrificed to the progress of wealth from which they will receive no profit'.[29] It had always been recognised that the capitalist and the landlord tended to be much better off than the workers, but the misfortunes of the latter had hitherto been attributed to their Malthusian tendencies to excessive reproduction, thus depressing themselves into ineluctable poverty for which their social superiors could not be blamed. Sismondi's analysis suggested, on the contrary, that it was the rapacity and greed of capitalists and landlords that might be responsible for the condition of the labouring classes – an important addition to the radical agenda which was beginning to emerge. Sismondi's solution was a retreat from industrialisation to agriculture and artisanship,[30] using the state to slow up technical progress.[31] This proposal was not in the mainstream of future thought, although his perceptions about the instability of demand turned out to have lasting substance. He was one of the last important writers to express concern about the lack of effective demand before the views of Say and Ricardo became the received wisdom.[32]

From an entirely separate source came an altogether different influence on writers critical of British economic development at the time. This was the work of David Dale (1739–1806) and his son-in-law, Robert Owen (1771–1858), who established a model industrial environment in New Lanark, showing what could be done to civilise living and working conditions. Even for those with as philanthropic a bent as Dale and Owen, however, conditions were still very harsh. To start with, the children employed in the New Lanark textile mills were required to work for 13 hours a day, though this was subsequently reduced, when Owen took over, to no more than 11.[33] Robert Owen was a writer as well as a doer, and particularly critical of Malthus who, he said, 'has not told us how much more food an intelligent and industrious people will create from the same soil, than will be produced by one ignorant and ill-governed. It is, however, as one to infinity'.[34] That scarcity of goods and excessive numbers of people were not a necessary part of the human condition, but the result of defective institutional arrangements was a point of view that many later socialists shared with Owen. They also agreed with his emphasis on the need for more widespread education, and the benefits of co-operative forms of industrial and commercial organisation.[35]

Owen's views on the merits of co-operation were shared by Pierre Joseph Proudhon (1809–1865), who produced even more radical dissent. 'Le propriété, c'est le vol' – property is theft – was his rallying cry, although he was not opposed to private ownership as such, which he realised was essential to the liberal society he wanted.[36] He was against what he saw as the abuse of property by landlords and capitalists, as opposed to the justice which he thought was society's most important objective. The solution he advocated was co-operative or voluntary associations of workers, financed by a special bank with note issuing powers, which would not charge interest. The state, by then superfluous, would disappear – a notion which turned out to be just as impractical and unhelpful as the equally utopian proposals put forward by some of the German romantics.[37] This did not, however, stop anarchism becoming a significant component of left-wing thinking in Europe. It shaded into the conspiracies which were a regular feature in the despotic Russia from whence came anarchism's chief advocate – and a close rival to Marx for the leadership of the Second International – Michael Bakunin (1814–1876).

Proudhon's distaste for the conditions produced by the Industrial Revolution was shared by a number of other significant French writers. Claude-Henri Saint-Simon (1760–1825) advocated that the study of society should be conducted on a scientific basis, leading to politics becoming the 'science of production',[38] an idea with some similarities to those being developed in Germany at the time. Charles Fourier (1772–1837) believed that the poverty which accompanied the 'colossal' advance of industry constituted the main cause of social disorders, leading to a mercantile feudal system.[39] Like Owen and Proudhon, he saw the solution in co-operation. Louis Blanc (1811–1882) believed that poverty and suffering had their origins in competition. By allowing the business for which they worked to fight against each other, the workers lowered their wages, while competition between manufacturers led them to bankruptcy. Blanc, the originator of one of the great rallying cries of the left 'From each according to his ability, to each according to his needs', believed that the solution was not so much co-operation as state socialism.[40] Auguste Blanqui (1805–1881), a professional revolutionary, added the concept of the *coup d'état* or *Putsch* to the armoury of those who believed that the capitalist state would have to be overthrown.[41]

Meanwhile, in Germany there was a similar ferment of ideas to that which was taking place in France. Ferdinand Lassalle (1825–1864), saw co-operation as the only way out of the trap set by the 'Iron Law of Wages'.[42] Ludwig Feuerbach (1825–1872), for a while one of Marx's close associates, promulgated the notion, which Marx took over, that by recognising the primacy of economic forces and conditions rather than the currents of conventional history, Hegel 'should be stood on his feet instead of his head'.[43] In Britain, too, there was a steady development of radical ideas, though the more important of them were much more influenced by the Labour Theory of Value, and the Ricardian legacy than those on the continent. Charles Hall (c1740–c1820), a generation older than the other members of his group, was a physician who had seen from his own medical practice the degradation to which working people were subjected during early industrialisation. He campaigned against the inequality he reviled in his book *The Effects of Civilisation*, published in 1805.[44] William Thompson (1783–1833), a model Irish landlord, John Gray (1799–1833) a clerk in a London wholesale house, John Francis Bray (1809–1895), a printer, photographer and farmer, and Thomas Hodgskin (1787–1869), a naval officer who became a journalist, all subscribed to and developed, in one form or another, the concept of surplus value. This was the notion that the capitalist system necessarily involved the wages paid to the workers always being less than the value of the products they produced. It thus gained wide currency, and became a well-established explanation for the exploitation, oppression and misery which the system exhibited. The solutions advocated were generally co-operation and syndicalism.[45]

While the mainstream of early British socialism was rationalistic and atheistic in outlook, shading into open hostility to religion in the case of Owen,[46] there was also a long-standing Church tradition of care for the community which flowered briefly in the middle of the nineteenth century. Its leaders were Frederick Denison Maurice (1805–1872), Charles Kingsley (1819–1875) and John Ludlow (1821–1911). While the involvement of individual members of the Church in left-wing politics has remained a long-standing tradition, the effectiveness of the Christian Socialists was limited by political divisions among them. Their opinions varied from Maurice's conservative leanings to the considerably more militant approach taken by Ludlow, who had spent time in France where the impact of Christian thinking on social and economic issues had developed a characteristically radical hue. Christian Socialism failed, however, to generate a significant following among British working people, and it withered away before the end of the 1850s.[47] Yet another form of antipathy to the materialism and ugliness of much that the Industrial Revolution produced came in the form of a reaction back to more traditional craftsmanship and concern for past methods of production, exemplified particularly by the life and work of William Morris (1834–1896).[48]

Opposition to the ideology of Classical Economics and the practical implications of the Industrial Revolution thus sprang from many sources. There was no uniformity in the solutions propounded. It took Karl Marx to pull together as many strands of dissent as he could, and to weld them into a coherent programme foretelling the downfall of capitalism and its replacement by socialism and then communism.

Karl Marx

Karl Marx (1818–1883) was born in Trier, in Germany, into a well-to-do and respected family. His father, who had recently converted from Judaism to Christianity under pressure from the Prussian state, was one Trier's leading lawyers, and an officer of the High Court. Marx moved comfortably among the social elite in his home town. Jenny, his wife and faithful, if sometimes sorely tried, companion for the rest of his life,[49] was the daughter of Baron Ludwig von Westphalen, Trier's first citizen.[49] After some years as a student at Bonn, Marx moved to the University of Berlin, where he came under the enduring influence of Hegel, describing himself in the preface to the second edition of *Das Kapital* as 'the pupil of that mighty thinker'.[50] He then moved to Jena, where he earned a doctorate in philosophy, covering the idealistic and materialistic elements in the doctrines of Democritus and Epicurus. Marx might then have secured a university teaching position, and settled down to a relatively uneventful academic life, but for a clamp-down on Hegelian thinking by the Prussian authorities which deprived him of his sponsor. He therefore took to journalism, only to fall foul of the Prussian authorities again. The newspaper he was then editing in Cologne was closed down by the censor, following its attacks on the policies of the autocratic Russian régime, which the Prussians were reluctant to offend.[51]

Thereafter, Marx never had a steady job. He moved to Paris, the centre of intellectual life at the time, where he absorbed the opinions of the French left, and met his life-long friend and supporter, Friedrich Engels (1820–1895). The combination of German philosophy and French revolutionary socialism transformed Marx in the 1840s from being a radical journalist to a campaigner for communism. After further moves, he eventually settled in London, where he soaked up the third formative influence on his intellectual development, British Classical Economics. He lived in London until his death, reading, writing and organising the international communist movement. He made a precarious living mostly by writing for the *New York Tribune*, subsequently to become the pillar of American Republicanism, as their London correspondent, though he was helped out financially from time to time by Engels. Later in life he was left a substantial bequest by an admirer, with which he bought a comfortable house in Hampstead.[52] It was thus that the liberal ideas which allowed capitalism to flourish independently of the state sheltered capitalism's most effective critic and antagonist.[53]

Marx's work, perhaps more than that of almost any other writer, is a mixture of brilliant insights, and a pedestrian style, encompassing a dense, academic structure of ideas, most of which, at least as regards economics, have stood the test of time poorly. A major reason for this is that the same fate has befallen all three of the major influences on his work.[54] Neither German romanticism, nor French socialist idealism, nor the elements of

Classical Economics on which Marx relied most heavily, provided him with a solid foundation. The reason why Marx has had such an enduring influence is not, therefore, because either the economic analytical framework he used and developed was sound or because the conclusions to which he came proved workable. The strength of Marx's legacy, on the contrary, derives from his effectiveness as a critic both of the way in which industrialisation had been allowed to proceed, and the way its outcome had been justified. The really successful part of Marx's critique of nineteenth-century British capitalism relies on the extent to which he managed to expose its weaknesses, of which four were pre-eminent.

First, Marx homed in on the distribution of power within the capitalist system, a problem which was simply ignored by Classical Economics, which had nothing of consequence to say about the manifest unfairness of unbridled free enterprise. Marx recognised the enormous achievements of the Industrial Revolution. 'During its rule of scarce one hundred years, [it] has created more massive and more colossal productive forces than have all preceding generations together'[55] and 'it has created enormous cities, has greatly increased the urban population as compared with the rural, and has thus rescued a considerable part of the population from the idiocy of rural life ... The cheap prices of its commodities are the heavy artillery with which it batters down all Chinese walls.'[56] He also emphasised, however, that the resulting class and ownership structure was one which gave the capitalist overweening power over his workers, generating conditions where exploitation and degradation were all too easily found. The capitalist 'strides in front ... the possessor of labour-power follows as his labourer. The one with an air of importance, smirking, intent on business; the other, timid and holding back, like one who is bringing his own hide to market, and has nothing to expect but – a hiding.'[57] Marx had no doubt that the class structure was to blame for this state of affairs. 'The executive of the modern state is but a committee for managing the common affairs of the whole bourgeoisie', he declared, and 'The ruling ideas of each age have ever been the ideas of its ruling class.'[58]

Second, he focused on the unequal distribution of income and wealth which the capitalist system generated, and for which Classical Economics again provided no convincing justification. To Marx, the explanation was clear, although his exposition, founded as it was on Ricardo's Labour Theory of Value, was flawed and inconsistent. The capitalist was usurping surplus value which rightfully belonged to the worker.[59] It did not, however, need the Labour Theory of Value to persuade a large section of the population that they were getting a raw deal out of nineteenth-century British capitalism. The lack of any welfare provision, the poverty of most working people compared to their social superiors, and the insecurity of almost all aspects of their lives were enough to convince them that they were badly treated. It was Marx, however, who proclaimed that this was not an immutable state of affairs, but one which could and should be changed.[60]

Third, Marx homed in on the instability of the capitalist system, and its propensity to crises. Here again, Classical Economics, in thrall to Say's Law, was on weak ground, claiming, as it did, that the system had an automatic and prompt capacity to correct itself.[61] Successive booms and recessions throughout the nineteenth century, accompanied every time there was a downturn by increased unemployment and hardship, made this look increasingly improbable, especially to those on the receiving end of falling economic activity. Marx's explanation for the process which caused this instability, and where it was leading, involving greater and greater competition among the capitalists, and the increasing misery of working people – 'the industrial reserve army of the unemployed'[62] – turned out, on the whole, to be wide of the mark. Marx was right and the classical economists were wrong, however, in believing that there were good reasons why demand deficiency was an inbuilt hazard which needed to be treated as a serious problem.

It was this instability which led Marx to his fourth major critique of the productive system, its tendency to concentration and monopoly, which Marx saw as the reason why it was destined eventually to collapse.[63] Marx's writing is often prolix and difficult, but some of his passages are deathless, as his description of the final *dénouement* of capitalism:

> Along with the constantly diminishing number of the magnates of capital, who usurp and monopolise all advantages of this process of transformation, grows the mass of misery, oppression, slavery, degradation, exploitation; but with this too grows the revolt of the working-class, a class always increasing in numbers, and disciplined, united, organised by the very mechanism of the process of capitalist production itself. The monopoly of capital becomes a fetter upon the mode of production, which has sprung up and flourished along with, and under it. Centralisation of the means of production and socialisation of labour at last reach a point where they become incompatible with their capitalist integument. This integument is burst asunder. The knell of capitalist private property sounds. The expropriators are expropriated.[64]

This clarion call to action was based on a great deal of theorising, for Marx was a hugely learned man. From Hegel he drew the idea that economic, social and political life is in a constant process of transformation, in contrast to the essential social stability implied by Classical Economics.[65] He also adopted Hegel's concept of thesis, antithesis and synthesis, but did not accept his conservative conclusions, claiming, following Feuerbach,[66] that Hegel's concept lacked a material content, and needed to be stood 'on its feet' instead of on its head.[67] Combined with the theory of classes and the class struggle, which came from the ideas developed by Sismondi, and his economic interpretation of history, derived from Hegel, Marx set out to show the extent to which economic relationships heavily influenced prevailing ideas.[68] This was an original and particularly important perception which has not only stood the test of time well, but has now become part of the intellectual mainstream.[69]

From British Classical Economics came Marx's theories of value, surplus value, capitalist development, declining profits and the increasing misery of the working class. Based, as they were, on concepts whose flaws became increasingly apparent as the nineteenth century wore on and, especially when the Marginal Revolution overtook them, these ideas have not fared well, and their value in foretelling the future turned out to be very poor. On the other hand, Marx's predictions about economic crises and the concentration of ownership, though derived from theory which had its faults, proved in fact to be more accurate than those of the more conventional economists of the time.[70] Interestingly, Marx had a high opinion of Smith and Ricardo, but thought that British economics had gone downhill since then, describing John Stuart Mill's work as 'shallow syncretism'.[71]

The strength of Marx's contribution, therefore, derived from its accurate assessment of the manifest deficiencies in the conditions which the Industrial Revolution had produced and the unconvincing justifications for them provided by Classical Economics. The weaknesses lay in much, though not all, of his theorising, which was mostly based on unsound foundations. Generally, therefore, Marx was right where he found fault but on much more insecure ground in either predicting the general outcome of events or in proposing remedies. The workers were not 'immiserised', as he had said they would be; on the contrary, their standard of living was generally on a long-standing rising trend. The business cycles did not become substantially more acute during the nineteenth century, though it did look to a significant number of people as though the 'crisis of capitalism' might have arrived when the Great Depression struck the world around 1930. Nor was there any absolute increase in the number of the unemployed again, at least, until the 1930s, nor a general fall in the level of profits, nor the gradual elimination of small and medium-sized businesses.[72]

There was, however, a further grave and even more deep-seated problem about Marx's economic and political work. Because of his fundamental beliefs in the unworthiness of the capitalist system, he wanted to conclude that it was doomed, and that its internal contradictions would bring it down. While constructing an exceedingly complex series of theories to prove that this would be the outcome, he was therefore inclined to ignore the scope there was for improving the system from within rather than pulling it down and replacing it with something else. He thus cut himself off from the route which was eventually chosen by most of the working people whom Marx wanted to lead in a different direction. In the end, it was rising living standards, better education, trade union activity and parliamentary action, particularly as the franchise widened, which proved to be the way chosen by the vast majority of working people to improve their lot.[73]

Where does this then leave Marx's contribution to the development of economic theory? The answer is that it was is not very great. Marx's teaching made a large difference to political perceptions, and his thinking was hugely influential on the development of historical and sociological studies. Outside those who took seriously his admonitions to overthrow the capitalist system altogether, however, his impact on the development of economics was limited. He produced no important new ideas which took the subject much beyond the point reached by Ricardo fifty years earlier, relying, as he did, on existing Classical Economics to provide most of his Labour Theory of Value-based conclusions. Where he undoubtedly did have an impact, as writings as early as those of John Stuart Mill exemplify, was in making it clear that if capitalism did not reform and tame itself by taking on board all the developments which eventually produced the welfare state, the risk of subversion was likely to be unacceptably high. This was a challenge to which, however, industrial capitalist régimes responded remarkably successfully. Future revolutions were seldom, if ever, found to have industrial capitalists as their main target. It was landlords in despotic agrarian countries, especially those which had been ravaged by war, against whom revolutionary action appeared in the end to be the only remedy likely to work.[74] We turn now to see how successful those who took this road were at running the economies they inherited.

Lenin, imperialism and revolution

Marx left a rich, if flawed, legacy to his successors. There was, of course, the passionate distaste and distrust of capitalism, and all that it produces both materially and socially – a tradition which has never been short of adherents. There were the critical and often deeply perceptive insights into the ways in which societies operate, and in particular the extent to which they are moulded and characterised by economic interests, which now helps to underpin much of the work done in the social sciences. There was also the large quantity of theory which Marx developed both to justify his views, and to assist in predictions as to what the future would hold. As we have seen, this has turned out to be the less successful part of his accomplishments. Not least was the problem that Marx had very little to say about how the state would operate once capitalism had been overthrown – if there was a state at all, as, at his most optimistic, Marx believed that the state apparatus would wither away, and no longer be required at all.

In communist society, where nobody has one exclusive sphere of activity but each can become accomplished in any branch he wishes, society regulates the general production and thus makes it possible for me to do one thing today and another tomorrow, to hunt in the morning, fish in the afternoon, rear cattle in the evening or criticise the dinner, just as I desire, without every becoming hunter, fisherman, shepherd or critic.[75]

Marx's successors were therefore faced with the challenges not only of developing his ideas as circumstances changed, but also of coping with the practical problems, once they had gained power, of dealing with a world where capitalism no longer existed. How did they fare?

During the 34 years between Marx's death in 1883 and the Russian Revolution in 1917, there were no communist governments in power, and the development of Marxism was therefore largely theoretical. Its main nineteenth-century extension was in reaction to the scramble for colonies exhibited mostly by the European powers, and the establishment of size-able colonial empires. By far the largest was the British Empire which, at its peak, covered about a quarter of the land surface of the globe.[76] These events led to the development of Marxist Theories of Imperialism, though neither Classical Economics nor Marx had had much to say about imperialism, and Marx had once opined that the British in India were a progressive force.[77] John A. Hobson (1858–1940), on the other hand, had argued that imperialism was primarily driven by the selfish interests of financial and commercial groups,[78] a view which was taken up by Marxists such as Rudolf Hilferding (1877–1941) and Rosa Luxemburg (1871–1919).[79] They maintained that shortage of investment opportunities in the aging capitalist states drove finance capital to imperialist rivalry, to provide new markets.

It was a short step from there to the proposition that imperialism was responsible for the prosperity of the European powers, as Lenin (Vladimir Ilyich Ulyanov) (1870–1924) argued in *Imperialism: the Last Stage of Capitalism*, published in 1917.[80] 'In backward countries profits are usually high, for capital is scarce, the price of land is relatively low, raw materials are cheap ... The necessity for exporting capital arises from the fact that in a few countries capitalism has become "over-ripe" and ... cannot find "profitable" investment.'[81] The relatively high standard of living in the developed countries, and notably also that of their workers, depended on exploitation of the deprived masses of the colonial territories,[82] providing markets for surplus production on the one hand, and cheap sources of supply of raw materials on the other.[83] This is a powerful and appealing argument, which explains the gap in development between the rich and the poor countries in the world in terms of the dynamics of investment strategy, and the political initiatives which this drives towards acquisition of overseas territories.

This was never a theory, however, which stood up to any significant empirical investigation. While no doubt greed and selfishness had as much to do with the establishment of the nineteenth-century European empires as is the case with most human enterprises, there were certainly other motives for imperialism, including national prestige, sense of mission and military strategy, which were probably more significant. Nor was the economic case persuasive. The proportion of trade which all the European powers did with their colonial territories was a small fraction of their total trade by the end of the nineteenth century, although it had been higher during the earlier phases of empire building. In 1720, 80% of all British exports went to elsewhere in Europe. By the 1780s this had fallen to 45%, and colonial exports were dominant. By the early twentieth century, however, the vast proportion of the trade of all the developed nations was among themselves, and not with their colonies.[84] The same was true of investment. Nor is there much evidence that colonies were of any significant direct benefit to the mother country. Germany's outgoing on its colonies, not counting defence, were greater in the twenty years before the First World War than the whole of the value of its colonial trade.[85] Some parts of the British Empire did better than this, not least those concerned with South Africa with its mineral riches, but Britain's poor growth performance compared with other competing countries during the heyday of its exceptionally large empire, suggests that overall the direct benefits were small, if not negative.[86]

The relative stability of most of the industrialising world during the decades running up to 1914 provided few opportunities, other than a brief and unsuccessful interlude during the 1971 Paris Commune,[87] for Marxist revolutionaries to put their ideas into practice. The turmoil generated by the First World War, however, provided the occasion for the establishment of the first régime dedicated to carrying out a full Marxist programme, including the abolition of capitalism, by Lenin and the Bolsheviks following the 1917 Russian Revolution. The economy which they inherited had expanded substantially during the late nineteenth and early twentieth centuries, with growth rates of 2.0% per annum between 1870 and 1900 and a rather more impressive 3.2% per annum between 1900 and 1913.[88] Mostly as a result of state initiatives, by the start of the First World War, there was a reasonably extensive railway system,[89] and some heavy industry. The standard of living in Russia was, however, well below the level of most of the rest of Europe, although slightly above that of Japan.[90] The Russian economy was severely disrupted by the First World War, and there was heavy loss of life. Another 10 million died in the course of the Revolution and the subsequent civil war and attacks on the new régime from Western powers, fearful of what the successful replacement of capitalism might presage. As a result, it was 1930 before the Soviet economy recovered the same level of output as it had enjoyed in 1913,[91] providing its rulers with a poor, backward and fractured economic base on which to build.

Although initially relatively liberal, during its New Economic Policy phase, the Soviet régime soon toughened its stance. Lenin died in 1924, to be succeeded by Joseph Stalin (1879–1953), who introduced the system of five-year plans, the first two of which covered the period from 1928 to 1939. Heavy and light industries were developed, and agriculture collectivised. The country began to be transformed as industrialisation proceeded and the urban population quickly doubled.[92] The cost, however, was prodigious not only in human terms, as millions died in the Ukraine and Kazakhstan famines of 1932–34 and in political purges and liquidations, but also in economic terms as state policies drove down the current standard of living to enable more and more resources to be mobilised for investment in the future.

The result was that the Soviet economy grew during the 1930s relatively quickly but, as a result of high capital to output ratios, much more slowly than would have been achieved if Western standards of return on the use of capital had been attained. Between 1928 and 1940, Soviet GDP rose by an estimated 81%, with an average growth rate of 5.1% per annum.[93] This was, of course, in sharp contrast with the slump and slow recovery evident in much of the West, prompting a substantial measure of support for the Soviet economic system among some Western economists, notably Maurice Dobb (1900–1976), a Cambridge economist, and John Strachey (1901–1963), an influential figure from outside the academic world.[94] Russian industrial output probably overtook Britain's at the end of the 1930s, enabling the Soviet Union to achieve prodigious output of tanks, ammunition and aircraft in the struggle which was about to start.[95] Until 1941, the USSR had staved off being involved in the Second World War as a result of the non-aggression pact negotiated with Germany in 1939 but, once the German invasion began in August 1941, the USSR embarked on four traumatic years of carnage and physical injury. About 25 million Soviet citizens are believed to have lost their lives as a result of the German invasion,[96] and the damage done to the area occupied by the Germans was immense. As a result, in spite of huge continuing investment in new production facilities, the output of the Soviet economy was over 20% lower in 1946 than it had been in 1940.[97]

The post-Second World War period, however, saw a steady increase in output, which rose every year until the end of the 1950s at an average rate between 1947 and 1958 estimated at 7.3%, a considerably higher pace than was being achieved anywhere else except in Japan and Germany.[98] This began to cause mounting concern in the West, particularly in the USA, whose growth rate was barely half that of the Soviet economy, prompting Nikita Khrushchev (1894–1971) to promise at the United Nations that the USSR would shortly overtake the American standard of living.[99] This threat, however, gradually appeared to be more and more empty. As the years wore on, it became increasingly clear that, although the Soviet economy had responded reasonably well to large-scale investment in basic industries, running a consumer-orientated economy was much more difficult to manage without a market framework within which to do it.

Although valiant attempts were made to get the Soviet economy to produce more consumer goods of reasonable quality, after Stalin's influence had worn off and following Khrushchev's speech in 1956 denouncing his excesses, the results were remarkably unsuccessful. The Soviet economy continued to have a high proportion of its GDP devoted to investment, but the growth rate in the economy slowed, and consumers remained dissatisfied. Between 1959 and 1973, the Soviet economy grew at a still more than respectable estimated 4.9% per annum, but thereafter, during the Brezhnev era, expansion slowed to 1.9% per annum.[100] During the whole of the period between 1973 and 1989, before the USSR began to disintegrate, GDP per head in the Soviet Union increased at a cumulative rate of less than 1% per annum.[101] Allowing for the military build-up which was taking place, the disposable income for the average Soviet citizen stopped rising after 1973, and stabilised, of course, at a far lower level than in the USA, where nevertheless a remarkably similar stagnant real income phenomenon was to be found among most of the population.

Unquestionably, part of the reason for the relatively poor performance in the later years of the USSR was the exceptionally heavy military burden which the economy had to bear, particularly from the mid-1960s onwards when the Cold War intensified.[102] After making all allowances for this, however, the root problem with the system proved to be the impossibility of running a more and more complex economy on the basis of central plans, with market signals largely suppressed. This led not only to the rate of growth slowing down, but to increasingly serious misallocation of resources, as their appropriation became ever more complicated, thus reducing the real value to the final consumer of the goods and services which were produced.

The problems of the Soviet economy were mirrored in varying degrees of intensity among all the East European countries which were obliged to adopt command economies at the behest of the USSR after the installation of communist régimes following the Soviet occupation after the Second World War. A particularly interesting example was the German Democratic Republic, which was long regarded as being the most successful of the Soviet satellites. Prior to reunification, Western estimates of East German per capita GDP levels had put them at about three-quarters of those in the Federal Republic and about two-thirds of those in the USA. When in 1990 the Berlin Wall came down, however, and East and West Germany were reunited, these estimates were found to be about 50% too high. The actual East German level of GDP per head was only about two-thirds of what it had been thought to be, confirming strongly the deep-rooted inefficiency of even a comparatively well-run command economy,[103] and emphasising the weaknesses in economic performance from which the erstwhile USSR had suffered.

What went wrong? Enrico Barone (1859–1924), a colonel in the Italian General Staff, and a pupil of Pareto whose contribution to economic theory will be discussed in the next chapter, had established long before 1917 that it was possible to calculate the optimum distribution of resources in a socialist society.[104] It was not, therefore, the theoretical but the practical problems of running a non-market-orientated economy that proved over-whelming. Initially, the successes achieved by the First World War belliger-ents in mobilising their economies for total war appeared to provide an appealing model, leading to the state control of all production advocated by Nikolai Bukharin (1888–1938).[105] Thereafter, economic policy drifted rapidly towards a relentless drive for increased output, favouring capital goods over consumer goods to whatever extent was practical, allowing for political, psychological and incentive considerations, with scant concern for welfare calculations.

One of the major problems in the Soviet Union was that the highly oppressive nature of the régime, especially during the Stalinist era, made it almost impossible for there to be any rational discussion about how to cope with the economic problems faced by the state. Even the relatively innocuous long economic cycle theories produced by N.D. Kondratieff (1892–c1931) were denounced, leading to their author's disappearance and the uncertainty of the date of his death.[106] Meanwhile other Russian economists, such as E.E. Slutsky (1880–1948), who had made significant contributions to welfare theory prior to the 1917 Revolution, simply stopped publishing.[107] Those who did try to contribute, such as Eugene Preobrazhensky (1886–1937), tended to pay with their lives, notwith-standing their high reputations as Marxist-Leninist theoreticians and their long-standing revolutionary credentials. Preobrazhensky, who had done much to show how to establish the forced saving regime subse-quently adopted by Stalin, was shot dead in 1937.[108] About the only major figure to survive was L.V. Kantorovich (1912–1986), a mathematician, who published a paper on linear programming in 1939, which became the basis for Soviet planning and resource allocation in subsequent years, not least after the Second World War, where Kantorovich's ideas were further developed by two other important innovators in this field. They were Oskar Lange (1904–1965) and Michal Kalecki (1899–1970), both of whom worked in senior positions in Poland, but whose work also influenced allocations policies in other East European economies.[109] Generally, however the Soviet period was one of dismal, though all too understandable, intellectual caution. For 25 years, from the late 1920s to the early 1950s, no one wrote an economic text book in Russia, although Stalin himself wrote an economic essay in 1952 – a thin apologia for the Soviet system.[110]

The well-known comment 'I have been over into the future, and it works',[111] made by Lincoln Steffens to Bernard Baruch after he had visited the Soviet Union in 1919, turned out to be wide of the mark. It was achieving reasonably efficient resource allocation, without the use of market signals, that turned out to be the insuperable problem, especially once the Soviet economy moved towards the production of consumer goods. In 1962, a leading Soviet mathematician and expert in cybernetics calculated that the personnel requirements for planning and administration increased as the square of the national product. His conclusion was that by 1980, the entire adult population would need to be employed in planning and administration to cope with the scale of problems involved in allocating resources effectively in the Soviet economy.[112] These sorts of extrapolations are easy to do, but in this case the point was a telling one. Getting rid of capitalism and abandoning the market economy turned out not to be the way to solve the world's economic problems.

Welfare reform

In the end, the major impact from the left on the way economic policy and practice developed was not the abandonment of capitalism, but taming it to produce a more acceptable distribution of income and life chances generally. Some of this was achieved by working-class self-help movements, such as syndicalism, co-operation and trades unions. Universally, however, other than increasing the national income, the most efficient way to improve welfare was found to be through the use of the state's power to tax and spend. The extent to which it was possible to produce a less unequal society by these methods, however, at least in the absence of other complementary economic policies, proved to have significant limitations. The results actually achieved were therefore less comprehensive and effective than some of their proponents thought and hoped they would be.

Syndicalism involved the use of trade union power to wrest a larger share of the fruits of labour for the workers rather than the capitalists. At least in the view of Georges Sorel (1847–1922), the leading theoretician, the approach to be taken was not simply one of pressing for higher wages. The struggle was against both the employers and the state, with the intention of undermining the capitalist order, and replacing it with trade union- rather than community-based co-operation.[113] Syndicalist ideas had a stronger following in France than most other countries, but were generally overtaken everywhere by more moderate trade union policies, orientated to improvement in wages and working conditions, but not to radical change in property ownership. Syndicalism had a brief resurgence in Britain between 1915 and 1925 as 'Guild Socialism', under the leadership of a leading socialist academic, G.D.H. Cole (1889–1959), before interest waned as it became clear that such ideas were gaining little ground among working people.[114]

Considerably more influential were the revisionist versions of Marxism, for whom Eduard Bernstein (1850–1932) was the early leader. Bernstein came from Germany, where Marx had his greatest number of followers. He left Germany in 1878, shortly before the passage during the same year[115] of Bismarck's anti-socialist legislation, first for Switzerland and then for London where he was based from 1888 to 1901. The liberal conditions in Britain, combined with the extension of the franchise, made it clear to him that there was an alternative and non-revolutionary way ahead to a more egalitarian society. This view also reflected much more accurately the way social and political conditions were evolving – a view increasingly shared by the British Fabian Society members. Bernstein therefore set out, despite his background as a major figure in a political party owing undivided allegiance to Marxism, to explore 'just where Marx is right and where he is wrong'.[116] He did this in his major work, originally published in German in 1899, and subsequently translated into English under the title *Evolutionary Socialism*.[117]

Bernstein had a profound sense of realism and a pronounced practical bent. He was not afraid to tackle Marx's predictions about rising concentration of industrial ownership, increasing misery for the workers, the growing intensity of the class struggle and ever more severe crises, none of which were greatly in evidence at the end of the nineteenth century. Instead, he advocated peaceful and lawful efforts by trades unions and socialist political parties to wrest benefits for those who were less well off from the capitalist system which was performing sufficiently well to be able to afford them. Bernstein thus established himself as the prophet of democratic socialism, which was taken up across the whole of the developed world, becoming the mainstream approach of all moderate left of centre political parties.[118]

The influence of ideas such as those advocated by Bernstein was not, however, confined to the left in politics. Apart from a combination of altruism and fear of the effect of excessive intransigence which have always motivated the 'haves' to be willing to make concessions to the 'have nots', three particular developments pushed them more strongly in the same direction. One was the spreading of Marxist ideas, proposing the overthrow of the existing bourgeois states, which those in established positions, particularly in Germany where Marxism had its greatest hold, realised needed to be counteracted. The second was the extension of the franchise, which both gave the disadvantaged and discontented more power to take political action to deal with their complaints, and provided a compelling argument for making sure that they were well enough educated and informed to use this power responsibly. The third was the need, as industrialisation proceeded, to ensure that there was a more thoroughly educated and trained work force, as well as one which was cared for better.

An important example of the second of these influences was the Forster Education Act of 1870,[119] which established district school boards throughout Britain shortly after the Conservative administration had widened the franchise in 1866. Perhaps more significant, however, were the reforms introduced in Germany by the Chancellor, Count Otto von Bismarck (1815–1898). Bismarck was an authoritarian figure, opposed to liberalism, who appears to have drawn his inspiration not from mainstream academic circles, but from a relatively obscure socialist writer, Karl Marlo (1810–1865).[120] In 1884 and 1887, after considerable controversy, legislation was passed in the Reichstag which provided the first steps towards a state-run scheme for accident, sickness and disability insurance, moves towards social insurance which were emulated, albeit in fragmentary form, in the Austro-Hungarian Empire.[121] Two decades later, similar steps were taken in Britain by the Liberal Government elected in 1905, with the lead being taken by the then Chancellor of the Exchequer, David Lloyd George (1863–1945). He introduced old age pensions in 1908 – not available in Germany until 1927[122] – and health and unemployment insurance in 1911, while his 1909 budget, which provoked its rejection by the House of Lords, contained provisions for graduated direct taxes and taxation of land values.[123] Over the following decades, similar reforms were introduced across the whole of the developed world.

Much of the inspiration of the reforms introduced by Lloyd George came from the work done by the Fabian Society, and in particular the contributions made by Sidney Webb (1859–1947) and his wife Beatrice Webb (1858–1943), assisted by other well-known Fabians, such as H.G. Wells (1866–1946) and George Bernard Shaw (1856–1950).[124] A formative influence, in turn, on the thinking of the Fabian Society – probably greater than that of Marx[125] – was the writing of the American Henry George (1839–1897) whose book *Progress and Poverty*, published in 1879, had articulated the social protest of the time. It was based on George's personal experiences as a sailor, printer, publisher and journalist, which had brought him face to face with dire poverty.[126]

Indeed, it was a lecture given in London by Henry George which impressed on Shaw the importance of economic problems, and which got him interested in the work of the Fabians.[127] 'When I was swept into the great socialist revival of 1883', Shaw later wrote, 'I found that five-sixths of those who were swept in with me had been converted by Henry George'.[128] George's solution to the inequalities generated by the capitalist system, like Marx's, lay in the legacy left by Ricardo, although whereas Marx relied on the Labour Theory of Value, George homed in on Ricardo's Theory of Rent. George was not in favour of the abolition of capitalism and drastic changes to the social order. Instead, he proposed a 'Single Tax' on land, which he believed would be able to provide both a sufficient flow of income to fund all necessary government expenditure, while at the same time playing a major role in promoting equality, by appropriating to the state the 'unearned increment' in rising land values.[129]

Henry George's ideas still have a vocal minority in their support, although they have never persuaded most mainstream economists of their practicality. In Victorian times, however, when taxation was much lower, and there was still a substantially agrarian society with high concentrations of ownership, a good deal of which was in the hands of absentee landlords, a significant anti-landlord tradition was available to be tapped.[130] George's proposals were thus fed into the Fabian melting pot of ideas when the Society was formed in 1884. Gradualness was the watchword, with the Fabian Society deriving its very name from Quintus Fabius Maximus Cunctator (260 BC–203 BC) – the Roman general whose delaying tactics won him battles and made him famous.[131]

The Webbs became masters at the art of social engineering and economic experimentation, with a heavy emphasis on historical and empirical studies – not, at the time, a conspicuous feature of much of the work done in other academic economic circles. Their poor opinion of the discussion of economic issues in the abstract, without adequate factual input, led the Webbs to establish their own university with a tradition much more to their taste, when they founded the London School of Economics in 1895.[132] To the Fabians, the trend towards socialism meant the achievement of as much social justice as possible, using the powers of planning and control available to democratic governments. Though they did not advocate the complete overthrow of the capitalist system, they believed that municipal and state enterprises might offer such effective competition that they would gradually take over a larger and larger share of the economy.

The extension of state enterprise has not, on the whole, stood the test of time particularly well, but the other main plank of Fabian thought, the development of the Welfare State, has done much better. In the Minority Report of the Poor Law Commission, their first blueprint, published in 1909, the Webbs proposed a 'national minimum standard of civilised life'. Although some of their proposals were implemented by Lloyd George, and other relatively minor improvements were made during the 1920s and 1930s, the full implementation of the Welfare State in Britain had to await the end of the Second World War. It was then that the proposals in *Social Insurance and Allied Services*, written by William Beveridge (1879–1963) and published in 1942, were put into effect by the post-Second World War Labour government. Meanwhile, somewhat earlier, similar proposals had been put forward in the USA, particularly by a group of economists centred round John R. Commons (1862–1945) at the University of Wisconsin.

This group, which worked closely with the Wisconsin state government, drew up the Wisconsin Plan, which aimed to combat the effects of the inter-war depression with widespread intervention, culminating in a state income tax, and, in 1932, a state unemployment compensation scheme.[133]

This led on to the federal Social Security Act, which introduced nationally the principles of unemployment insurance and pension entitlements, although not with universal approval. Among other weighty business figures who denounced the proposals were Arthur M. Schlesinger, Jr (1888–1965), who wrote that 'With unemployment insurance, no-one would work; with old-age and survivors insurance no-one would save; the results would be moral decay, financial bankruptcy and the collapse of the republic.'[134] The popularity of social security was such, however, that rearguard rhetoric of this sort cut little ice, and the trend in the USA continued in the same direction as it did elsewhere. Health insurance, aid to families with dependent children, housing help for lower-income families, and many other programmes were to follow, although the USA has never achieved the levels of social security prevalent in almost all of Europe.[135]

The development of the Welfare State was mirrored by an increasing academic interest in what became called Welfare Economics. Generally, the academic economist's world had not had a great deal to say about the practicality of welfare programmes as they were gradually introduced in all the developed countries. A considerable literature grew up, however, about the theoretical benefits which might be secured by greater welfare expenditure, much of which turned on the issue, to be covered in the next chapter, as to whether inter-personal comparisons were legitimate. An early exponent of the problems was Arthur C. Pigou (1877–1959) whose *The Economics of Welfare* was published in 1920. Although a relatively establishment figure, he was evidently influenced by Bacon's distinction, which he enjoyed quoting, between scientific works that bear fruit and those which shed light, his preference being with the former.[136] In any event, he argued against the classical notion that inter-personal comparisons about the benefit secured from extra spending were impossible, and in favour of the proposition that welfare could be increased by transferring funds from rich to poor.[137] This conclusion certainly reflected political realities, although a highly abstract economic debate about the rationality and justification for income transfers has continued ever since.

Of greater significance, judged by the criteria set out at the beginning of this book, is the extent to which the Welfare State, as it has manifested itself across the world, has contributed to the improvement of the lot of humanity. Whatever theories may say, few would argue against the view that, in practice, at least some redistribution of income from rich to poor has an important role to play in producing a civilised society which is reasonably at ease with itself. The problems have been not so much with this principle, but with the practicality of large-scale redistribution and to what extent, if it is achieved, the side effects offset the benefits.

The main problem in achieving redistributive taxation and expenditure is that so much of taxation, direct and indirect, tends to fall on those with relatively low incomes, while a high proportion of public expenditure tends to benefit everyone, and often those who are better off more than those who are poorer. Calculations suggest that the overall effect of government taxation and expenditure in most developed countries is to transfer resources from roughly the top 5% of earners to the bottom 20%, but to leave everyone else with about the same net income, after taxation but including the benefit of public expenditure, as before.[138] The fact that a significant proportion of services are provided publicly – whether health, public transport, pensions or education – may well improve the average quality of everyone's life. It is not, however, necessarily redistributive at the same time, particularly taking into account the well-known ability of those who are better informed and in a stronger position to influence the allocation of resources to manipulate state provision to their advantage.

More serious still have been the trends seen in most developed countries, especially since the early 1970s, towards lower rates of economic growth and higher levels of unemployment. These have had a massive impact on the distribution of income, wealth and all associated life chances throughout the developed world, swamping the effects of the best intended redistributive policies, even in countries, such as Britain, with left of centre governments committed to trying to ameliorate social divisions.[139] Successful achievement of the goals set by the architects of the Welfare State thus depend heavily on appropriate macro-economic policies being implemented to secure reasonably high growth rates combined with something much closer to the full employment enjoyed by Europe in the 1950s and 1960s than is the current experience.

The adverse impact of recent macro-economic policies in widening out the distribution of wealth and income both within and between countries has also in some ways made it more difficult to unwind the impact of what has been done. Despite all the steps which have been taken, especially in Britain and the USA, to deregulate the market, partly as a result of globalisation, in some respects there are more restrictions and distortions than there were. Inevitably, the reaction of those threatened with unemployment, or redundancy leading to early and unwanted retirement, has been to put up defences, both at a personal and at a political level. These have characteristically taken the form of many more people getting themselves classified as suffering from long-term sickness, and the creation of ever more complex welfare systems which too easily trap those benefiting from them into making it not worth their while looking for work. In much of Europe, though not so much in Britain, there have been changes to employment law, protecting those in employment from being dismissed, but in ways which impact adversely on those with no jobs. All these reactions make it more difficult to create conditions where full employment can be re-established, however understandable all these defensive reactions may be. Hopefully, however, it ought to be possible to achieve better economic performance despite these problems, as confidence in the availability of jobs increases, and dependency, with all its burdens on the tax system consequently decreases, providing a backdrop against which more rational use of the resources of the Welfare State can be delivered.

The contribution of the left to economics

How, then, are we to assess the contribution made by the attack on establishment views from the left to the development of a system of ideas in economics capable of delivering the results which the world needs?

Inevitably, the answer is that, like so much in human endeavour, it is, like the curate's egg, a mixture. The great achievement of the major dissenters in the nineteenth century, particularly Marx, was not to re-create a new and better understanding of economics. It was to awaken the conscience of some, the fear in others, and the realisation among large sections of the population, that the quietist, establishment approach of Classical Economics was not the only possibility. In particular, the heavily one-sided distributions of power, wealth and income, for which Classical Economics had no justification, were not necessarily inevitable. Nor was the system as stable and rational as its proponents claimed it was. In retrospect, the fundamental mistake made by Marx and his followers was not to realise that the market-driven, capitalist system may have had well-known drawbacks, but that it also had within itself the capacity for reform and change to make its impact less harsh, which became key features as it matured. Much more positively, it turned out that welfare state capitalism was the only framework within which social democratic forms of government could exist. These, in turn, provided much the most effective route to organic, acceptable change, allowing economic growth to flourish and living standards to rise.[140]

It is not, perhaps, wholly fair to condemn, with the benefit of a great deal of hindsight, the theorising, particularly from Marx, which underpinned his critique of capitalism. Without the theory, it is very doubtful whether the criticisms he produced would have become as effective as they were. Nevertheless, the cost of this theory has been massive, not least for all the countries most affected by them, particularly the Soviet Union, which tried the most determinedly over a long period to put their implementation into practice. The Soviet model also played a large and negative role in the development of many Third World countries, as their leaders came to realise as they surveyed their bankrupt state enterprises, generating little or no value added, which were the sad legacy of too much state-sponsored industrial development. It was not, however, just the developing world which suffered from this sort of waste of resources. Across the developed world, too, there were too many cases of state-run activities failing to provide satisfactory services to their clients or customers as a result of poor management or because they were captured by producer interests. While state involvement in the economy could be used to blunt the harsher outcomes of the market place, there were found to be increasingly serious and unacceptable costs involved in weaving away too far from the discipline and consumer orientation which the market required and which public enterprise too often inclined to forget.

Less costly, although still expensive in some cases, have been some of the other by-products of left-wing dissent. Syndicalism has generally failed. Co-operation has had mixed success, though some of its achievements have been impressive. Trades unions have generally been a positive factor when they have concentrated on pressing for better working conditions and moderate redistribution of income. Their contribution has surely been a negative one, however, as is generally the case with all rent seekers, when they have been responsible for inflationary wage claims and defended unreasonable restrictive practices. On the wider scene, left-led revolts, mostly in undeveloped countries and nearly always against corrupt and self-serving rural landlords rather than urban industrialists, have generally not had a good record in the promotion of increased economic growth and improved welfare. It is often the case that they have been triggered by intolerable conditions, but extreme left-wing ideology, fomenting resentment and dissent, has too often led to oppression and civil and economic breakdown, making conditions even worse than they were before. More recently, the Green movement, which has a distinct left of centre pedigree, has emerged, with another critique of capitalism which finds wide echoes, but with different, but still heavy, trade-offs between their immediate environmental objectives and the broader picture.

Of much greater long-term benefit have been the efforts to create social security systems across the world, although these too have not been without their costs and disbenefits. We have seen that their capacity for redistribution is limited, although they have other advantages in making life generally more civilised for those who live in countries where they operate on an extensive scale. It also needs to be stressed that welfare states are not a universal panacea. They can be made to work well in countries with fairly high living standards where there are large numbers of well-educated people available to operate them, and reasonable standards of public probity. If these conditions are not fulfilled, as sadly is the case in much of the Third World, the implementation of social security proposals is all too likely to make a bad situation worse. They can all too easily suck scarce talent into systems which benefit only those who are already relatively well off, especially if they are open to corruption and manipulation. This is not, of course, an argument against public provision of services, such as health programmes, where they can be run effectively. It is, however, a warning that welfare states are not the solution in countries which are too poor to afford them, where self-help, for all its failings, is often a better overall remedy than state welfare systems. The only real solution in cases such as these is a much higher growth rate, to enable levels of GDP per head to be achieved as quickly as possible, providing a sufficiently large resource base to ensure that in future a social security system will be able to operate effectively and fairly.

Perhaps the major general charge to be levelled against the left's contribution to economic progress has been that there has been much too much concentration on how the cake is to be divided up rather than on increasing its size. Even Marx, as we have seen, had no doubts about the capacity of the capitalist system to generate wealth. Focusing too hard on the division of the spoils, as opposed to making the total to be divided up greater, has not, however, proved to be the best way of creating better living standards for all. This is not, of course, to deny that redistribution has an important role to play, nor that public expenditure can be used to produce a more civilised society. The lesson to be learnt, however, is that if, especially on a world scale, living standards are to be raised, and the very poor brought into the fold where they have a reasonable GDP per head, the only real solutions are higher growth rates and the fullest and most productive employment possible. Redistribution through the tax and expenditure system has an important role to play, but still a relatively small one compared to what can be achieved by vastly improved economic policies.

The key role thus played by those from the left of centre in influencing the way economic theorising has developed has been in driving the concern to find practical ways of spreading the benefits from industrialisation and economic expansion to as wide a number of people as possible. This has not turned out at any stage to be as easy a task as some of its more optimistic proponents thought it would be. Neither radical institutional change nor welfare programmes have provided panaceas, but the fact that this is the case does not detract from the importance of the objective of evening up life chances as much as is practically possible. If humanity is to have a reasonably stable and long-term future, it is hard to see this happening without the redistribution of wealth and income playing a significant role. The increasing disparities which recent decades have witnessed, and the tensions which these have evidently created, are an ominous sign that the humanitarian agenda of the left still needs to have a major influence on future policy. The key is going to be to find ways of getting it implemented sufficiently efficiently to carry majority opinion with it. No doubt, this will be as difficult to achieve in the future as it has been in the past. The major contribution of the left has been both to flag up the need for this agenda, and to provide what, on balance, has been a patchy but vital and very significant input towards the alleviation of at least some avoidable poverty and blighted lives.

6
Technical Development

Perhaps it is a sense of history that divides good economics from bad.

John Kenneth Galbraith (born 1908)

About 1870, economics moved away from being a subject which was largely in the hands of non-professionals – businessmen, administrators and civil servants, as well as politicians, revolutionaries and even soldiers – and became largely, though not exclusively, the province of academic economists. The subject changed from being called 'Political Economy', and became 'Economics'. It was, however, more than an alteration in name that took place. The impact of economics becoming a subject in the hands mostly of academics rather than people with other jobs to do had a marked effect on where the main emphasis and focus of interest of the major participants henceforward was to be found. The character of the subject changed subtly away from its practical roots – trying to explain the world so that it could be changed – to a more abstract approach, where explanation was all, or nearly all, and prescription counted for much less. Whereas political economy was primarily concerned with influencing policy, economics, with relatively few, although important, exceptions, was from now onwards intended mainly to be more like a scientific subject, concerned with providing convincing theories about relationships, but with less and less of a normative and prescriptive, policy-orientated content.

These constraints did not stop a large amount of theoretical development occurring, some of it providing much more convincing explanations of the way the world worked than those available previously. Some of this work had important practical implications, and other parts of it shaped political opinions and provided a greater or lesser justification for the status quo. Generally, however, the impact of the change in role which the subject experienced was to increase markedly the number of people with some degree of familiarity with conventional economic theory, while at the same time reducing the influence that economic ideas had on most of the practical decisions which had to be taken. This was not true of the Keynesian Revolution, nor of the advent of Monetarism, both of which had major impacts on what happened in the policymaking world, but it applied to most of the rest of the developments which took place in economics from 1870 onwards. Especially from then until about 1930, governments and others concerned with deciding what had to be done did what they thought best, without much practical help from theoretical economics, which generally had little to say about the merits of adopting one policy rather than another.

Unfortunately, especially after the First World War had upset the delicate balance which had been largely responsible for the relative stability and success of the pre-war world, policymakers badly needed sound economic guidance. Except from Keynes, they did not receive it as the Versailles Treaty, concluded after the end of the war, stored up trouble for the future. Still less was mainstream economic theory in any position to provide useful advice as the world plunged into the slump in 1929. The reality was that economics had by then, and for a long time previously, largely divorced itself from providing solutions to real world problems. This did not stop worthwhile work being done, and the tools used for economic analysis being improved. The overall value of what was achieved, however, needs to be set in the context of the disastrous economic situation which was allowed to develop during the inter-war period, for which conventional economics had no useful prescriptions. For its failings, the world was to pay a very heavy price, and arguably, at least in the case of the outbreak of the Second World War, one which could probably have been avoided.

The Marginal Revolution

The most significant change to economic theory towards the end of the nineteenth century was the replacement of the Labour Theory of Value by what has come to be called the Marginal Revolution. This was a change in perception which swept the board when it was fully developed in the early 1870s, although its roots went a long way back into the past.

As we have seen, until the Marginal Revolution materialised, the Labour Theory of Value had maintained its place as the mainstream explanation for values and prices. There had, however, for a long time been a series of thinkers who had been less than satisfied with this formulation. They believed that there was more to the way in which price and value were established than the costs of production, however calculated. The essential principle embodied in the Marginal Revolution was that prices were determined not just by supply side costs but by the interplay of both supply and demand, with the actual price of any commodity being fixed by the marginal buyer and seller. As each buyer considers further purchases, the marginal utility of each additional unit falls, while the marginal cost rises. The price is determined when demand and supply are in balance, and equilibrium is reached.

The concepts which in the end were to flower as the Marginal Revolution had a long history. Ferdinando Galiani (1728–1787), a Neapolitan priest, had published a book in 1751 called *Della Moneta*, which anticipated a substantial proportion of the later theory.[1] During the eighteenth century, both Law and Turgot had developed subjective theories of value, implying that the value of anything depended on its utility as well as its cost.[2] Condillac and Say had both suggested that the Labour Theory of Value was defective, and that the demand for goods and services ought also to be taken into account in determining prices as well as the supply costs – a view with which Malthus also had some sympathy.[3] Auguste Walras (1801–1877), father of Léon, made the first attempt to deal systematically with the relationships between 'value in use' and 'value in exchange', proposing scarcity as an additional source of value.[4] Johann Heinrich von Thünen (1783–1850), a learned German estate owner, whose main work, *The Isolated State* was published in instalments over a long period from 1826 to 1863, applied the marginal principle in his study of land values. Thünen was mainly concerned with the determinants of the use to which successive rings of land round a city would be put, taking into account the cost of production of varying forms of agriculture, with intensive market gardening close in, and extensive pasture further out. His analysis culminated in the concept that net revenue is maximised when the value of the marginal product is equal to marginal factor cost.[5]

Further progress was made by Richard Whatley (1787–1863), later to become Bishop of Dublin, but obliged, while teaching at Oxford University, to produce at least one lecture a year.[6] This requirement led to the publication in 1831 of Whatley's *Introductory Lectures on Political Economy*, in which he expressed the view that economics was primarily the 'science of exchanges'. His main contribution was to reject the idea that labour was essential to create value, and, in a passage which has been quoted many times, he expressed what he thought to be the real relation between cost and price. 'It is not', he said, 'that pearls fetch a high price *because* men have dived for them; but, on the contrary, men dive for them because they fetch a high price'.[7] An even fuller exposition of almost all aspects of marginal utility doctrine is to be found in the *Lectures on Political Economy* published in 1834 by Mountiford Longfield (1802–1884), the first holder of the Chair of Political Economy at Trinity College, Dublin, endowed by Whatley after his appointment to the archbishopric.[8] Longfield was in no doubt that price is determined by supply and demand, with the cost of production behind the former and utility behind the other.[9] Further work was then done by William Nassau Senior who, in 1836, defined wealth as 'everything which is susceptible of exchange or which possesses value. Three qualities are necessary to this end: transferability, relative scarcity and utility.' He also noted that as the supply of all commodities rises 'the pleasure diminishes in a rapidly increasing ratio'.[10]

Until well into the nineteenth century, not much use had been made of sophisticated mathematical techniques to illuminate economic problems, though Malthus had suggested as early as 1814 that differential calculus might have applications in economics and related subjects.[11] The first person to use this technique extensively was Augustin Cournot (1801–1877), a French mathematician and philosopher, in a book published in 1838 entitled *Researches into the Mathematical Principles of the Theory of Wealth*.[12] This contained the first systematic elaboration of the marginal principle applied to the theory of the firm. Its style was highly abstract and deductive, in the Cartesian tradition, setting a trend which many were to follow. It was in this book that demand schedules and functions and downward sloping demand curves entered the literature of economics, as did the related concepts of marginal revenue and marginal cost.[13] Cournot's book did not have a great impact at the time when it was published, but its significance was gradually recognised by later writers. The first person to develop a fully fledged theory of consumption, grounded in the marginal principle, was Hermann Heinrich Gossen (1810–1858), a native of the Rhineland, in a book which he published in 1854, characterised by 'determined utilitarianism, a consumption approach, and mathematical method'.[14] Unfortunately, despite the author's high hopes, the book received almost no attention, although, again, its contribution was later recognised and acknowledged.[15]

Perhaps remarkably, it was not for almost another 20 years after the publication of Gossen's book – and 40 years after the work done by Whatley, Longfield and Senior – that three separate people, working independently in different countries, all realised at almost exactly the same time where the solution to the determination of prices and values lay. It was not to be found in the balance between supply and demand for any one product but in the general equilibrium in the market between the supply and demand for all products at the same time. William Stanley Jevons (1835–1882) published his *Theory of Political Economy* in Britain in 1871.[16] Karl Menger (1840–1921) published his book *Grundsätze der Volkswirtschaftlehre* in Austria in the same year.[17] Only a short time later, Léon Walras, of French origin but by then living and working in Switzerland, published his *Eléments d'Economie politique pure* in two parts, the first in 1874 and the second in 1877.[18]

While all three writers came substantially to the same conclusion, their routes to finding it were as varied as the traditions within which they worked. Jevons, whose education had been interrupted by the bankruptcy of the family business, and who, after a period working in the mint in Sydney, Australia, returned to London to complete his education, took up academic appointments first in Manchester and then in London, before he was killed in a drowning accident, aged only 47.[19] His starting point was the theory of utility – that objects had value because of their usefulness – from which he derived a theory about how the values attributed to them were established when they were exchanged. His book, rounded out with chapters on labour, rent and capital, contains frequent references to Bentham and Utilitarianism. Jevons held that economics required mathematical treatment, because it dealt with quantities and, because he was dealing with continuous variations, he believed it especially lent itself to differential calculus and graphical representation. With his earlier training in natural science, Jevons was keen to apply to economics the same methods which had proved so fruitful in physics and chemistry.[20]

Karl Menger, by contrast, was a law graduate, who held the Chair of Political Economy from 1879 to 1903 at the University of Vienna, still, at that time, the political and cultural centre of a large and diverse empire. He was also the tutor and confidant of the heir to the Hapsburg throne. The intellectual traditions he inherited were very different from those prevailing in Britain. In developing his theoretical approach to the questions of prices and values, he faced much more serious methodological opposition from the determinedly inductive German historical economists. They had no use for abstract economic analysis, in contrast to the intellectual climate in which Jevons worked in Britain, though their influence was weaker in Austria than in Germany. Menger was also much more influenced by the strong tradition which stemmed in all German-speaking countries from the philosophic idealism of Immanuel Kant (1724–1804). Kant's writings interpreted the phenomena of the external world as creations of the human mind, providing a bridge to the subjective view of the theory of value.[21] He had the additional advantage of having access to the work, written in German, of Thünen and others, on which he drew extensively.

Léon Walras came from yet another intellectual background, much more influenced by Cournot, and the long-standing French tradition of abstract thought, going back to Descartes. Originally a student at the School of Mines in Paris, he subsequently became a journalist and businessman before deciding – encouraged by his father – to devote himself to economics, though for a while he maintained his business interests. Because he lacked the necessary educational credentials, he failed to secure an academic appointment in France. This was why he eventually moved to Switzerland, where he became a tenured professor in 1871.[22] Walras's theoretical contributions went beyond those of Jevons and Menger in the development of the idea of general economic equilibrium, and in its expression in the form of a system of simultaneous equations. It was this feature of his work which came to be seen as his greatest achievement, as he produced a formulation capable, at least in principle, of linking all the markets making up an economy together in a quantitative way, and showing how equilibrium in all of them could be established at the same time.[23] Whether this construct was as capable of producing results as definitive as he hoped they would be, even in theory, was, however, subsequently challenged, particularly by Abraham Wald (1902–1950), echoing doubts which Walras himself had expressed.[24] Its influence, nevertheless, was immense.

Once the marginal principle had been established, it was possible to push out the boundaries further. Important new developments included the indifference curve, which was originally devised by Francis Ysidro Edgeworth (1845–1926), and explained in his *Mathematical Psychics*, published in 1881, and the marginal productivity theory covered in various publications by Philip H. Wicksteed (1844–1927). The significance of the indifference curve was that it enabled the balance in supply and demand for one product or service to be related to any other, the points of indifference being reached when the consumer believed that an additional unit of any product or service available was equally desirable. Wicksteed's main contribution was the notion that the selection between alternatives was the key to understanding all aspects of allocation, emphasising the opportunity costs involved every time a choice is made.[25] Meanwhile, John Bates Clark (1847–1938), a Professor at Columbia University in the USA, was the leading publicist for the Marginal Revolution in America. Although his main work was published some ten years later than those of Jevons, Menger and Walras, it appears that the ideas they contained may have been developed independently, though Clark had studied in Germany, and may have picked up at least some of the rudiments of his subsequent exposition there.[26]

Significant further advances were made by Vilfredo Pareto (1848–1923), an Italian nobleman and engineer, who succeeded to Léon Walras's chair at Lausanne in 1893, comparatively late in life, after a successful career as a business executive in railways and heavy industry.[27] Pareto's major contribution was to remove the last vestiges of Utilitarianism and subjective value judgements from Walras's system. By using Edgeworth's indifference curve concept, Pareto was able to show that equilibrium could be reached without any assumptions being made about utility – shorthand for a measure of how useful any particular product or service was thought to be by a consumer. Instead, there were simply empirical statements about which combinations of goods were equally acceptable. The major advantage of this approach is that it by-passed the awkward problems of comparing one person's perception of usefulness with another's, though an important implication of Pareto's formulation was that it made interpersonal comparisons impossible.[28] Pareto's work led on to important work on Welfare Economics, influencing both the socialist tradition, through Enrico Barone, whose work was referred to in the last chapter, and to mainstream economic thinking. Here, Pareto's indifference curve analysis lent strong support to the notion that markets, when left to themselves, ought to produce an optimal distribution of resources, and therefore should not be subject to more than minimal state interference.[29]

Pareto's enthusiasm for empirical research, on the basis of which he hoped to establish general rules, also led him to formulate another influential concept, known as Pareto's Law. Based on statistical information drawn from many countries, and relating to widely varying periods of time, this claimed to show that the distribution of income conforms to an invariant pattern. The implication was that any attempts to alter the way in which incomes are distributed by taxation and public expenditure were doomed to failure – inevitably an attractive proposition to those who had other reasons for wanting redistributive taxation to be discouraged. In fact, this view, and the statistical procedures from which it was derived, attracted sufficient criticism to undermine the Law's validity, but the quantitative and empirical approach exemplified techniques which became increasingly widely recognised in the twentieth century.[30]

The impact of the Marginal Revolution was certainly to dethrone the Labour Theory of Value, which had underpinned the mainstream view of prices and values for a century and more, but its influence on the way in which economics developed in the succeeding years went much wider than this. The emphasis shifted away almost completely from regarding economic growth and the increase in wealth as the main issues with which economics ought to be concerned, which had been the main thrust behind the work of Adam Smith. Instead the focus of interest moved to a much more static approach, designed to determine the equilibrium and optimum positions within a framework within which the total quantity of resources was given. Economics became a science, deliberately excluding normative statements, which dealt largely with the allocation of a given quantum of resources, meaning that little attention was paid to how this quantum was determined, and how it might be increased.[31] The Marginal Revolution thus completed the move away from the policy orientation which characterised Smith's work, and which was steadily attenuated by the development of the Classical tradition. By the end of the nineteenth century economics was almost entirely what would now be called 'micro-economics', with much of its present shape. It was highly abstract, much more mathematically orientated than it had been previously, and even weaker on policy prescription than nineteenth-century Classical Economics had been.

Mainstream Neo-Classicism

The period following the Marginal Revolution was followed by a reformulation of Classical Economics into what came to be known as Neo-Classicism. The first major synthesis between Classical Economics and the Marginal Revolution was to be found in *Principles of Economics*, written by Alfred Marshall (1842–1924), first published in 1890. The fact that seven subsequent editions followed during Marshall's lifetime, the last in 1920,[32] confirms how influential this work was. Marshall's background was as a mathematician, though he was much more cautious about the usefulness of mathematical abstractions than many of his contemporaries, advocating that 'the right place for mathematics in a treatise on Economics is in the background'.[33] He acceded to the Chair of Political Economy at Cambridge in 1885, and succeeded in turning his university into a world-renowned centre of economic studies.[34] Marshall was an ardent philanthropist and humanitarian. The pragmatic urgency with which he approached his subject made his work more realistic and less abstract than the utility theory of the Austrians or Walras's general equilibrium system. Nor was Marshall inclined to ignore or disparage the tradition he had inherited. Continuity was his watchword, demonstrated by the inscription *'natura non facit saltum'* – nature does not leap – which appeared on the title page of his *Principles*. His intention was to continue as seamlessly as possible the traditions established by Ricardo and John Stuart Mill.[35]

Marshall's range of interests ran wide. As well as synthesising the knowledge of economics which had been accumulated so far, he also made significant advances himself. He had an exceptional capacity for explaining clearly the ideas and concepts with which he was concerned. He refined them, for example, by considering different time frames such as the short, medium and long term, and by recognising the significance of both production techniques and consumer preferences in determining relative prices. The Neo-Classical approach was in some important ways a major advance on Classical Economics. Labour was included in marginal analysis, allowing wages to be well above subsistence level,[36] while fitting into the same framework which allowed all factors of production, including capital, to flow to where they obtained their best returns. Marshall's work suffered, however, from the malaise which affected the whole of economics at the time. While it was clear that Neo-Classics had a rigorous and elegant explanation of the way in which prices were determined in long-run stationary equilibrium conditions, the remoteness of this analysis, as Marshall was well aware, provided an inadequate substitute for the policy-orientated economics which he would have liked to have produced.[37]

An important imperfection in the Neo-Classical view of the world was that price determination was clearly not going to be optimal if restrictions on demand or supply were imposed by those in a position to exercise monopoly powers, whether producers or trades unions.[38] In these circumstances, prices would not reflect the untrammelled balance between supply and demand, but would be biased in favour of the monopolist. This was a condition which Marshall, who expected declining returns from natural sources of wealth, but increasing returns from industry, hoped could be avoided as a general condition among firms, as these two trends balanced out.[39] This being the case, monopolies needed to be opposed, although monopolistic restriction was not a consideration to which a great deal of practical significance was given in Europe. The situation was different in the United States, however, where Marshall's work was heavily influential, particularly as a result of the publication in 1911 of a book covering very similar ground to Marshall's. This was *Principles of Economics*, written by Frank W. Taussig (1859–1940), who was on the Harvard Faculty, and for half a century one of America's most influential economists.[40] In the USA, the threats to the optimal distribution of resources from monopolies or trusts were taken much more seriously than was the case the other side of the Atlantic. Indeed, one of the major practical results of Neo-Classicism has been to make anti-trust activity a significant component of US policy-making to this day. Whether monopoly was or was not in the general interest, however, is an issue which has never been persuasively resolved, whatever the theory might be. While there has been support for competition in principle, the general thrust of policy in Europe, particularly on the continent, has tended to be much more favourable to combines and cartels, on the grounds that these produced stronger companies. The bias has always been heavily the other way in the USA.

Marshall's concern with falling costs, whose benefits were obstructed by monopoly, set in motion another train of thought, which in time came to fruition with the development of theories of imperfect or monopolistic competition. These concern conditions – evidently widely prevalent in the real world – where there are a relatively small number of firms competing against each other, all of whom are able to collude with each other to a greater or lesser degree to avoid competition. The first key step was taken by a young Italian economist, Piero Sraffa (1898–1983), then at Cambridge, who published in 1926 a seminal article called *The Laws of Returns under Competitive Conditions*.[41] The gist of Sraffa's article was a plea for analysis of the firm in terms of monopoly rather than competition. In the real world, mass production, where costs went down with rising output, was becoming increasingly common, especially in manufacturing. At the same time advertising, the development of brands, and product differentiation were becoming more and more widespread. It was clear that at least some degree of monopoly, far from being the exception, was becoming the norm.[42] With decreasing production costs widely prevalent in many industries, the obstacle to an increase in the sales of a firm was not the threat of rising costs as production increased, but the unwillingness of the market to absorb larger quantities.[43] The fact that costs were falling rather than rising as output rose – the opposite to the conditions posited by the conventional static analysis – suggested that a whole new approach was needed to explain how markets would react to these conditions.

The accepted resolution of this problem was achieved in another example of more than one person coming to essentially the same conclusion at the same time, though the validity of their approach has recently been comprehensively attacked.[44] In this case, the two people concerned were Edward H. Chamberlin (1899–1967), at Harvard in the USA, and Joan Robinson (1903–1983), at Cambridge in Britain, both of whom published their findings in 1933.[45] The key was the realisation that, in the real world, most businesses did not operate either as complete monopolies or in conditions of unfettered competition with undifferentiated products. In most cases there were a limited number of suppliers of products, which were only partial substitutes for each other. This condition was called 'oligopoly' by Chamberlin, an apparently new term which soon passed into the common currency of economics,[46] although interestingly both the word and the concept are to be found in Thomas More's *Utopia*.[47] In these circumstances, firms would have a limited, but not necessarily insignificant ability to control their prices. Furthermore, in oligopolistic conditions, the rational policy for each firm to pursue would be to limit competition, so that all could benefit from higher prices, whether or not this was done by formal collusion, which, at least in the USA, was strictly forbidden. The outcome, however, with price leadership often being exercised by one firm, with others falling in behind, was generally similar to what would have happened if a cartel had existed. Nor did this appear to have caused the public any great harm, at least during the 1920s, when the American economy boomed, although more doubts were expressed in the 1930s as to whether oligopolistic pricing might be partly responsible for the Depression.[48] In general, however, the development of partial monopoly theories made it common knowledge that monopolistic conditions were much more pervasive than had previously been supposed, making them more difficult to attack.[49] They might be wrong in principle, but they were acceptable in practice.[50]

While this analytical work was proceeding, there were other steady improvements in economic techniques in other fields, of which some of the most important were in the collection, organising and dissemination of statistics. Early work in Britain was done by Arthur Bowley (1869–1957) who, in 1919, became the first holder of the new Chair in Statistics at London University, and was one of the first proponents of sample surveys.[51] His main book was his *The Division of the Product of Industry*, published in 1920.[52] His work was followed up by Colin Clark (1905–1989), who, over half a century of work, established himself as one of the pioneers of national income estimates. He was the first to use the term Gross National Product, and to break it down into what are now treated as its standard components. In an article published in 1937, he produced one of the first comparative estimates of national product in different countries. He followed this up in 1940 with his *Conditions of Economic Progress* which both sparked renewed interest among economists in long-term economic growth, and also supplied the first substantial statistical evidence for the width of the gap in living standards between the rich and poor countries in the world.[53] A consequence of the work of Bowley, Clark and others was the establishment in Britain of an Economic Advisory Council to oversee the gathering of statistics and, in 1941, originally within the Cabinet Office, the Central Statistical Office.[54]

Similar work done by Clark in Britain was carried out by Simon Kuznets (1901–1985) in the USA, although there were some earlier precedents there, set by Irving Fisher, of whom more in Chapter 8, who, in his *Nature of Capital and Income*, published in 1906, had explicitly set himself the task of evolving concepts suitable for economic accounting.[55] Kuznets was born in Russia and had spent a brief period as head of the statistical office in the Ukraine under the early Soviet régime, before moving to the USA. Like Clark, he began by organising US economic statistics in the way in which they are now universally presented, and went on from there to produce international studies of growth and development, for which he was awarded his Nobel Prize in 1971.[56] Kuznet's defining article was written in 1933, followed by the publication in 1941 of his *National Income and its Composition 1919–1938*.

Other important technical developments which took place during the inter-war period, to some extent paving the way for Keynes, included a gradual revival of interest in monetary policy. The Neo-Classical system, which was dominant from about 1870 to 1914, consisted almost wholly of micro-economics, based squarely on the equi-marginal rule.[57] This involved detailed investigations of the circumstances in which demand and supply were in balance for all goods and services across the whole economy, generally with the assumption that there was perfect competition. The influence of changes in monetary conditions were almost entirely ignored. Partly as a result of this limited approach, the Neo-Classical system never challenged the validity of Say's Law, because it had very little to say about business cycles and monetary economics. Indeed, Marshall himself said of his *Principles* that 'we may throughout this volume neglect possible changes in the general purchasing power of money'.[58] Even as late as 1932, Lionel Robbins (1898–1984), by then Senior Economics Professor at the London School of Economics,[59] had written in an influential *Essay on the Nature and Significance of Economic Science*, that 'economics should be defined as a science treating of the allocation of scarce resources'.[60] Others, however, took a different view, particularly as conditions deteriorated during the inter-war period. Under the leadership of Ralph Hawtrey (1879–1975), Keynes and Dennis Robertson (1890–1963), increasing attention was paid to the relationship between prices and monetary and credit policy, and the consequences of changes in both on business conditions. Even before the outbreak of the First World War, Hawtrey had anticipated the core of later macro-economics, stating that 'all costs of production are someone's income', stressing the impact that changes in monetary policy had on the level of activity in the economy. In Hawtrey's view, business cycle downturns were attributable to the policy of the banks, which would contract credit once they found themselves exposed to a shrinking cash position.[61] This was an important advance towards the formulations to which Keynes was moving.

What assessment then needs to be made of the Neo-Classical period? In an important sense, its teachings reflected the temper of the age in which it was dominant, especially in Britain which was then at the peak of its power relative to other countries. Its quietist tenor suited a country whose success appeared to be evident for all to see, although in fact the signs of at least relative decline were becoming apparent as Britain's growth rate slowed compared with those of continental competitors. Its continuity with the older classical tradition was in line with the social stability of the country, despite shifts in emphasis, again perhaps reflecting the changing times. Its descriptive rather than normative character mirrored the long-standing tradition, heavily influenced by the Newtonian concept of equilibrium and successful developments in science, that economics ought to have more of the character of physics, chemistry or astronomy than history or biology.[62] Although both claimed to be universal systems, Classical Economics had been primarily concerned with production, supply and cost, and with the structure of society – landlords, labourers and capitalists – whereas the Neo-Classics were more orientated to consumption, demand and utility, and the role of the individual.[63] In any event, Neo-Classical economics – pre-eminently developed in Britain – provided no effective analysis about why the British lead in the world was slipping away, or prescriptions to stop this occurring, although there was widespread awareness of the adverse trends which were materialising. For example, British exports fell in value from £256m in 1872 to £192m in 1879. Much of this fall was compensated for in volume terms by lower prices, but not all. The 1872 export figure was not exceeded until 1890. In the case of manufactures, the ground lost was not recovered in terms of value until 1903, over 30 years later.[64] The practical consequences of these developments were well known in policymaking circles, as is clear from *The Final Report of the Royal Commission on the Depression of Trade and Industry*, published in 1887. The gulf between harsh business reality and academic economics by the late nineteenth century, however, was too wide for the relative decline in British industrial performance, and the absolute distress caused to significant parts of it, to make much impact, if any, on the scholastic and other-worldly subject which economics had by this time become.

The reality was that the system for which Marshall was such an eloquent advocate was simply not orientated to dealing with such problems, or their consequences. Despite its analytical sophistication, it had nothing to say about economic growth, denied that structural unemployment could exist, assumed away changes in the price level, had no message about the alleviation of poverty, and did not see capacity constraints on earth's ecology, even on the horizon. Of course, any view of the world is inevitably heavily coloured by the perceptions of the time. Nevertheless, economics needed to move on a long way from the complacency of late Victorian Britain if it was going to make a worthwhile, policy-orientated contribution to the betterment of the human lot.

Dissident voices

While the economic mainstream was broadly content with the Neo-Classical formulations, there were always dissidents who, in varying degrees, disagreed with them. Criticism, attacks and new approaches came from a variety of different directions.

One was led by Herbert Spencer (1820–1903), who, as a young man, had been a civil engineer with the London and Birmingham Railway. Largely self-educated, he was an early and enthusiastic supporter of Darwin's evolutionary ideas, which he used for his own purposes, culminating in his book *The Man versus the State*, published in 1884.[65] One of the largely unresolved problems faced by both Classical and Neo-Classical Economics was to explain and justify the large disparities of wealth and income thrown up by the market-orientated economies of the nineteenth century. Spencer's solution to this problem – Social Darwinism – was to assume that this had to be the natural order of things. The publication in 1859 of *The Origin of Species* by Charles Darwin (1809–1882) had undermined the Christian certainties about creation, putting forward a totally different explanation to the one in the Bible for the diversity of flora and fauna throughout the world.[66] Instead of the beneficence of God, the reason for the evolution of different plants and animals was a relentless competitive process, with nature 'red in tooth and claw' as Alfred Tennyson (1809–1892), very much the poet of the age, aptly described it.[67] This allowed only 'the survival of the fittest', which was Spencer's phrase, not Darwin's,[68] to provide a justification for avoiding pity for those who failed to thrive under the industrial system.

The poor, in Spencer's view, were the weaklings, and their failure to survive and prosper was nature's way of improving the species. 'I am simply carrying out the views of Mr. Darwin in their applications to the human race ... Only those who *do* advance under [the pressure imposed by the system] ... eventually survive ... [These] must be the select of their generation.'[69] It was a short step from propositions like these to the conclusion that this process, being natural, should be allowed to run its course. 'Partly by weeding out those of lowest development, and partly by subjecting those who remain to the never-ceasing discipline of experience, nature secures the growth of a race who shall both understand the conditions of existence, and be able to act up to them. It is impossible in any degree to suspend this discipline.'[70]

These ideas had a ready hearing in some quarters, especially in the USA where, as the nineteenth century progressed, wealth was increasingly flaunted, in contrast to the harsh conditions often experienced both by those at the receiving end of American industrialisation and the millions of poor people who were migrating to the USA at the time. While Spencer, with some reluctance, accepted that charity might have a role to play in alleviating the suffering of the poor, the implication of Social Darwinism was that state initiatives to do so were off limits. On the other hand, those who had done best out of the system needed to feel no qualms about having done so. As William Graham Sumner (1840–1910), a Yale University professor, and the most eminent of the American Social Darwinists, put it 'The millionaires are a product of natural selection ... the naturally selected agents of society for certain work. They get high wages and live in luxury, but the bargain is a good one for society.'[71]

This was not a view of the world, however, which commended itself to one of the more trenchant critics of the way the US economy operated around the turn of the twentieth century. This was Thorstein Veblen (1857–1929), who, although coming from a farming background in Minnesota, spent all his adult life on the faculty of a variety of American universities. His family was Norwegian by origin, and was looked down on by the surrounding Anglo-Saxon settlers. This early experience may have been a factor affecting Veblen's later attitudes to the rich and powerful.[72] He began his publishing career with a series of short papers produced around 1900, in which he attacked the established economic ideas as being not the product of a search for truth and reality, but a cloak for the self-interest of those already well off. He described economic theory as an exercise in static 'ceremonial adequacy',[73] ignoring the dynamic nature of real economic experience. From this beginning, Veblen developed a general critique of established motivations, querying any ideas which were accepted, and challenging public action even it appeared to be done with the best of intentions. His style was almost entirely destructive. Practical recommendations for improved perform-ance were not Veblen's forte.[74]

1904 saw the publication of his *The Theory of Business Enterprise* in which he contrasted the professional skill and productive potential of engineers and scientists with the apparently parasitical control of their activities by those primarily concerned with maintaining prices and profits.[75] In 1914, he produced *The Instinct for Workmanship*, which was an attack on the industrial system's capacity for suppressing the ordinary worker's or artisan's artistically motivated concern for the quality of his performance.[76] *The Higher Learning in America*, published in 1918, exposed the extent to which teaching in American universities was controlled by business inter-ests, who guided the curriculum to ensure that the teaching accorded with their views of the world. The book for which Veblen is best known, however, was his first major work, *The Theory of the Leisure Class*, which was published in 1899.

The subject of this book was the American super-rich, with whom he identified the leisure class, whose behaviour he ruthlessly analysed in a sufficiently scientific manner to make the case he put forward a compelling read. Taking a lead from anthropology, he declared that 'The institution of a leisure class is found in its best development at the higher stages of the barbarian culture.'[77] Both in primitive societies and in New York and Newport 'Costly entertainments, such as the potlatch or the ball, are peculiarly adapted to serve the end.' 'As the latter-day outcome of this evolution of an archaic institution, the wife, who was at the outset the drudge and chattel of man, both in fact and in theory – the producer of goods for him to consume – has become the ceremonial consumer of goods which he produces.' It was Veblen who invented the term 'conspicuous consumption',[78] and who half admired and half despised the rich for whom 'The only practical means of impressing one's pecuniary ability ... is the unremitting demonstration of ability to pay.'[79]

The impact of Veblen's diatribes against the behaviour of the rich, and – more damaging still – his ability to make them look ridiculous, had a lasting impact on the discretion with which those who were very well off in America spent their money. An equally long-lasting tradition was established by Henry George, whose influence on the Fabian Society has already been mentioned. George's formative experience was on the west coast of the USA, where, especially during the years following the 1849 California Gold Rush, he saw enormous sums of money being made by those who owned land, in many cases whether or not they did anything to improve it. This, he believed, was at the root of much of the inequality he saw all round him. 'So long as all the increased wealth which modern progress brings goes but to build up great fortunes, to increase luxury and make sharper the contrast between the House of Have and the House of Want, progress is not real and cannot be permanent.'[80]

George's solution was the Single Tax, to mulct away the unearned gain in land values which did not derive from any positive contribution from the owner, but from the general expansion of population and wealth.[81] George believed that this could be pitched at a sufficiently high rate to provide all the funds required by the state, thus relieving everyone but landowners of the obligation to pay taxes. The appeal of such a proposal is obvious, and has lasted to this day, although the problems with it were manifest from the beginning. Increasing land values were not the only way in which people became rich without having to work for their good fortune. There was an inescapable element of confiscation in the Single Tax proposal, which led to overwhelming political opposition to it. As state expenditures increased, it became increasingly obvious that the proceeds from only one form of taxation would be inadequate, although George – a pioneer in tax limitation despite his left-wing credentials – claimed that land tax proceeds should set an upper limit on state expenditures.[82] Nevertheless, the appeal of the Single Tax remains, and its legacy still exists in a residual distrust of property speculation, and support for publicly owned land and the planning system which has created spaces such as London's Green Belt.[83] Single Tax parties have seldom been successful at the polls, although Henry George, who stood twice for the mayoralty of New York, might have won the second time in 1897, if he had not died a few days before election day.[84]

If the influences on the development of economic thought of Spencer, Veblen and George were significant but minor, those who attacked the Classical and Neo-Classical systems frontally, and eventually with considerable success over the issue of Free Trade, were considerably more effective. Removal of tariffs and other barriers to trade had been advocated by mainstream economists, especially in Britain, ever since the time of Adam Smith, although such ideas had generally had considerably less appeal elsewhere, both on the continent of Europe and in the USA. Since the time of Alexander Hamilton and the American Declaration of Independence, the US market had always been heavily protected. Partly under the influence of Britain, the major continental countries in Europe had reduced their tariff barriers from around 1860 onwards, but had raised them again from the mid-1880s.[85] As the nineteenth century moved to a close, public opinion became aware that Britain was losing ground, at least relatively to the major economies on the continent. In particular, during the 1870s, the total value of British exports to the rest of Europe and the USA fell, whereas those to the rest of the world, and especially to the British Empire, increased considerably.[86] This led to the creation in 1881 of the Fair Trade League, with comparatively modest demands for retaliatory tariffs against countries which had raised new restrictions on the importation of British goods. At this stage, however, Britain was still exporting almost five times more manufactured goods than were being imported, so the Liberals, then the governing party, had little difficulty in opposing moves to protectionism.[87]

By the early twentieth century, however, the five to one ratio had shrunk to two to one, with the bulk of the surplus coming in trade with territories within the British Empire. This led Joseph Chamberlain (1836–1914), who, as President of the Board of Trade, had previously opposed the League's policies, to change his mind. In 1903 he launched what became the Tariff Reform League, favouring what was still a comparatively modest form of protection, with a reciprocal preferential system for the Empire. This led to a counter-attack on behalf of the Treasury by Alfred Marshall, exemplifying all too clearly the mainstream mindset of the time:

> On the other hand, it is not merely expedient – it is absolutely essential – for England's hopes of retaining a high place in the world, that she should neglect no opportunity of increasing the alertness of her indus-

trial population in general, and her manufacturers in particular, and for this purpose there is no device to be compared in efficiency with the plan of keeping her markets open to the new products of other nations and especially to those of American inventive genius and of German systematic thought and scientific training.[88]

The Tariff Reform League was not successful in changing British tariff policy prior to the First World War but, in the much more difficult period between the wars, opposition to Free Trade increased, culminating in the change to a much more extensive system of tariffs and imperial preference which were introduced as Britain came off the Gold Standard in 1931. British policymakers were slow to learn – as were many in other countries – that there is much to be said for free trade, but only if exchange rates are correctly aligned.

Developing techniques

During the period between the 1930s and the beginning of the twenty-first century, economics went through two major upheavals. One was the Keynesian Revolution, which is the subject of the next chapter, and the other is the monetarist counterblast, which is the subject of the chapter after that. While these large-scale changes in perception were taking place, however, techniques in economic analysis continued to evolve, providing a more comprehensive, but in some ways more daunting and recondite backdrop to the work which was being done. This section highlights some of the more significant of these developments, and the contributions which they made to the evolution of economics theory.

First, there was a group of economists on both sides of the Atlantic who developed econometrics, a term originally used by the Norwegian economist Ragnar Frisch (1895–1973), a co-founder with Irving Fischer of the Econometric Society in 1930.[89] This is a technique which involves the setting-up of mathematical models describing economic relationships, and then testing the validity of such hypotheses against empirical data. The way that this is done is to use mathematical techniques, particularly tests for correlation, to establish the extent to which one variable is dependent on another. Is it, for example, true that in most cases the demand for any particular good rises as its price falls?

The pioneers of this technique in the USA, apart from Irving Fisher, whose main work will be covered in Chapter 8, were Henry L. Moore (1869–1958), Henry Schultz (1893–1938) and Paul H. Douglas (1892–1976).[90] Douglas worked with a professor of mathematics, Charles E. Cobb, to produce the so-called Cobb-Douglas Production Function. In 1928,[91] they used this to estimate the effects on the US economy of increased labour and capital inputs, showing that, broadly speaking, a 1% increase in labour input would raise national output by about two-thirds of 1%, whereas a 1% increase in capital input would raise it by one-third of 1%.[92] In Europe, the leading figures were Jan Tinbergen (1903–1994) in the Netherlands, and Richard Stone (born 1913) in Britain. Tinbergen's specialities were business cycle research[93] and, later, development in poorer countries,[94] while Stone's work at the beginning of the Second World War in determining the resources which could be mobilised for the war effort, mirrored similar accomplishments at the same time in the USA. In 1969 Frisch and Tinbergen shared the first Nobel Prize in economics for their pioneering work.[95] In 1984 Stone was similarly honoured,[96] preceded in 1980 by the American Lawrence R. Klein (born 1920), who had led the way in using computers in the 1950s and 1960s to build much more complex models of the US economy than had existed previously.[97] Tellingly, during the interwar period, the use of econometrics spread more slowly in Germany than in other parts of Europe. As with their lack of adequate national statistics, of which more later, this must have contributed to the difficulty which the Germans had in mobilising their economy as effectively as they might have done during the Second World War.[98]

Particularly interesting applications of econometric studies were those concerned with the relationship between unemployment, growth and inflation. In the USA, Arthur Okun (1920–1980) discovered that, during the 1950s and 1960s, a 1% increase in unemployment was associated with a 3% drop in the ratio of actual compared to potential national income, a relationship which became known as Okun's Law.[99] Meanwhile, an even more influential apparent correlation was reported by Alban Phillips (1914–1975) in an article in *Economica* in 1958. This set out empirical evidence to show that there was a significant relationship between the percentage change of money wages and unemployment: the lower the number of unemployed, the higher the average wage increases which were recorded. This became known as the Phillips Curve. Its implication was that there was an inconsistency between aiming both for low levels of unemployment and low levels of inflation, and that a policy choice had to be made between the number out of work and the rate at which prices would be allowed to rise.[100] In due course, this became an important component of the monetarist attack on Keynesianism.

Another part of economics in which considerable refinement of both theoretical and practical techniques took place was in growth theory. Sir Roy Harrod (1900–1978), who had also made important contributions to ideas about partial monopoly,[101] explored the relationships between the growth intentions of individual firms and the availability of capital and labour to show that there was no theoretical reason why growth should not continue exponentially, despite the intuitive sense that this might not to be possible. In fact, the ratio between savings and investment on the one hand, and consumption on the other, as a proportion of the national income has remained remarkably stable in all advanced countries at least over the last 130 years during which reliable statistics have been available. So too has the growth rate of GDP per head, at about 2% per annum.[102] The Harrod-Domar model showed the conditions which had to be fulfilled for this balanced growth to happen,[103] with the output from new productive capacity, generated by investment, being absorbed by the additional income generated from the same source.[104] This work was further refined and extended by Sir John Hicks (1904–1989), who also made significant contributions to Welfare Economics.

While the work of writers such as Harrod and Hicks was highly abstract and theoretical, and thus difficult to relate in any practical sense to the real world, others were taking the lead in investigating empirically the way in which economic growth appeared to be generated. During the period following the Second World War, this was a matter of particular concern in countries such as Britain and the USA, which were evidently growing more slowly than most other developed countries at the time. This state of affairs triggered extensive studies on the contribution to economic growth from different factors of production, especially, in the US case, in the work of Edward F. Denison (1915–1992). Similar concerns were voiced in Britain by writers such as Andrew Shonfield (1917–1981), who was particularly concerned about the relationship between the public and the private sectors, and the framework in which they could best be made to co-operate.[105]

In between those with a theoretical approach to economic growth and those with a largely empirical bent came attempts to impose a pattern on the way the advanced economies of the world had evolved, which both took account of empirical data and also explained the processes at work in enabling sustained growth to occur. The best known of the writers who attempted this kind of synthesis was Walt Whitman Rostow (born 1916), who proposed in his *Stages of Economic Growth*, published in 1960, that societies passed through five stages of development. These were: the traditional society; the pre-conditions for take-off; the take-off, when growth becomes a normal feature of the economy; the drive to maturity; and finally, some sixty years after take-off, the advent of an age of mass consumption.[106] While it was agreed that this kind of analysis provided useful insights into the process of economic evolution, it was criticised on the grounds that not all growth and development took the same uniform path.

Other significant influences on economic thinking over the last few decades have come from developments in related fields of inquiry, especially those to do with mathematics. John von Neumann (1903–1957), one of the many extraordinarily talented people to emerge from the period when the Austro-Hungarian Empire broke up as a result of the First World War,[107] was the original inventor of game theory. This was not concerned with games of chance, in which mathematicians had long been interested, but with games of strategy, the outcomes of which depended not only on

individual choices, but also on the actions and reactions of other participants. In such circumstances, rational behaviour does not rest on each par-
ticipant attempting to achieve the maximum benefit from the available
choices in isolation, because the outcome will also depend on the actions
of others.[108] This was a theory which provided particular insights in circumstances, such as partial monopoly, where traditional marginal analysis
was liable to lead to inconclusive results. In order to demonstrate the rele-
vance of game theory in contexts of this kind, von Neumann joined with
Oskar Morgenstern (1902–1977), a Princeton economist, to publish, in
1944, their *Theory of Games and Economic Behavior*.[109]

A contribution from a different direction was supplied by Ronald Coase
(born 1910), who received a Nobel Prize for his work in 1991. Its main
significance was encapsulated in an article published in *Economica* in 1937,
entitled *The Nature of the Firm*,[110] which was, in turn, based on an essay
which he had written as an undergraduate some years previously, while on
a scholarship visit to the USA.[111] In this paper Coase asked why, in a free
enterprise economy, workers should voluntarily submit to direction by
being employed in a firm rather than selling their output directly to customers in the market. His answer was that the firm was more efficient
because it reduced the costs of operating in the market place, allowing
economies of scale in discovering prices, sources of supply, and other information. These benefits were not, however, ones which increased
indefinitely, as in at least some cases, the rising costs of running ever more
complex organisations outweighed the gains from shared knowledge.
Although the term 'transactions costs' was not coined until the 1960s,[112] it
was from these insights that he developed what came to be known as the
Coase Theorem, which was published in an article in 1959.[113] This deals
with social costs, and concerns the efficiency of property rights as a way of
allocating them. The Theorem states that, provided there is a completely
free market, the optimum distribution of benefits will be achieved by
trading between these rights,[114] for example by polluting factories compen-
sating those who suffer the pollution up to a point where no further
exchanges can produce a better outcome.

Another way in which mathematical theory had a significant impact on
economics came from the work pioneered by Trygve Haavelmo (born
1911), a Norwegian economist, and yet another Nobel Prize winner, on this
occasion in 1989. His most important paper *The Probability Approach to
Econometrics* was published in the USA during the Second World War.[115] In
it, he stressed the inexactitude of economic data, and the extent to which
any figures were, in most cases, the central estimate around which one of a
range of possible results might actually be the correct one.[116] This was an
important warning, particularly about over-reliance on projections of
future outcomes, such as next year's national income. While such forecasts
were always in demand, they were invariably based on past estimates

which were not necessarily correct, compounding errors in projecting the future, which was also an uncertain process. Haavelmo showed how the likelihood of error could be quantified, and the risks attached to such forecasts contained by appropriate use of mathematical probability analysis.

The past decades have also seen important reformulations of economic theory as well as the creation of new analytical tools. By general consent, the most important and influential synthesis of economic concepts during the twentieth century was the one entitled *Economics* by Paul A. Samuelson (born 1915) which was first published in 1948; 50 years later, it was in its twelfth edition.[117] For this, and many other contributions to economic thought, Samuelson was also a Nobel Prize winner, in his case in 1970.[118] Yet another winner of the same prize, in 1973, was Wassily Leontief (1906–1999), who used matrix algebra and modern computers to build input–output tables showing the interactions and inter-relationships between the components of the modern economy. These were set out in two editions of his book *The Structure of the American Economy*, one published in 1941 covering the years from 1919 to 1929, and the second in 1951 a more extended period from 1919 to 1939.[119]

Other developments took place in international trade theory. Bertil Ohlin (1899–1979), originally from Sweden, and James Meade (1907–1995), from Britain, shared the 1977 Nobel Prize for their work in this field. Ohlin attained worldwide recognition with his reconstruction of the theory of international trade in his book *Interregional and International Trade*, which was published in 1933. Whereas Ricardo and James Mill had concentrated on the gains from trade, Ohlin's point of departure was to ask why it took place at all. He argued that it came about because of the unequal endowment of productive resources among regions and countries.[120] Jointly with his former teacher at Stockholm University, Eli Filip Heckscher (1879–1952), he developed the Heckscher-Ohlin Trade Theory, which essentially stated that the exports of any country would tend to be biased towards output made up of factor inputs – land, labour and investment – for which they were well endowed, with the reverse applying to imports.[121] Subsequent empirical research, however, showed that actual patterns of trade frequently did not follow the predicted pattern,[122] highlighting the danger of drawing complex conclusions from plausible first principles, which may not be able to stand the weight put upon them. Meade's main contribution, made in a series of books, was to highlight the problems associated with attempting to achieve multiple objectives to do with foreign trade at the same time, including a satisfactory trade balance, modest inflation and full employment. He emphasised the need, originally formulated by Tinbergen, for there always to be at least as many policy instruments available as there were objectives to be attained.[123]

Robert Solow (born 1924), the Nobel Prize-winner in 1987 for his work on the theory of economic growth in which he emphasised the significance of improving technology as opposed to simply measuring the scale of capital investment, also had an important influence on linear programming theory. This is a technique which was originally used for the logistical planning and deployment of military forces, but which now has a wide range of applications in both industry and elsewhere. Its tenets are equally appropriate to a market or non-market economy, which was one of the reasons why some of its early development took place in the Soviet Union.[124] While linear programming is primarily a discipline for determining the best way of solving problems such as finding the optimum mix of inputs to achieve a given output at the lowest possible cost, it also sheds light on the way the economy as a whole operates, not least for those concerned with central planning.

The twentieth century, therefore, saw a steady development of economic theory and techniques. To what extent they made it easier to see what really needed to be done to make economics a more effective discipline, is, however, much more debatable. To a large extent, modern economics has inherited from both Classical and Neo-Classical Economics assumptions about pure competition, perfect knowledge, and the ability of factors of production to find their optimum allocation. These make it easy to create models which can then be subjected to mathematical treatment, but with at least two heavy costs. The first is that, in the real world, pure competition seldom, if ever, exists. The general rule in the real world is that nearly everyone lacks important and relevant information on decisions that have to be taken. As a result of this, and the fact that the allocation of resources is generally subject to many other factors than those attributed to rational economic man or woman, the way the economy actually operates often bears little resemblance to what ought to happen in theory, and seldom corresponds at all exactly to it in practice. The second is that the abstruseness and difficulty of much economic model-making effectively excludes all but those thoroughly familiar with advanced mathematical techniques from understanding fully what it is trying to achieve, let alone being able to make much use of its results.

The outcome has been that, as with so much of the development of economics in earlier periods from the beginning of the nineteenth century onwards, most of the huge amount of work done in recent decades to refine economic techniques has not produced a corresponding increase in the capacity of policymakers to understand more clearly the range of choices in front of them. Nor has most of it been of as much value as it might have been in assisting them to take an informed view on economic decisions. Some of it, particularly the organisation of reliable statistical information, has unquestionably been of substantial worth, though whether economists have used all this data as effectively as they might have done is yet another matter to which the response is by no means an obviously positive one. The issue is how to find a way ahead which will relate economic theory much more immediately to the solution of practical policy problems.

The case argued in this book is that only to a limited extent does the future of economics, if this is to be worth having, lie in refining mathematical models. Far more pressing is the need to find more intelligible ways of relating the major economic issues which urgently need to be resolved to the data which is available, and to developing relatively simple and straightforward ways of interpreting and using it. It is vitally important that this is done in such a way that it can be understood both by policy-makers and the general public. This is not an argument for over-simplification, nor for ignoring the important need for a quantitative approach. There is, however, a very strong case for simplifying issues as much as possible, so that anyone who wants to follow them can appreciate what they are, and can understand the arguments surrounding the critical choices which need to be made.

7
The Keynesian Revolution

Ideas shape the course of history.

John Maynard Keynes (1883–1946)

Whereas the decades running up to the First World War had seen rising living standards and reasonably stable conditions almost everywhere, especially in the economically developed world, by no stretch of the imagination could the same be said for the period between the wars. The First World War, and the Treaty of Versailles which followed it, had seen the delicate network of relationships which made up the pre-war world damaged, apparently beyond repair. Different rates of inflation during the war among the major belligerents – 50% in the USA, 80% in Britain, 100% in France and 200% in Germany[1] – had wreaked havoc with the relative competitiveness, which could only be remedied if major, but unwelcome, exchange rate changes took place. Reparations – forcing the defeated Germany to pay the victorious allies compensation for war guilt and damage – provided a profoundly destabilising influence. All the countries which had been engaged in the war suffered from recessions as hostilities ended. France's industrial production fell by over 40% between 1913 and 1919,[2] and it was not until 1927 that German GDP rose again to its immediate pre-First World War level.[3] Germany suffered a catastrophic hyperinflation in 1923.[4] Unemployment in Britain, one of the least successful of the world's economies in the 1920s, averaged nearly 8.5% throughout the period from 1920 to 1929.[5]

Worse, however, was to follow. In 1929, the boom which had gathered pace in the USA from the beginning of the 1920s, fuelled towards the end of the decade by more and more feverish speculation, broke as the New York stock market began a precipitous fall. The Dow-Jones, which had peaked at 381, reached its nadir of 41 in July 1932.[6] The German economy, which, during the 1920s had been kept reasonably prosperous by loans from the USA, despite reparations payments, found itself suffering the same fate as the US as loans were withdrawn, and confidence tumbled. Between 1929 and 1932, German GDP fell by almost a quarter, and industrial production dropped by nearly 40%.[7] By 1932 over 30% of the labour force was out of work in Germany, and 25% by 1933 in the USA.[8] In Britain, the situation was not quite so bad, partly because the Gold Standard had been abandoned in 1931, causing sterling to lose a third of its value against gold in three months.[9] Despite this, however, a year later, 3.2m members of the insured labour force had no work.

As this disaster overtook the world, dismally bad advice came from all quarters of the professional economic mainstream. Leading figures such as Joseph A. Schumpeter, now at Harvard, Lionel Robbins of the London School of Economics, and Irving Fisher, then the USA's leading economic theorist, all urged that nothing should be done. The Depression must be allowed to run its course. Only time would cure the disequilibrium in the system. Recovery would come of its own accord and, said Schumpeter, 'this is not all: our analysis leads us to believe that recovery is sound only if it does come of itself'.[10] Irving Fisher declared that 'with the stamina of the American people fortified by prohibition there was no need to be afraid of a severe depression'.[11] Still imprisoned by the implications of Say's Law, economists in the classical tradition, which at that time was almost all economists, had nothing useful to say about the slump and no remedies to offer other than waiting for better times to turn up.[12]

This great malaise, however, far from convincing an initially small number of economists, particularly Keynes himself, that there were no solutions to the world's pressing economic problems, stimulated them to further action. Although the Keynesian Revolution had its antecedents well before the Great Depression overwhelmed the world, it was the magnitude of the downturn which occurred around 1930 that provided the urgency with which new policies were formulated and promulgated.

Precursors to Keynes

The history of economics has been shaped to a remarkable extent by the work of people from two relatively small countries, though each has a proud past. One is Austria, where until the collapse of the Hapsburg régime at the end of the First World War, Vienna had been the capital of a large empire. The other, Sweden, although a small country in population terms at least since relinquishing its union with Norway in 1905, had been a substantial military power in previous centuries.[13] The Austrian legacy was mainly of the right in political terms, whereas the Swedish tradition was mainly of left, or in American terminology, liberal persuasion. With this goes another paradox. A good deal of the reason for the bent of Austrian thinkers was a reaction against Marx, who wrote in German, and the

Marxist tradition which he established. Most of the remarkably impressive economic liberal practitioners in Sweden, on the other hand, were taught by Gustav Cassel (1866–1944), Professor of Economics and Public Finance at Stockholm University,[14] and the pillar, in his time, of Swedish, and to a considerable extent, European economic conservatism.[15]

Among the most important of Cassel's pupils were Gunnar Myrdal (1898–1987), Bertil Ohlin (1899–1979), Erik Lundberg (1907–1987) and Dag Hammarskjöld (1905–1961), later to be Secretary General of the United Nations, in whose service he died in an aircrash in Africa. One of the important ingredients to the changes in economic perceptions associated with Keynes was the remarkable series of reforms that this group helped to engineer in Sweden during the inter-war period. Among these was the deliberate use of the government budget to sustain demand and employment in a counter-cyclical manner, specifically designed to offset the effects of the Depression, and buttressed by a well-developed social welfare system.[16] The result was that many of the policies subsequently advocated by Keynes as a cure for depressions had already been implemented during the inter-war period in Sweden, and could be seen to be successful.

In the background of the thinking of the Swedes, who coped so much better with the Depression in their country than did almost everyone else, was the work of an earlier Swedish economist, Knut Wicksell (1851–1926), who had originally made his reputation in marginal utility studies. He believed that monopoly and competition were at opposite ends of a spectrum, with many forms of market organisation in between, anticipating the work subsequently done by Chamberlin and Robinson.[17] Later, Wicksell turned to interest rate theory. While he was more concerned with policies which would stabilise prices than raise employment, he was particularly interested in the relationship between changes in the price level and the extent to which the general monetary demand for goods exceeded or fell short of their supply.[18] The work which he did on the role played by interest rates in monetary policy, and the influence they had on investment and on the total level of activity in the economy, nevertheless laid some of the ground for the interventionist policies pursued in Sweden during the 1930s. On a theoretical level, they also led to the work done by Ohlin, Myrdal and Lindahl in the 1920s and 1930s on the relationship between savings and investment, which was to be so crucial to the Keynesian analysis. In particular, they homed in on the fact that savings plans might not be matched by corresponding investment intentions, thus opening up the possibility that Say's Law might not hold.[19] Gunnar Myrdal's book, *Monetary Equilibrium*, published in 1931, foreshadowed many aspects of Keynes' *General Theory*.[20]

There were other antecedents to the Keynesian Revolution in Britain. Mention has already been made of the work of Ralph Hawtrey in realising that money did not play the almost entirely neutral role assigned to it by

Marshall and the Neo-Classicists. Hawtrey believed that changes to income and expenditure affected the price level, and the amount of activity in the economy, and that interest rates played an important part in determining how much money the public wanted to hold – the 'cash balance' – and hence how willing people would be to spend whatever money they had available.[21] More work along these lines was done by Dennis Robertson (1890–1963), whose investigations centred round trade cycles. He believed that their causes were a combination of monetary factors and market phenomena such as good and bad harvests, partial overproduction, and the temporary exhaustion of investment opportunities.[22]

There were also precursors to Keynes in the USA. In the 1920s William Trufant Foster (1879–1950) and Waddill Catchings (1879–1967) published a series of books in which they strongly urged government intervention to sustain and augment demand. Their target, in their book *The Road to Plenty*, published in 1928, was Say's Law: 'These Lords of the domain of economic theory [the Classical Economists] merely assumed, without even an attempt at proof, that the financing of production itself provides people with the means of purchase.'[23] Foster and Catchings were not in the economic mainstream, but others who were closer to it had also anticipated Keynes in important respects, particularly Lauchlin Currie (1902–1993), whose *The Supply and Control of Money in the United States* had been published in 1934.[24] Once the Depression started in earnest, however, practical necessity brought into play the remedies which Keynes was subsequently to rationalise and make respectable. Despite the canons of orthodox economic thinking, it proved impossible, as the Depression deepened, to cover government expenditure with receipts. As a result, *de facto* deficit financing began to play an important role in counteracting the slump. By 1936, the year in which Keynes' *General Theory* was published, US federal receipts covered only just under 60% of outlays, and the deficit represented 4.2% of GNP.[25]

The Keynesian Revolution also needs to be seen against the background of events in the Soviet Union and in Germany. Largely divorced from the capitalist world, the Soviet economy was expanding rapidly in the 1930s, and unemployment was almost non-existent. Whatever the charges which could be levelled against the Soviet system in terms of its cruelty and inefficiency, its achievements in generating growth and employment made it harder to argue that there was no alternative to the dismal performance in both respects of the main Western economies at the time. Two economists who had moved from Poland to the West, Oskar Lange (1904–1965) and Michal Kalecki (1899–1970), both of whom were to return to their native country after the war in important administrative positions, were in a better position than many to appreciate the contrasts in performance between the Soviet Union and the USA.[26] Lange's special expertise lay in his study of business cycles,[27] while Kalecki independently discovered the essential ideas in Keynes' *General Theory*, and published them in his *Essay on Business Cycle Theory*, published in 1933.[28]

The position in Germany, after Adolf Hitler (1889–1945) and his Nazi Party came to power in 1933, provided an even more potent example of what could be done if conventional economic policy was abandoned. However much their racist, militarist and nationalist policies are to be condemned, the record of the new régime in turning round the German economy was remarkable. Unemployment, which stood at over 30% of the working population in 1932, was reduced to just over 2% by 1938.[29] Over the same period, industrial production rose by a cumulative 14% per annum, and GNP by 9% a year.[30] Military expenditures were responsible for some of this increase, but they represented no more than 9.6% of GNP as late as 1937.[31] Average living standards rose markedly. Between 1932 and 1938, consumer expenditure rose by almost a quarter.[32] Nor was inflation a problem. Consumer prices rose by a total of only 7% between 1933 and 1939 – about 1% per annum.[33] Most of this economic achievement was secured by huge increases in expenditure by the state, financed by large-scale borrowings, some through bonds, but much of it from the banking system, instigated by the Reichsbank President, Hjalmar Schacht (1877–1970).[34] Meanwhile, similar developments were taking place in Japan. The policies pursued by Nazi Germany could not have been in sharper contrast to those of the Chancellor, Heinrich Brüning (1885–1970) – subsequently on the Harvard faculty – whose period in power immediately preceded the arrival of the Nazis. With the support of the Social Democrat opposition, he had presided over the economic downturn in Germany, putting forward no effective policies designed to reverse it. On the contrary, his government reduced public expenditure, thus making the slump worse, and precipitated the arrival of Hitler by cutting unemployment benefits.[35]

The problems thus faced by the liberal democratic countries of the West, as the Depression deepened, were therefore not just that their resources in terms of output were being wasted and their social capital run down. There were also alternative, and perhaps more successful ways of running economies for all to see, some menacing enough soon to engulf the world again in war. The post-First World War consensus had been that the only way to restore the stability of the pre-war period was to re-establish the Gold Standard, and that the markets, left to themselves, would thereafter return the world to the steady rise in prosperity which had prevailed before the First World War began.[36] Experience had shown that this was a recipe for disaster. The market showed no adequate capacity to correct itself. The Depression had brought falling prices and disinflation, unemployment, poverty and distress. Prescriptions were urgently needed to counteract the baleful outcome of laissez faire, pursued in circumstances where there was no sign of equilibrium being attained naturally. The liberal democracies thus badly needed the revolution in economic policies which Keynes, more than anyone else, was responsible for bringing about.

John Maynard Keynes

John Maynard Keynes (1883–1946) was born into a distinguished academic family. His father, John Neville Keynes (1852–1949), was a significant economist in his own right, and the administrator – called the Registrary[37] – for Cambridge University, to which his son returned after being at school at Eton.[38] After he had taken his degree in 1905 in Mathematics, which he combined with being President of the Cambridge Union,[39] the younger Keynes spent a year studying economics under Alfred Marshall. He then sat for the Civil Service examinations, and spent two years in the India Office, from which experience came his first book *Indian Currency and Finance*, published in 1913. In 1908, he returned to Cambridge to lecture in economics.

Shortly after the outbreak of the First World War, Keynes moved back to the Civil Service, this time to the Treasury, where his outstanding ability led him to be, by 1919, the principal Treasury representative at the Peace Conference at Versailles.[40] His violent disagreement with the terms of the Treaty, however, led to his resignation from the British delegation, and to a book entitled *Economic Consequences of the Peace*, whose success – the British edition alone sold 84,000 copies[41] – provided him overnight with a worldwide reputation. Apart from severe criticism of the major participants at the Peace Conference – Woodrow Wilson (1856–1924), the American President, was described as a 'blind and deaf Don Quixote' and Georges Clemenceau (1841–1929), Prime Minster of France as having 'one illusion – France; and one disillusion – mankind' – Keynes' book denounced the impracticality of the Treaty's conditions. Germany would never be allowed to run a sufficiently large export surplus to pay the reparations demanded and, even if this were permitted, the resulting financial and trade dislocation would penalise the whole of Europe.[42]

No longer a civil servant, Keynes spent the 1920s and 1930s carrying out an exceptionally wide range of activities. Apart from writing, he was involved with the arts, helping to establish the Arts Council[43] and, in 1925, marrying the Russian ballerina Lydia Lopokova[44] (1892–1981). He was chairman of an insurance company and of the governing body of the influential weekly magazine, *The New Statesman and Nation*. He served on a major Committee of Enquiry into Finance and Industry. He was also Fellow and Bursar of King's College, Cambridge,[45] though no longer a lecturer there. To augment the relatively small sums he earned from these activities, he speculated on the stock exchange. In this capacity, he enjoyed mixed success, having at one stage to be rescued by his father and City friends, though later he did much better.[46] In 1921 he published *A Treatise on*

Probability, a revised version of a dissertation he had prepared 12 years previously, followed in 1923 by *A Tract on Monetary Reform*.[47] These books reinforced Keynes' academic reputation, helping to prepare the ground for the next major brush he had with convention. This was over the restoration of sterling in 1925[48] by the then Chancellor of the Exchequer, Winston Churchill (1874–1965) to the Gold Standard at the same parity – $4.87 to the pound – as had prevailed prior to the First World War. In a pamphlet entitled *The Economic Consequences of Mr Churchill*, Keynes attacked this policy as being bound to lead to further deflation on the grounds that sterling was by then over-valued by some 10%. He railed that Churchill had 'no instinctive judgement to prevent him from making [such] mistakes ... [He] was deafened by the clamorous voices of conventional finance; and ... gravely misled by his experts.'[49]

In 1930, Keynes published his two-volume *A Treatise on Money*. This contained some of the key ideas which were to appear in the *General Theory*, in particular an attack on Say's Law. 'It might be supposed – and has frequently been supposed – that the amount of investment is necessarily equal to the amount of saving. But reflection will show that this is not the case.'[50] The full exposition of Keynes' ideas had to wait another six years, however, following a good deal of criticism of the *Treatise*,[51] during which further refining took place. It was not until 1936 that his *General Theory of Employment, Interest and Money* appeared.

When war broke out again in 1939, Keynes returned to the Treasury, publishing in 1940 an influential pamphlet entitled *How to Pay for War*. Its major purpose was to present a programme for financing Britain's war effort without generating inflation, the main method he advocated being compulsory savings.[52] Already by 1943, he was beginning to look forward to the post-war era, writing in a memorandum on *The Long Term Problem of Full Employment* that it might be necessary for 'two-thirds or three-quarters of total investment [to be] carried out or ... influenced by public or semi-public bodies',[53] a reference to his continuing concerns that there would not be sufficient demand to maintain full employment. For the remainder of his life, however, Keynes' main contribution to British policy was his leading role in negotiations with the Americans. These began with discussions on lend-lease support which continued throughout the Second World War, and then shifted to the terms on which a special post-war loan from the USA to Britain in 1945 should be granted. He combined these tasks with his role as one of the major architects of the Bretton Woods agreement of 1944, which established the International Monetary Fund and the Bank for Reconstruction and Development (the World Bank), and created the international economic framework for the post-1945 world.[54] Exhausted by unremitting hard work, and never having enjoyed the best of health, Keynes died in the spring of 1946.[55]

Although the volume of writings that Keynes produced in his lifetime was immense, and there is no doubt that the ideas which are indelibly associated with him were evolved slowly and sometimes painstakingly through them, the key economic message which he eventually delivered to the policymaking world was a comparatively simple one. It was essentially the reverse of Say's Law. There was no reason why economies should always generate sufficient demand to keep everyone in employment. In particular, while everyone's current expenditure had to be someone else's revenues, the same was not the case with income which its recipients planned to save, unless this was exactly matched by intentions to invest. If investment plans fell short of saving intentions, there would be a mismatch, which would lead to a shortfall in demand. In the end, investment and savings – or, more strictly, borrowing and lending[56] – would have to match, as an accounting identity. They might well do so, however, at a level which left the economy failing to use its full productive capacity, with both significant numbers of people without work, and with factories, machinery and other productive assets underemployed. The solution was to ensure that the state made good the shortfall in demand, by borrowing from those intending to save more than the private sector wanted to invest, and spending the proceeds on current consumption. In this way, the full use of the economy's productive capacity could be secured.

It is worth stressing where this formulation differs from the traditional Neo-Classical view. The fact that there were business cycles was, of course, accepted by the Neo-Classicists but, in their view, they were temporary disruptions of a full employment equilibrium to which market conditions would necessarily return of their own accord. This would happen as the result of a natural combination of falling wages and lower interest rates, which would encourage both increased employment and higher levels of investment. If unemployment and under-consumption persisted, the reason was that there was insufficient downward wage flexibility, the solution to which was to persuade the labour force to accept wage cuts.

Keynes, by contrast, argued that while this might make sense for an individual worker or industry, there was a fallacy of composition if the same approach was used for the whole economy. Far from matters being improved by reducing wages, the effect might well be to decrease still further the total amount of demand in the economy, making any shortfall still greater than it had been previously. Keynes admitted that, if the overall price level fell as fast as wages, this effect might be mitigated as lower prices and wages together would restore the status quo ante. This was the so-called Pigou effect, which would be augmented by the fact that falling prices would increase the value of any idle cash balances in the economy, thus encouraging them to be spent. Keynes still averred, however, that this might not be sufficient and that, while businesses responding to lower wage and interest costs might help expansion, there would still be likely to be a role for the state in augmenting demand by borrowing from the public, and then spending the money on public works and other forms of expenditure. Furthermore, falling prices entailed rising real costs of repaying borrowings, providing an additional significant deflationary element which needed to be offset by the state's intervention.[57]

This proposal from Keynes grated on another long-held tenet, supported by Neo-Classical economists, that the government's budget ought to be in balance, mirroring that of a prudent household, a view which went back to Adam Smith, who had argued that 'What is prudence in the conduct of every private family can scarce be folly in that of a great kingdom.'[58] While many economists of the time accepted that increased government expenditure might assist in the short term, they were concerned that this was a palliative which would provide no long-term solution. This approach was reinforced by the so-called Treasury View that public works would merely divert savings and labour from the private sector. As there was a consensus in the Treasury that the former was almost always less productive than the latter, the effect would be overall to worsen the situation.[59] Keynes showed that, on the contrary, attempts to balance the budget by cutting expenditure, as business confidence fell away and recession loomed, would simply make a bad situation worse, as indeed manifestly had happened at the time of the onset of the slump.

As to the benefit being secured by a fall in the price level increasing the purchasing power of cash balances, Keynes agreed that this might assist by increasing the amount which people were willing to lend by affecting their 'liquidity preference' in a positive direction, thus lowering interest rates and encouraging investment. He argued, however, that this could equally be done by state action to increase the money supply, thus lowering the rate of interest. There were, however, limits to how far on their own, these would be effective policies. If there were no investment opportunities, the result might be simply the accumulation of more idle balances. With or without wage cuts, the economy would fail to be stimulated, with chronic unemployment and underused resources,[60] unless expenditure by the state was used to fill the gap.

In the classical system, fluctuations in the national income were determined by the level of employment, which in turn was set by the level of real wages, while the quantity of money in circulation determined the price level. Savings and investment were brought into balance by the rate of interest, a balance which Say's Law maintained would always be achieved without unused resources, given the fluctuations round the mean caused by the trade cycle. In Keynes' system, no such balance could be assumed. Saving and investment, although as a matter of accounting always *ex post* equal to each other, would only be on a sufficient scale to maintain full employment if independent steps were taken to make sure that there was adequate demand in the economy to keep all the factors of production fully employed. Achieving this state of affairs would be made easier by the fact that any changes which helped to increase demand would have a knock-on stimulating effect through the 'multiplier' – a contribution to Keynes' thinking made by Richard Kahn (1905–1989) – as any increase in expenditure generated further additional rounds of spending. Furthermore, the rate of interest was determined by the money supply, Keynes argued, and not by the balance between the demand for investment funds and the availability of savings.[61]

The revolutionary nature of Keynes' analysis was apparent. Far from the Depression being the consequence of temporary imbalances in a self-correcting system, Keynes had shown them to be the consequence of structural deficiencies, but not ones without a cure. On the contrary, once it was apparent what the defects were, the remedy was both comparatively simple and painless. Keynes' influence, however, also went well beyond simply altering economic policy prescriptions. It also caused a major shift in the way in which economic theory affected the real world. Before him, economic analysis was concerned largely with describing the efficient allocation of resources, under the headings of price theory, value and distribution, all subject to partial and general equilibrium. In summary, it was almost entirely about micro-economics. Thereafter, macro-economics, a term coined – but not until the 1930s – by the same Ragnar Frisch who had invented the word econometrics,[62] was to dominate, with the focus on the make-up of the national income and the attainment of full employment. Before Keynes, most economic theory had only a formal validity, in that it could claim to be logically consistently developed from a series of assumptions, but its analytical remoteness from reality made it difficult to test empirically. These characteristics explained all too clearly why it lacked value for the purposes of policy prescription. After the Keynesian Revolution, macro-economics, at least, became much more closely coupled to the policymaking world. The main aggregates with which it was concerned were easy to relate to national accounting concepts, and thus well within the bounds of measurement, and correspondingly useful to those who had to make decisions about how the economy was to be run.[63]

Nor was this all. Before Keynes, economic policy was primarily aimed at the stabilisation of prices, and was pursued largely by means of self-regulating monetary action, with reductions in the real wage seen as the way in which labour resources would price themselves back into the market, in the event of a recession occurring. After him, the notion that there was a process of automatic stabilisation at work disappeared. Instead, the maintenance of full employment by state action – at least until the arrival of monetarism – became the primary policy objective. Changed too, was the attitude to monetary policy. In the past, the role of money had been regarded as being largely neutral, at least in the sense that there was no clear connection between the amount available through the money supply and the level of output, with the balance between savings and investment being a function of the rate of interest. After Keynes, it was realised that the volume of money in circulation was a prime determinant of the amount of activity in the economy, with the level of interest rates being a function much more of policy decisions than anything which balanced the supply and demand for funds in the market place. There were also changes to social attitudes, particularly those to do with thrift. Long regarded as a primary virtue, with a concomitantly favourable view of balanced budgets, Keynesian analysis showed that expenditure generates income, and that when there are unused resources and unemployment, public and private thrift ceases to be a virtue.[64] Similarly undermined was the argument, sometimes used under the classical system to justify a skewed distribution of income, that the rich would save more than the poor, thus necessarily freeing up more resources for investment.[65]

It was the scale of all these changes which makes clear the breadth of Keynes' achievement. There were others before him who had anticipated many of the ideas which came to fruition in the *General Theory*. The impact that their ideas had had on the vast body of economic practitioners, let alone those in charge of public affairs either as politicians or civil servants, had, however, been relatively insignificant except in one or two special cases such as in Sweden. The extent of the problems caused by the Depression, especially in countries such as the USA and Germany, which were worst affected, had led those faced with coping with them to adopt some of the remedies which Keynes proposed as practical necessities. These included policies such as deficit financing, which occurred largely because there were pressing reasons for expenditure, combined with an insufficient tax base from which to raise the funds to pay for it. They were implemented, however, without any clear intellectual justification for what was being done. The result was that much of the remedial action taken – though of evident practical benefit – was disparaged and attacked as being without theoretical justification, and still, therefore, misguided and wrong. Even as late as 1936, Franklin Roosevelt (1882–1945), the American New Deal President, alarmed by a $3.5bn federal deficit, cut government expenditure and deflated the American economy,[66] causing GDP to fall by 4% between 1937 and 1938, while industrial output fell back nearly a third and unemployment rose from 14.3% to 19%.[67] Once the full import of Keynes' ideas had been absorbed in the USA during the early post-Second World War decades, this would never have been allowed to happen. It was Keynes' great achievement that he not only formulated the ideas associated with his name as powerfully as he did, but that he also had the connections, held the pivotal positions, and had the ear of those in power, to enable him to get his ideas across to the world at large.

Spreading the word

One of Keynes' great strengths had always been his ability to work with other people. Although he was the mastermind behind the revolution which he inspired, he had been greatly helped along the way by a host of associates, many, but not all, from Cambridge University. These included Richard Kahn, James Meade, Joan Robinson and Piero Sraffa, Ralph Hawtrey and Dennis Robertson, all of whom, as we have seen, made other contributions of significance to economics in their own right.[68] These contacts helped to spread Keynesian ideas, but only relatively late on in relation to the most serious of the economic conditions experienced between the wars. By the time that the *General Theory* was published in 1936, the worst of the Depression was over, and the Second World War was looming. Only, therefore, to a limited extent did the Keynesian Revolution lead to a recovery from the slump. The countries which had seized a competitive advantage relatively early by devaluation – Britain in 1931 and the USA in 1934 – did much better than the Gold Bloc economies, which ploughed on into further stagnation with the gold exchange standard, until the advent of the Popular Front government of Leon Blum (1872–1950) in 1936.[69] To a large extent, however, the policies pursued in all the Western democracies were adopted by force of circumstances rather than with any clear intellectual backing to them.

The 1930s, nevertheless, saw a gradual conversion especially of younger economists to Keynes' way of thinking, a process which was particularly marked in the USA. Partly, this was a result of the scene having already been set by a widening debate in Washington about the causes of the slump, led by people such as Rexford Guy Tugwell (1891–1979), whose approach was much more pragmatic and statistically orientated than that of traditional economists. Keynes' influence therefore grew more rapidly in the academic world than it did within the US government, at least during the early years of the New Deal. An appeal by Keynes to Roosevelt, in the form of an open letter in the *New York Times* at the end of 1933 in which he placed 'overwhelming emphasis on the increase of national purchasing power resulting from government expenditure, which is financed by loans' produced little more response than a subsequent not very successful face-to-face meeting with the US President.[70]

The reaction to Keynesian ideas, particularly at Harvard, was however, much more favourable, with a particularly important role being played by Alvin Harvey Hansen (1887–1975). He had originally been a sceptic, describing the *General Theory* as 'Not a landmark in the sense that it lays a foundation for a "new economics" ... more a symptom of economic trends than a foundation stone upon which a science can be built.'[71] On further reflection, however, he changed his mind, and became one of the staunchest advocates of Keynes' thinking, summarising his views with great clarity in his *Fiscal Policy and Business Cycles*, published in 1941. Even more important in carrying the message to millions of economics students was the publication of Paul A. Samuelson's *Foundations of Economic Analysis* in 1947, followed by *Economics* in 1948,[72] later editions of this book, starting with the 12th edition published in 1985, being written jointly with William D. Nordhaus (born 1941).[73]

Much conventional opinion in the USA – and elsewhere – on Keynes' approach to economic policy remained, however, either unconvinced, or definitely hostile, especially before the outbreak of the Second World War. Whereas socialism had never materialised as a serious threat to Republican sentiment in the USA, Keynes' views were seen from an early stage to provide an unwelcome rallying point for collectivism and state interference. This helped to promote an alternative explanation of the Depression, which partly depended on an important book which was published in 1932 called *The Modern Corporation and Private Property*. Written by a lawyer, Adolf A. Berle (1895–1971) and an economist, Gardiner C. Means (1896–1988), this showed how far the USA had moved from being an economy with any resemblance to the perfect competition conditions posited by classical theory. The two hundred largest non-banking corporations were estimated to own almost one half of the non-banking assets in the country – almost a quarter of the entire national wealth. Their management was mainly in the hands of self-selecting boards of directors, leaving shareholders with a passive or even insignificant role. These incontrovertible facts prompted the response that the explanation for the continuing stagnation in the 1930s might be found within the existing orthodox canons in the form of corporate concentration and monopoly. This view was reinforced by the fact that layoffs and unemployment had tended to be much greater among major corporations than in highly competitive agriculture. The practical outcome was a considerable revival of antitrust enforcement, dissipated during the Second World War, but revived thereafter, and still a notable feature of American industrial and commercial policy.

There was also considerable disagreement about whether the Depression had been caused by too much credit creation rather than too little. An influential school of thought believed that too much cheap credit had fuelled excessive speculation, setting the stage for the 1929 crash. They were concerned that, if the central bank were to intervene to increase the money supply again when prices had only begun to fall, the outcome might be another round of excessive speculation, to be followed by another depression. The cure, then, was to allow a purge by liquidating over-extended enterprises.[74]

Despite these reactions among conventional economists as the Keynesian Revolution took place, some initial converts assumed positions of power and influence early enough to start making a difference in the 1930s. One was Robert Bryce[75] (born 1910), who had studied at both Cambridge and

Harvard, and whose impact on Canadian policy helped Canada to achieve something of the same success in combating the Depression as had been accomplished in Sweden. Another was Lauchlin Currie (1902–1993), whose book, *The Supply and Control of Money in the United States*, published in 1934, had anticipated Keynes in important respects.[76] It was the advent of the Second World War, however, more than anything else which propelled Keynesian thinking, and economists who knew how to implement it, into positions of authority. This was partly caused by the development, simultaneously to the Keynesian Revolution, of far better national statistical techniques, as we have already seen. The combination of macro-economics and detailed knowledge about the make-up of the national product turned out to be an extremely powerful one. The availability of accurate and intelligible statistics was a massive benefit to the Allied cause during the Second World War.

Prior to the First World War, there had been almost total ignorance, even in relatively advanced economies, of their size and structure. Even on matters of pressing topical concern, figures were often lacking. For example, until well into the Depression years, the USA had no reliable data on the level or distribution of unemployment.[77] The rapid remedying of these deficiencies was to be one of the major planks in making the best use of the US economy's potential in the Second World War. Once the statistics were available, the Victory Program, prepared by Robert Roy Nathan (born 1908) made clear the enormous extent to which the US economy had under-performed in the 1930s, thus showing how it would be possible to achieve the huge increases in output which did in fact materialise from 1939 onwards.[78] Similar developments in Britain were in sharp contrast to those in Germany, where the absence of any comparable data meant that the Nazi régime had no way of gauging accurately their economy's full production potential. The result was that they greatly underestimated it.[79] In the absence of knowledge of how resources were being used, both civilian consumption and the use of civilian manpower remained uncontrollably high in Germany during the Second World War.[80] As Samuelson said in his *Economics*, without 'this great invention of the twentieth century ... macro-economics would be adrift in a sea of unorganised data',[81] as was indeed to a substantial extent the position under the Nazi régime.

The successful prosecution of the war effort in both the USA and Britain therefore greatly enhanced the acceptability of Keynes' ideas, which were well suited to the collectivist sentiments of the time. In both countries, inflation was much better contained than had been the case during the First World War, while large increases in output were achieved – spectacularly so in the case of the USA. The expectations raised by the war were reflected on both sides of the Atlantic in declarations that full employment should in future be a major policy plank, although these were watered down in the US Employment Act of 1946, with no more than 'employment' being the target, and then only for those 'able, willing and seeking to work'.[82] Meanwhile, in London, preparations were being made to implement the Beveridge Report, which William Beveridge (1879–1963) himself supplemented in his book *Full Employment in a Free Society*, published in 1944, in which he suggested a target level of 3% unemployed. This was a figure which soon became a reference point for subsequent government policy.[83]

The high noon for Keynesian policies was then to follow during the 1950s and 1960s. Across almost all the developed, as well as the developing world, much higher growth rates were achieved, combined with far lower levels of unemployment, than had ever been seen before for any sustained period. The countries whose economies had been badly damaged recovered rapidly, and soon surged ahead, attaining significantly faster expansion rates than those seen in the USA and Britain. Overall, the cumulative growth rate in Northern Europe between 1950 and 1973 was 4.6%. It was 3.9% in the USA, and 5.2% in the main countries in Asia.[84] Meanwhile, over the same period, unemployment averaged respectively 2.4% and 4.6% and 1.6%, although the last figure relates only to Japan.[85] These were much better levels of performance than had been achieved previously. Between 1870 and 1913, the cumulative growth rate of world output had been 2.1%, and between 1913 and 1950 it had been only 1.9%. From 1950 to 1973 it was 4.9% – about two and a half times the rate which had been achieved over the previous 80 years.[86]

These figures are perhaps the best measure of what the Keynesian Revolution achieved, although the downturn which was to follow showed that there were weaknesses as well as strengths in the system which had been developed. Some of the reasons for the change in sentiment which came so obviously to the fore in the 1970s were ones with an intellectual background – from people who had never been convinced that the reforms which Keynes had been so important in promulgating had been in the right direction. Even at the height of the collectivist wartime effort, Friedrich A. von Hayek (1899–1992), seeing in government intervention a threat to liberty, had warned in his *The Road to Serfdom* that 'The price system will fulfil [its] ... function only if competition prevails, that is, if the individual producer has to adapt himself to price changes and cannot control them.'[87] Part of the problem lay in the fact that most of Keynes' adherents put more of a leftward tilt on his ideas than Keynes himself would have supported.[88] As a result, when confidence in left of centre remedies began to decline in the 1960s, the ground was prepared for abandonment of Keynesianism as well in the decade to follow. More pressing reasons for the loss of confidence in Keynesian remedies, however, came from the way in which events developed, especially after the American devaluation of the dollar in 1971, which led to the break-up of the Bretton Woods international monetary system. If Keynes had still been alive, he might have been able to steer policy round the rocks to come, but he had died a quarter of a century previously. The problems which most urgently required attention then were different from those which the world confronted as it moved into the last quarter of the twentieth century.

The Keynesian legacy

With the achievements of the Keynesian Revolution as manifest as they were, how did it come about that so much of the thinking which seemed eminently well established during the 1960s and 1970s was swept away so quickly and – at least as far as most policymakers were concerned – so completely in the first half of the 1970s? Some of the reasons were to do with the powerful appeal of the monetarist ideas, which came to the fore just at the time when external events had caused the previous consensus to start to break up. This was not, however, the whole explanation. Although the Keynesian system had great strengths, it also had weaknesses, some of which had been becoming increasingly apparent during the quarter-century following the end of the Second World War. Others only became clear much later, as the post-Second World War monetary settlement disintegrated at the beginning of the 1970s.

The earlier concerns centred largely round inflation. In the 1930s, excessive price rises had barely been a problem anywhere. On the contrary, for much of the time the major policy concern had been dealing with the disinflation caused by both falling prices and money incomes. There were serious inflationary problems in several countries during the period immediately after the end of the Second World War, but these were attributed largely to the inevitable dislocations as hostilities ended. When growth got under way in earnest, however, after the immediate post-war recovery period, continuing inflation began to look like a considerably more serious challenge. There was a sharp increase in price rises in Britain in the early 1950s as the economy became over-taxed by re-armament for the Korean War, although inflation then fell back again to more modest levels.[89] Increases in the price level were a particular problem in France throughout the 1950s and 1960s. All over the developed world – and elsewhere – there was a steady rise in prices which had not been seen before on such a consistent basis.

Between 1950 and 1973, prices rose cumulatively by an average of 4.2% in Europe, and by 2.7% in the USA, and even faster, at 5.2%, in the strongly resurgent Japanese economy.[90] These figures were in marked contrast to the apparent rough stability of prices for long periods in the past. It was true that there had been severe inflation during the First World War, and to a lesser extent in the Second. Furthermore, some countries, particularly Germany in 1923, had seen their currencies losing all their value in hyper-inflations. These were regarded as isolated events, however, explicable by the special circumstances which triggered them. Otherwise, while there had been considerable fluctuations in the price level, generally the rises had been offset by subsequent falls, as the stability of the Gold Standard had both ordained and exemplified. The continuous rise in prices experienced in the 1950s and 1960s, to which there seemed to be no end, was a different matter.

Moreover, there appeared to be some signs, especially in Britain, where relatively poor economic performance had generated a less consensual wage climate than prevailed in most other developed countries, that wage cost pressure was increasing and becoming a serious problem. Between 1950 and 1970, Britain had higher average levels of consumer price inflation than any other major European country except France. Partly to contain these pressures, Britain had experienced two periods of decline in year-on-year growth, in 1952 and in 1958, and another series of years in the mid- to late 1960s when growth was very slow.[91] Britain's poor performance exemplified the extent to which international comparisons showed other substantial variations. In some developed countries, particularly France, price rises were uncomfortably high, as already noted, averaging 5.0% per annum between 1950 and 1973, while in Germany they were much lower at 2.7%. A cumulative difference of 2.3% per annum between the rates of inflation in these two countries over almost a quarter of a century inevitably required exchange rate adjustments, although using increases in the consumer price level on its own as a guide to international competitiveness turned out to be full of pitfalls. In Japan, at one extreme, with consumer prices increasing on average at 5.8% per annum between 1952 and 1979, export prices rose at 1.2% a year, whereas over the same period in Britain, consumer prices increased by 6.5% and export prices by 6.0% per annum.[92] It was small wonder that, in these conditions, Japanese exports, and hence the whole economy, grew far more quickly than was the case in Britain. It was also, however, not so obvious what exchange rate adjustments needed to be made. In fact it was export prices which were the key to international competitiveness, not inflation in the economy as a whole, but this appeared not to be an easy point for policymakers to grasp.

This leads on to the second major problem with the post-war settlement, with which Keynes was irrevocably associated, although the final terms of reference for the main institutions were not entirely of his choice. These organisations were the International Monetary Fund and the World Bank, established as part of the Bretton Woods agreements in 1944, with the IMF in particular charged with stabilising exchange rates.[93] There were pressing reasons why policymakers at the time wanted to ensure the maximum exchange rate stability after the experiences of the 1920s and 1930s. The devaluations between the wars had helped to fuel the protectionism which the new arrangements were designed to inhibit. Exchange rate flexibility had encouraged destabilising capital flows. The United States, by far the largest economy, but with comparatively small foreign trade exposure in relation to the size of its GNP, needed to be locked into the system.[94] The way in which the International Monetory Fund operated, however, involved imposing sanctions on countries which ran into balance of payments difficulties much more effectively than it did on discouraging countries running balance of payments surpluses from accumulating larger and larger reserves. Since all surpluses – accumulated without much restraint particularly by Germany and Taiwan in the 1950s and 1960s[95] – were necessarily reflected in deficits elsewhere, the strain on the deficit economies, of which Britain was for much of the time the largest, became increasingly acute. When the US balance of payments began to deteriorate sharply in the late 1960s, going into deficit in the early 1970s,[96] it became clear in turn that the dollar had become overvalued. It was this state of affairs which led to the Smithsonian Conference, held at Washington DC in 1971, at which the USA announced that it was no longer maintaining the link between the dollar and gold, upon which the whole Bretton Woods system relied.[97] The USA in consequence suspended its commitment to provide gold to official foreign holders of dollars at $35 an ounce, or any other price.[98]

The result was the break-up of the fixed but movable peg exchange rate system which had prevailed for the previous quarter of a century, and in its place there came into being the managed floating system, which has operated over most of the world ever since. Unfortunately, however, after decades of discipline exercised by the Bretton Woods arrangements, many governments reacted to their disappearance by expansionary policies which led to a huge surge in the world's money supply, a sharp increase in world output, and rapid rises in commodity prices. The Yom Kippur War between Israel and the surrounding Arab States then triggered the recently established OPEC[99] – the Organisation of Petroleum Exporting Countries – into raising the price of oil from about $2.50 to $10 a barrel.[100] The result was to plunge the world into an inflationary spiral, for which the Keynesian system had no answers, opening the way to the monetarist ideas which were to follow.

These structural problems with the Keynesian settlement showed why there were fissures in the Keynesian system which meant that it began to stand the test of time less well than many people had hoped it would. Perhaps the most fundamental of these was that the Keynesian Revolution did not provide a path to continuing high growth rates, and was never really designed to do so. If it had, it might have been able to deal with the exceptional problems of the 1970s. The fact that it did not do so explains why Keynes' followers lost their intellectual pre-eminence as economic problems mounted, after the collapse of the Bretton Woods settlement, for which they were unprepared. The ground thus ceded was taken over by the monetarists, for whom high growth rates were never as important as the conquest of inflation. The result was that the world's economic growth performance declined from 4.9% per annum compound between 1950 and 1973 to 3.0% between 1973 and 1992.[101] The problem was particularly acute in the most developed Western countries, where the decline was steepest – from about 4.4% per annum growth rates to barely half this figure.[102]

The truth was that the Keynesian system was not designed to achieve a consistent high rate of growth, although it did do this in the 1950s and 1960s, but largely as a by-product of its real orientation, which was to avoid unemployment. Keynes' main preoccupation was to prevent the waste and misery of the inter-war slump recurring, not to produce continuing high growth thereafter, about which he was in fact very sceptical. As he stated in the *General Theory*, Keynes believed that the marginal efficiency of capital – or the ability of advanced economies to find productive use for investment – was bound to decline in a wealthy community because 'owing to its accumulation of capital being already large, the opportunities for further investment are less attractive'.[103] Indeed, Keynes thought that a plateau in economic outlook would be reached before too many decades had passed, when economic growth had ceased, by which time he thought that most wants would have been satisfied, a perception which has certainly not turned out to be correct. 'The economic problem is not', he wrote, ' – if we look into the future – *the permanent problem of the human race*'.[104] Indeed, Keynes even went so far at one point as to speculate that the role of economics might become much less significant, as wants were satiated, and shortages diminished. 'If economists could manage to get themselves thought of as humble competent people, on a level with dentists, that would be splendid!'[105]

It is possible, however, that this wrong perception about how important economic growth was to continue to be had something to do with one of the stranger paradoxes concerning the Keynesian legacy, which was that the two countries with which Keynes was mostly strongly associated, Britain and the USA, ended up with the poorest growth performance in the developed world during the post-war decades. Britain, in particular, achieved a cumulative growth rate only two-thirds the average for Western Europe between 1950 and 1973, while the USA, although doing better than this, was still well below the average achieved by other developed economies.[106] As it became apparent, particularly in Britain, that performance was lagging, a number of influential writers very much in the Keynesian tradition, put forward explanations and remedies.

Andrew Shonfield (1917–1981) believed that Britain had been less successful than other countries in securing co-operative and supportive relationships between the public and the private sectors.[107] Thomas Balogh (1905–1985), of a more left-wing persuasion, saw the solution in greater public intervention, sustained by a strong incomes policy,[108] a view with which Nicholas Kaldor (1908–1986) broadly concurred. Kaldor, however, was more inclined to use innovative tax proposals such as his

Selective Employment Tax – well received at the time, but now generally reckoned to have had the opposite effect to what was intended[109] – rather than direct intervention to achieve his ends.[110] James Meade (1907–1995) favoured various forms of incomes policy to contain the balance of payments problems, which he saw as the main threat to achieving a better growth rate in Britain.[111] Anthony Crosland (1918–1977) wrote an influential book, *The Future of Socialism*, published in 1956, in which he took a more complacent view of the performance of the British economy, his main focus being on how a modern industrial economy should be run to achieve greater equality.[112] In this respect, his theme was mirrored by the work of John Kenneth Galbraith (born 1908) in the USA, who was critical of the way in which US society had developed, without suggesting any concrete plans for improving overall US economic performance.[113] Significantly, none of these writers put forward proposals that made any real difference to the growth rates or other measures of success for either of the economies with which they were concerned. Perhaps this is the best measure of the achievement for which Keynes himself was responsible, for no one could say the same of him.

Although it is, therefore, possible to produce important criticisms of the Keynesian legacy, they should be put in perspective. Keynes was necessarily primarily concerned with dealing with the problems which were most pressing in his own time. These were unquestionably the worldwide inter-war economic dislocations and the Depression, and not problems which materialised 25 years later. The fact that the world economy did so well for a quarter of a century after his death is testimony enough to the contribution Keynes made to the welfare of humanity. It was not Keynes' lack of foresight which led to the downturn in the world's economic performance from about 1973 onwards, but the absence of a successor of the calibre to deal a fraction as successfully as he had done with the new problems which arose in the last quarter of the twentieth century.

8
Hard Money

It is to be regretted that the rich and powerful too often bend the acts of government to their selfish purposes.

Andrew Jackson (1767–1845)

The history of hard money is a long one. Those who have had the good fortune to inherit or accumulate wealth have always had a strong interest in seeing its value retained, not least that part of it which has been held in the form of cash or its equivalents. There has always, therefore, been strong pressure from the rich and powerful within all societies to keep inflation low, and the price level stable. There has also, however, been a correspondingly continuous tendency for those who are the world's borrowers to see price inflation as a helpful way of reducing the real burden of their debts. Included among such borrowers have generally been found entrepreneurs, farmers, the young and the irresponsible, who have not always made up an easy coalition, as William Jennings Bryan (1860–1925) found out during the nineteenth century in the USA. The Frontier was in debt to the East Coast, whose bankers wanted repayment in gold rather than paper money – the Greenback. Bryan's rhetoric, 'You shall not press down upon the brow of labour this crown of thorns. You shall not crucify mankind upon a cross of gold',[1] has often subsequently been echoed, but it fell on deaf ears at the time, as frequently was to be the case in the future with similar exhortations. The United States adopted the Gold Standard rather than the softer Silver Standard favoured by Bryan's supporters. Prices fell and debts became correspondingly harder to repay.

Nor have borrowers just been individuals, or groups of them. They have also included states, particularly those engaged in war, who have nearly always had problems in raising sufficient taxation to finance their expenditures. The American, French and Russian Revolutions were all financed on paper money, as were the two major twentieth-century wars, and many smaller ones. Much of the history of economics and the evolution of economic policy has been forged by the enduring tension between, on the one hand, those who have money and want to lend it out at significant rates of interest without seeing the value of the principal being eroded, and borrowers, on the other, with exactly opposite concerns.

The main intermediaries between borrowers and lenders have always been banks, first established in their modern form in Italy in the thirteenth century, once double entry book-keeping became practical following the arrival of Arabic numerals. Banks were originally run by private companies independently of the state – although they frequently lent to royal borrowers, a significant number of whom turned out to be poor credit risks. Gradually, however, the practice grew up of establishing a leading bank substantially under the control of the state, to provide an anchor for other banks who dealt with businesses and the public. The first of these central banks was the Bank of Amsterdam, established in 1609,[2] followed some time later by the Bank of England in 1694.[3] From these beginnings, modern banking evolved.

The key role of banks, however, is not just to borrow from those with surplus funds, and to lend to those who need extra financial resources. Banks also create money. They do this because most bank transactions are not carried out with cash in the form of coins and notes, but with cheques and other money instruments. Provided that confidence is maintained, banks can create accounts on which cheques can be drawn, whose value amounts to a substantial multiple of the actual amount of cash they have deposited with them. This can be done because only a small proportion of the cheque payments will actually involve the redemption of coins and notes. Most will simply transfer balances from one account to another. Furthermore, even a significant amount of what counts as cash money is actually bank notes – usually, though not always, issued only by the central bank – which provide further leverage on the coinage at the base of the money pyramid. There is, however, an important limit to the extent to which banks can increase their lending without running the risk of becoming insolvent. They have to maintain a prudent ratio between their total credit creation and the monetary assets which they have available to meet calls for repayment. They have to be capable of paying out money not just by allowing further drawings on bank accounts which they have created, but in cash or, because they are immediately marketable, such equivalents to cash as government securities.

It has always been clear that such a system is open to abuse, if the need to maintain such precautionary ratios is ignored. Indeed history is replete with examples of poorly managed and reckless bank credit creation, from the collapse of John Law's Banque Royale in pre-Revolutionary France to such modern examples of bank failures as the collapse of the Bank of Credit and Commerce International in 1991 and the suspension of payments by the Nigerian Central Bank in the 1980s. It is, indeed, the need to provide control and regulation which has created both central banks at national level, and world institutions such as the International Monetary Fund. The primary role of central banks nowadays is to act as 'lender of last resort' – to provide enough liquid funds to keep the banking system solvent when it is under pressure – in return for which other banks have to maintain minimum reserves against deposits and comply with other precautionary requirements.

Monetary policy is primarily concerned with regulating the extent to which the banking system is allowed to create extra credit. This can be encouraged at any time by the central bank increasing the amount of eligible deposits held by the clearing banks, and thus raising their capacity to lend without the precautionary limits being changed. All the central bank, or the government, has to do to achieve this end is to sell more government bonds to the clearing banks. The additional government securities which the banks will then hold will increase the monetary base against which they can safely lend. Their resulting increased willingness to lend tends to be matched meanwhile by lower interest rates, which are both an encouragement to borrowers and the result of easier monetary conditions increasing the supply of money in relation to the demand for it. Easier credit conditions tend to produce higher rates of growth and a closer approximation to full employment but, especially if such policies are pursued to excess, may well increase inflation.

The major issue then raised is the extent to which economic policy affects the balance between borrowers and lenders. Where should the trade-off lie between lower inflation on the one hand, which broadly benefits most existing wealth holders, and higher rates of economic growth on the other, which by and large are inclined to favour everyone else? The answer to questions such as this tend in turn to be heavily coloured by perceptions about how well and responsibly the state can be expected to use the resources and powers at its disposal, and, in particular, how much it will give priority to maintaining the value of the currency in comparison to other priorities. This shades in turn into broader issues, such as the extent to which those who hold wealth ought to be able to use it to their own best advantage, untrammelled by state interference and control. Much of economic history can be seen as successive attempts to portray the way the economy works, with the interests of varying sections of the population being given most importance, and corresponding credit for the economy's performance. Monetarism and its antecedents are essentially the creed of wealth holders, just as Adam Smith's writings provided a doctrine which reflected the interests of the rising industrial classes. Classical Economics was the canon needed by the finance capitalism of nineteenth-century Britain, and Keynesianism was the salvation for those hardest hit by inter-war instability and depression. It does not follow that arguments which are heavily overlaid with self-interest are necessarily wrong, but they need to be treated with caution.

The idea that there was a relationship between the amount of money in circulation and movements in the price level has a history which goes back at least as far as Jean Bodin, who noted the impact of Spanish silver and gold on the price level in Europe. Locke, Law, Hume and Cantillon all recognised the validity of Bodin's concept, and it was part of the accepted background to the Classical Economists, such as Ricardo, Mill and Senior. During the nineteenth century, numerous attempts were made in Britain, France and Germany to define the relationship between money and economic activity more accurately, but it was an American, Irving Fisher (1867–1947), who eventually succeeded in producing a formulation which became the one which was generally accepted.[4] This was his Equation of Exchange.

Irving Fisher had a wide range of accomplishments to his name. He was a mathematician by background, a pioneer econometrician, and the inventor of index numbers and a card file system, which he sold for a considerable sum to Remington Rand. He was also a eugenist, an ardent enthusiast for prohibition, and a stock exchange speculator, losing, it is said between $8m and $10m by investing heavily in the New York stock market as late as the autumn of 1929.[5] In 1898, while only 31 years old, he had been appointed Professor of Political Economy at Yale, and it was in this capacity that, in 1911, he published his *The Purchasing Power of Money*. In it he set out the Equation of Exchange, which is as follows:[6]

$$P = \frac{MV + M'V'}{T}$$

In this equation, P stands for prices; M the amount of notes and coin in circulation; V its velocity, or rate of turnover; M' the funds available in chequing accounts; V' their velocity or rate of turnover, and T the number of transactions, or, more broadly, the level of activity in the economy. In much subsequent discussion, the distinction between MV and M'V' was often blurred, and the relationship made even simpler: P = MV/T. This formula then states that if the total volume of transactions, at least in the short term, is relatively constant, and the velocity of circulation remains stable, then an increase in the money supply, M, will automatically imply a more or less similar increase in the price level, leaving the volume of activity in the economy much as it was before. If this formulation is correct, all that has to be done to ensure stable prices is to run the economy's monetary policy in a way which keeps the relationship between M and T constant, or as close as possible to the trend rate of real growth in economic output.[7]

This was a very simple and very powerful idea. It was easy to grasp. It appeared to be relatively straightforward to implement. Its implications were policies with which large sections of the rich and powerful, but also many other people who depended on money retaining its value, were instinctively in sympathy. Whether such policies would work as well in practice as they did in theory, however, and whether they would advance the lot of humanity as a whole, as opposed to disproportionately favouring mainly those who were already well off, time was to tell.

The Austrian and Chicago schools

The major influences on the development of the ideas which eventually formed monetarism – a term coined as late as 1968 by Karl Brunner (1916–1989) – came together from a variety of different sources. Some originated in Europe, from such figures as Gustav Cassel, who, as Professor of Economics and Public Finance at Stockholm University, had had as his pupils the extraordinarily talented group of people who guided the Swedish economy through the inter-war slump. Cassel developed the Purchasing Power Parity Theory, which became an important component of international monetarism. This claimed to demonstrate that the equilibrium exchange rate between currencies had to reflect the domestic purchasing power of each of the domestic currencies concerned, the consequence being that any attempts to change parities would be self-defeating.[8] Other ideas came from the USA. Wesley C. Mitchell (1874–1948), a strong advocate of careful empirical work,[9] had produced an influential theory in his *Business Cycles*, published in 1913.[10] This implied that, although each of them had some features in common, every business cycle was essentially unique, thus denying that there could be any general theory to explain their existence.[11] If this were true, then there could be no corresponding generally applicable remedy, such as offsetting demand deficiency, which was likely to be effective in dealing with them. Much the most important influences on the development of monetarism, however, came from two distinct sources whose key figures came together in the USA. One was the University of Vienna and the other was the University of Chicago.

Following in the footsteps of Karl Menger, one of the framers of the Marginal Revolution, Austria had established a formidable reputation as an influential source of economic ideas. Gone was the detailed empiricism of the German historical economists. Instead, the principal Austrian practitioners were mainly concerned with pure theory, and more specifically the part of it covering comparative statics, the analysis of consumer behaviour, based on utility, and the marginal productivity theory of distribution. The requirements of perfect competition which were implicit in analysis of this kind encouraged them to be strongly opposed to state intervention in general, and to Marxism in particular. The leading thinkers in this school, Eugen Böhm-Bawerk (1851–1914) and Friedrich von Wieser (1851–1926), both had experience in senior government posts in the Austrian Empire, von Wieser as Minister of Commerce and Böhm-Bawerk during three separate periods in charge of the Ministry of Finance.[12] Their resulting familiarity with the autocratic Hapsburg administration no doubt also coloured their views.

Böhm-Bawerk's main contribution to economic theory concerned the relationship between capital and interest. In contrast to the Marxist view that interest was an unjustifiable imposition on borrowers by lenders, Böhm-Bawerk held in his book *The Positive Theory of Capital*, published in 1889, that it was a natural phenomenon. It was caused partly by time preference and partly by psychological factors such as uncertainty,[13] which would be just as relevant in a socialist state as they were in one which was run on capitalist lines.[14] Von Wieser produced an allied series of ideas on value in his *Natural Value*, also published in 1889, in which he set out to show that, in any rationally ordered society, similar relative valuations would have to be apportioned to all goods and services irrespective of whether they were provided by a market economy or the state.[15] It is notable that this theme – the way in which a non-market economy would have to be operated to achieve rational and, if possible, optimal outcomes – was one that continued to run though the school of thought that led to monetarism. Some of those concerned were eventually involved in putting these ideas into practice, particularly Oskar Lange (1904–1965), who returned to Poland from Chicago after the end of the Second World War, when the communist government had been established there.[16]

When the Hapsburg Empire was disbanded after the end of the Second World War, several of the more outstanding pupils who had been taught by Böhm-Bawerk and von Wieser left Austria and eventually found their way to Chicago University. There, they encountered similar views to those of their mentors in Vienna about the value of markets and the dangers of excessive state interference. Early American exponents of this view were Frank H. Knight (1885–1962), Henry Simons (1899–1946), Jacob Viner (1892–1970) and James Angell (1898–1986). Knight's main interests were in the history of economic thought, and in the theory of the firm, where his principal contribution, published in 1921 in his book *Risk, Uncertainty and Profit*,[17] was in making the distinction for those running businesses between risks which could be quantified and uncertainty which could not. He was a firm supporter of Neo-Classical pricing theory, and shared the Austrians' lack of interest in empirical investigation, but not their enthusiasm for mathematical formulations.[18] Simons took a more liberal view on state involvement, being prepared to support using the tax system to secure a more egalitarian distribution of income, and even to consider public ownership. He advanced these proposals in an influential pamphlet, published in 1934, entitled *A Positive Program for Laissez Faire: Some Proposals for a Liberal Economic Policy*. Otherwise, however, he was opposed to all interference in the operation of markets, while taking a strong line on the need for tight monetary discipline.[19] Viner shared Knight's interest in the history of economic thought, while his main original work was in the study of international trade. He contributed the phrase 'marginal revenue' to the economic lexicon, as he and Knight forged a substantial proportion of partial equilibrium analysis as it evolved during the first half of the twentieth century.[20] Angell also worked on international trade, stressing in his *Theory of International Prices*, published in 1926, that with the Gold Standard in operation, disequilibria in competitiveness could only be solved by changes in the relative price levels in competing countries. Angell also anticipated much of the later work done by Milton Friedman in his 1936 book *Behavior of Money*, advocating the same stern monetary control.[21]

While not all the leading lights in what came to be called the Chicago School shared every opinion with which they were associated, there emerged early on a strongly held core of views to which all of them in varying degrees subscribed, and with which those who came to America from Austria found a ready affinity. First, they believed strongly in the power of Neo-Classical price theory to explain observed economic behaviour. Second, they had faith in the efficacy of free markets to allocate resources and distribute income more efficiently than in any other way. Third, in consequence, they tended to support a minimalist role for the state in regulating the economy.[22] These were, of course, views which were widely shared within the culture and ethos of the USA, particularly among its business classes.

The four most significant Austrians to join the Chicago School, in turn, were Ludwig von Mises (1880–1973), Joseph A. Schumpeter (1883–1950), Friedrich A. von Hayek (1899–1992) and Fritz Machlup (1902–1983). Von Mises was the most austere. Condemning socialism because he believed it had no rational method of pricing, he was ultra pro *laissez faire*. He argued in *Die Gemeinschaft*, published in 1932, that even if, *per impossibile*, planning could stop short of serfdom, it could ensure neither as rational nor as stable a distribution of resources as the market economy. Schumpeter had wider interests and experience, including a period, for a few months in 1919, as Austrian Minister of Finance.[23] After early flirtations with socialist policies, he gradually moved to the right, his ideas culminating in the most significant of his books *Capitalism, Socialism and Democracy*, published in 1942 after he had moved to the USA. In this and in previous writings – a throwback to Cantillon and Say – he stressed the role of the entrepreneur, a figure largely neglected in most Classical Economics, as the most active agent in achieving economic growth. He regarded interest as a kind of tax levied by investors on entrepreneurs, upon whose 'gales of creative destruction'[24] innovation depended. He feared that, as business became more corporate, entrepreneurs would be extinguished and growth would falter, claiming that 'Dematerialised, defunctionalised and absentee ownership does not impress and call forth moral allegiance as the vital form of property did.'[25]

Consonant with these views, Schumpeter was sceptical about the benefits of the bourgeois state, tolerant of the kind of monopoly which he believed that entrepreneurs inevitably tried to create, and much inclined to prefer private initiative to collective policy. Like the rest of the Chicago School, he was highly critical of Keynes, whom he accused of being afflicted by 'the curse of usefulness'.[26]

Von Hayek was another able economist and mathematician, who made significant contributions to business cycle and capital theories, developing a hypothesis that capital shortage was the key factor in triggering the downturn from a boom to a depression. In later life, he became more concerned with broader issues, and particularly the extent to which any attempts to interfere with the freedom of the market might lead in the end to tyranny. This prompted him to publish in 1944 his *Road to Serfdom*,[27] a pessimistic but influential book, in which he appeared to underestimate the capacity of a powerful democratic tradition to stop a strong state necessarily becoming an oppressive one.[28] Von Hayek's main concern was that the state was a threat to liberty, not that it was necessarily inefficient.[29] Finally, there was Fritz Machlup, who had had experience of the business world in his family cardboard manufacturing partnership before taking up an academic career. His main interests were international monetary economics and industrial organisation, the latter particularly concerned with patents, round which Machlup developed a formal theory of invention.[30]

This, then, was the background against which monetarism was developed. It was an intellectually austere environment, where most of the tenets of the Neo-Classical system were still accepted much more readily than they were elsewhere. Even such developments as those on oligopoly produced by Chamberlin and Robinson were rejected by Knight, and a later generation, including George Stigler (1911–1991) and Milton Friedman, as lacking precision, though doubts on this score were also expressed by others closer to the Keynesian tradition, such as Roy Harrod,[31] and much more recently and radically by Steve Keen.[32] The Chicago School was never convinced by Keynes' views on economic policy issues partly on intellectual grounds, and partly because, as conservatives, nearly all members of it were unpersuaded by, and uncomfortable with, their collectivist bias. They had never believed that interference with the market would, in the long term, be of benefit. When, therefore, inflation suddenly became a major threat in the 1970s, and the Keynesians had no remedy for it, the time could hardly have been more propitious for the ideas which the Chicago School had so long nurtured to flourish. Codified and underpinned with new and impressive theorising, their culmination, now universally known as monetarism, came close to sweeping the board among both academics, commentators and policymakers in many, but not all developed countries, as well as within the international institutions charged with regulating and assisting the Third World.

Milton Friedman

We have seen that the appeal of hard money has a long history. Those with established wealth have always been in favour of it earning as substantial a return as possible. High rates of interest and low rates of inflation have an obvious appeal to them, a view of the world almost invariably shared by those with a banking background. A sense of prudence militates against deficit financing and easy money. Nor, as we have seen, is it just the well off who are inclined to favour the financial environment which monetarist policies generate. Many poorer people, particularly pensioners on fixed incomes, favour high interest rates, and therefore the relative scarcity of money which is necessary to ensure that they can prevail. A high exchange rate, which runs with high interest rates and a restrictive monetary policy, provides the benefit of lowering the cost of imports and making travel abroad cheaper, reinforcing the widely held view that people should be proud of their currency if it is perceived to be 'strong' rather than favouring a low, but competitive, international value. It was not therefore just the business community and academics of a right-wing persuasion who were ready to see the value of money protected as inflation soared out of control in the 1970s. Monetarist ideas, in their standard form, would not have become accepted as widely as they were, however, without the theoretical and statistical underpinning provided by Milton Friedman (born 1912) and his associate, Anna Jacobson Schwartz (born 1915), in their seminal book, *A Monetary History of the United States, 1867–1960*, published in 1963.

Milton Friedman came from a humble background. He was born in New York where his father was a poor immigrant dry-goods merchant, who died when Friedman was 15. Nevertheless, as a result of ability and hard work, by the time he was 24 Milton Friedman was on the economics faculty at Chicago University, where, apart from brief breaks as visiting Professor of Economics at Wisconsin and Minnesota, and on government service during the Second World War, he remained until he retired in 1979. In 1937 he started his long association with the National Bureau of Economic Research, which persisted until 1981, giving him an insight into the policy-making world as well as academic areas of study. During the Second World War, he made important theoretical advances in statistical techniques while working on the highly practical problems involved in developing methods of testing the reliability of wartime munitions production – a digression from his main focus of interest which was detailed analyses of income and expenditure. It was this latter subject which led to the publication in 1957 of what is regarded by most academic economists as Friedman's best work, *A Theory of the Consumption Function*, in which he showed that important assumptions in Keynes' analysis of the multiplier were statistically flawed. To do this, Friedman amassed and organised a formidable amount of empirical data, a process at which he excelled. This led on to his interest in the Equation of Exchange, and his production of much more thorough empirical data in relation to its performance than had been available previously in his *Studies in the Quantity Theory of Money*, published in 1956.[33] The way was then open to the development of the ideas in his most important and influential book, co-authored with Anna Jacobson Schwartz (born 1915).

In *A Monetary History of the United States, 1867–1960*, Friedman and Schwartz made three important claims which had a major impact on economic thinking all over the world. First, they said that there was a clear association between the total amount of money in circulation and changes in money incomes and prices, but not in economic activity until approximately two years later. Changes in the money supply therefore affected the price level, but not, except perhaps for a short period of time, the level of output in the real economy. Second, these relationships had proved to be stable over a long period. Third, changes, and particularly increases in the money supply, had generally occurred as a result of events which were independent of the needs of the economy. In consequence, they added to inflation without raising the level of economic activity.

The attractive simplicity of these propositions is easily recognised. The essence of the monetarist case is that increases in prices and wages can be held in check by nothing more complicated than the apparently simple process of controlling the amount of money in circulation. Ideally, a condition of zero inflation is achieved when the increase in the money supply equals the rise in output in the economy. Since both wages and prices can only go up if extra money to finance them is made available, rises in either cannot occur unless more is provided. Thus, as long as the government is seen to be giving sufficient priority to controlling the money supply, everyone will realise that it is in his or her interest to exercise restraint, reducing the rate of inflation to whatever level is deemed acceptable. These simple and powerful prescriptions have attracted much support to the monetarist banner, reinforcing the view held not only by monetarists but many others that prudent management of any economy's finances is required at all times. Inflation, undesirable even at low levels, though perhaps tolerable, is a threat to everyone if it gets out of control. Excessive credit creation is the main cause of rapid price increases.

Monetarism, however, as adumbrated by Milton and Schwartz, went a good deal further than these broad and widely accepted perceptions. Their formulations were much more precise. They posited a great deal more rigid a link between credit creation and inflation than had been generally accepted at least up to the time of the publication of their book, and it was this seminal idea which grabbed the world's attention. Nevertheless, despite the support it received, and notwithstanding the intellectual rigour on which Chicago prided itself, it was never clear that this strong version of monetarism, and the statistical analysis on which it was based, would bear the weight which was put upon it.[34] As with so many of the most important ideas in economics, the underlying reality was much more complex and slippery than the simplified and, to many people, appealing headline message which cut such a swathe through both the academic and the policymaking world, carrying almost all before it.

It may be true that, over a long period, the total amount of money in circulation bears a close relationship to the total value of the economy's output. It does not follow, however, that as a general rule the money supply determines the money value of the Gross National Product, and hence the rate of inflation. It may well be, instead, that the total amount of money in circulation is a function of the need for sufficient finance to accommodate transactions. If this is so, then a rise in the money supply may well accompany an increase in inflation caused by some other event, simply to provide this accommodation. It need not necessarily be the cause of rising prices.

While large changes in the money stock clearly have an influence on the future course of inflation, it is much less clear that small changes are the only cause of movements in the price level. Nor is it easy to find the tight correlation between alterations in the rate of price increases and changes in the money supply some two years previously which monetarists maintain always exists. They also claim that the future course of inflation can be guided within narrow limits by controlling the money stock. Empirical evidence demonstrates that this contention is far too precise, substantially overstating the predictive accuracy of monetarist theories.

For this amount of fine tuning to be possible, an unequivocal definition of money is required. It is one thing to recognise a situation where clearly far too much money, or, more accurately, too much credit is being created. Monetarists are right in saying that if credit is so cheap and so readily available that it is easy to speculate on asset inflation, or the economy is getting overheated by excess demand financed by lax monetary conditions, then the money supply is too large. This is a broad quantitative judgement. It is another matter to state that small alterations in the money supply generate correspondingly exact changes in the rate of inflation. Yet this is the claim which monetarists put forward.

This claim is implausible for a number of reasons. One is the difficulty in defining accurately what is money and what is not. Notes and coins are clearly 'money', but where should the line be drawn thereafter? What kinds of bank facilities and money market instruments should also be included or excluded? Many different measures are available in every country, depending on what is put in and what is left out. None of them has been found anywhere to have had a strikingly close correlation with subsequent changes in the rate of inflation for any length of time. Often, different measures of the money supply move in different directions. This is very damaging evidence against propositions which are supposed to be precise in their formulation and impact.

Another major problem for monetarists is that there can be no constant ratio between the amount of money in circulation, however defined, and the aggregate value of transactions, because the rate at which money circulates can, and does, vary widely over time. The 'velocity of circulation', which is the ratio between the GDP and the money supply, is far from constant. In the USA, for example, the velocity of the money supply defined as M3[35] fell 17% between 1970 and 1986, but by 1996 it had risen 22% compared to ten years earlier.[36] It has been exceptionally volatile in Britain, where it rose by 7% between 1964 and 1970, and by a further 28% between 1970 and 1974, only to fall by 26% between 1974 and 1979. Since then it has risen by 82%.[37] Other countries, such as the Netherlands and Greece, have also had large changes in the velocity of circulation, particularly during the 1970s.[38]

Some of these movements were caused by changes in monetary policy, but a substantial proportion, especially recently, have had extraneous causes. They have been the results of radical changes to the financial environment, caused by the effects of deregulation on credit creation, and the growth of new financial instruments, such as derivatives. Variations like these make it even more difficult to establish and measure exactly what is happening to the money supply which monetarist policies require. In fact, the statistical record everywhere on the money supply and inflation shows what one would expect if there was little causation at all at work. Except in extreme circumstances of gross over-creation of money and credit, changes in the money supply have not had much impact on the rate of inflation, and generally less and more erratically than monetarists predicted. The need to provide enough money to finance all the transactions taking place has, over the long term, proved to be much more important a determinant of the money supply than attempts to restrict it to control inflation, although some countries have certainly had tighter monetary policies than others. In the short term, there is no systematic evidence that changes in the money supply affect subsequent inflation rates with high levels of precision.

It is not surprising, therefore, that the predictions of monetarists about future levels of inflation, based on trends in the money supply, have turned out to be no better, and often worse, than those of other people who have used more eclectic methods. Monetarists have not, however, kept their analysis and prescription solely on the subject of inflation. There are three other important areas of economic thought where their ideas have had a decisive effect on practical policy over the last quarter of a century. These are to do with unemployment, interest rates and exchange rates.

The monetarist view of unemployment is that there is a 'natural' rate which cannot be avoided, set essentially by supply side rigidities, such as restrictive practices and the power of trades unions to secure wage increases unconnected with corresponding rises in productivity. Any attempt to reduce unemployment below this level by reflation will necessarily increase wage rates and then the price level. This will leave those in employment no better off than they were before, while the greater level of demand, having been absorbed by rising prices, will result in the same number of people being employed as previously. Increasing demand only pushes up the rate of inflation. It will not raise either output or the number of people in work.

At some point, as pressure on the available labour force increases and the number of those unemployed falls, there is no doubt that a bidding-up process will take place, and wages and salaries will rise. This is a different matter, however, from postulating that unemployment levels like those seen over much of the developed world during the 1980s and 1990s are required to keep inflation at bay. Nor is it plausible that supply side rigidities are the major constraint on getting unemployment down. There is little evidence that these rigidities are significantly greater than they were in the 1950s and 1960s, and on balance they are almost certainly less. If, during the whole of these two decades, it was possible to combine high rates of economic growth with low levels of unemployment, while inflation remained reasonably stable, it seems hard to believe that it is impossible now for these conditions to prevail again. Indeed, sustained low levels of inflation have recently been experienced in all the developed world, while prices have recently been rising somewhat more rapidly in the euro zone of the European Union than elsewhere, despite the fact that unemployment there is still much higher than in the rest of the developed world. One of the unfortunate triumphs of monetarism has been to condition people to tolerating much higher levels of unemployment than would otherwise have been considered economically desirable or politically acceptable.

Monetarism has also had a considerable influence on interest rates. The tight control of the money supply, which monetarists advocate, can only be achieved if interest rates are used to balance a relatively low supply of money against the demand for credit which has to be reduced by raising the price of money. This requirement is deemed necessary to secure a positive real rate of interest, required to ensure that there are sufficient loanable funds available to cater for borrowers. It is alleged that any attempt to lower interest rates to encourage expansion may fail as lenders withdraw from the market until the premium they require above the inflation rate reappears.

Again, however, it is not clear that this is a proposition for which there is strong empirical evidence. Nor is it one which is congruent with practical experience in financial markets.[39] For years on end, in many countries, real interest rates paid to savers have been negative, sometimes even before tax. Lenders, of course, have never regarded negative interest rates as fair, and frequently complain bitterly when they occur. There is, however, little that they can do about them. Their ability to withdraw from the market is generally limited. It is undoubtedly the case, however, that high positive rates of interest are a discouragement to investment, partly directly, but much more importantly, because of their influence on driving up the exchange rate.

This leads on to the third major impact of monetarist ideas on practical issues, which has been on exchange rate policy. It is argued that no policy for improving an economy's competitiveness by devaluation will work, because the inflationary effects of a depreciation will automatically raise the domestic price level back to where it was in international terms. This will leave the devaluing country with no more competitiveness than it had before, but with a real extra inflationary problem with which it will have to contend.

This proposition is one which it is easy to test against historical experience. There have been large numbers of substantial exchange rate changes over the last few decades, providing plenty of empirical data against which to assess the validity of this monetarist assertion. The evidence is overwhelmingly against it. As we have seen exemplified in Table 2.3 on page 28, there are many examples to be found of large-scale devaluations failing to produce sufficient excess inflation, if any, to wipe out the competitive advantage initially gained. On the contrary, there is ample evidence indicating that exactly the opposite effect has been the experience in a wide variety of different economies. Those which devalue tend to perform progressively better, as their manufacturing sectors expand, and the internationally tradable goods and services which they produce become cumulatively more competitive.

Countries which have gained an initial price advantage therefore tend to forge ahead, with increasingly competitive import-saving and exporting sectors. Rapidly growing efficiency in the sectors of their economies involved in international trading gains them higher shares in world trade, providing them with platforms for further expansion. High productivity growth generates conditions which may even allow them, with good management, to experience less domestic inflation than their more sluggish competitors. In practice, monetarist policies have had pronounced effects on the exchange rates of the countries where they have been most effectively imposed, but almost invariably their impact has been to push them up. The economies concerned then suffer the worst of all worlds – a mixture of slow growth, low increases in output to absorb wage and salary increases, and sometimes higher price inflation than their more favoured competitors.

Monetarist theory therefore starts by appearing simple and straightforward, but ends by being much less convincing once all the complications its assertions entail are taken into account. There is a lack of clear explanation about the transmission mechanisms involved between what are claimed to be the causes of economic events, and the effects which it is declared will necessarily follow. Where monetarist theory can be tested against empirical results, its predictions have generally failed to achieve expected levels of accuracy, greatly reducing their value.

The strength of the monetarist case does not, therefore, lie in the detail of its analysis or its prescriptions. The precision with which the future course of inflation can be predicted from changes in the current money supply has not turned out to be nearly so great as its advocates hoped it would be. It does not follow from this, however, that the monetarists lack a powerful, but more general case. The real appeal behind monetarism rests in its assertions – undoubtedly true – that there is a strong correlation between excessive credit creation and subsequent inflation, and that lack of financial discipline very easily degenerates into waste and inefficiency as well as rapidly rising prices. These conditions are then likely to produce the worst of all worlds. Existing wealth holders lose out at the same time that everyone else gains little or nothing, as a result of economic misman-agement which would not have been possible if more restraint had been exercised.

Monetarist theories have nevertheless reinforced everywhere all the atti-tudes widely held in favour of cautious financial conservatism. It is no coincidence that monetarism came to the fore in response to the excessive credit creation in the early 1970s, and subsequent sour combination of stagnation and inflation, which resulted from the discipline provided by the Bretton Woods system being removed once exchange rates began to float after the devaluation of the US dollar. The need to find some solution to the inflationary problems which plagued the world in the 1970s appears, however, to have unbalanced the approach of policymakers across the world to the relative significance of different economic objectives. Curtailing inflation, and then making sure that it is not allowed to rise again exponentially is clearly an important goal, but it is not the only one. Furthermore, bringing inflation down to lower and lower levels impacts more and more adversely on other economic objectives. This is not to argue against financial discipline, which is the compellingly strong upside of monetarism, but merely to point out that too much of it can have griev-ously damaging results which those who are already wealthy will not feel nearly so harshly as others who are not so fortunate.

The monetarist legacy

Whereas the impact of much of the economic theorising of the nineteenth and early twentieth century on practical policymaking had been relatively small, this has been far from true either in the case of Keynesian thinking during and for the quarter-century after the Second World War, or following the arrival of monetarism as a serious force on the intellectual scene in the 1970s. Just as Keynes can take much of the credit for the success with which most economies – especially in the developed world – were run during the 1960s and 1970s, so monetarist ideas shaped the performance of the world economy for the last quarter of the twentieth century.

The speed with which the monetarist consensus took over from the one previously associated with Keynes, following the early 1970s inflationary experience, was remarkable. During both the Second World War and for the 25 years which followed it, little attention was paid anywhere to the money supply. Yet within a few months the view that the quantity of money has a major influence on economic activity and the price level, and that the objectives of monetary policy are best achieved by targeting the rate of growth of the money supply[40] became the talisman by which all else was judged.[41] By 1976, the British Prime Minister, James Callaghan (born 1912), could confidently assure the Labour Party Conference that it was no longer possible to spend your way out of a recession.[42] Even earlier, British commentators such as Peter Jay (born 1937) and Samuel Brittan (born 1933) came rapidly to assume that monetarist views about 'rational expectations' – the assertion that all wage claims tended to take existing levels of inflation into account and that increases ought to be on top of them – were necessarily correct. The consequence was a very pessimistic view about future price increases unless drastic deflationary action was taken.

While the concept that restraining the money supply would reduce inflation was widely accepted, it was, nevertheless, not particularly obvious what all the linkages which led to this happening might be. The nature of the transmission mechanisms which might be involved were explored by a number of influential economists sympathetic to the monetarist cause, particularly David Laidler (born 1938) and Harry Johnson (1923–1977). The fact that there was never a wholly convincing consensus about the detailed processes concerned might have been thought to have exposed an important weakness in the monetarist formulation, but largely failed to do so. The essential monetarist message continued to be the same. Only control of the money supply would force down inflation, allowing the world's economies to regain stability, primarily of prices but also in growth of output.

The result was a steep increase in deflationary policies both during the 1970s, and then their even more vigorous implementation in the 1980s, especially in Britain and the USA with the arrival in power of respectively Margaret Thatcher (born 1925) as Prime Minister in 1979 and Ronald Reagan (born 1911) as President in 1981. Both were wholly converted to the monetarist case. Neither flinched when interest base rates in Britain were raised to 17%,[43] and to 14% in the USA.[44] The results were immediately apparent in falling output and rising unemployment. In Britain, GDP fell in both 1980 and 1981,[45] while unemployment rose from 1.3m in 1979 to 2.5m in 1981.[46] In the USA, GDP fell in both 1980 and 1982,[47] and unemployment rose from 7.6m in 1980 to 10.7m in 1982.[48] These were relatively extreme examples of what monetarism in practice could do, but they set the scene for the linkages between the ideas behind the policies and the actual results which were achieved across the world as a result of their implementation.

Between 1950 and 1973, the world economy grew cumulatively by 4.9%[49] per annum, and income per head by 2.9%.[50] For the next two decades, the figures were 3.0%[51] and 1.2%.[52] For developed countries, the decline was even more marked. In Western Europe, the fall was from 5.7%[53] annual growth and 4.7%[54] increase in GDP per head to respectively 2.2%[55] and 2.0%.[56] In the USA there was a similar pattern. Growth fell from 3.9% to 2.5%,[57] and the increase in GDP per head 2.4% to 1.5%.[58] In Japan, growth went down from 9.2% to 3.5%,[59] and the rise in living standards from 8.0% to 2.8%.[60] Across the whole of the developed world, even more than among the Third World countries, growth in GDP fell on average to about half its previous level, while the rate at which living standards were increasing fell proportionately more, as a result of rises in the population.

At the same time as growth rates slackened, the numbers of people out of work, which had barely been a problem in the 1950s and 1960s in either the West or Japan, became a much greater matter of concern. During the 1950s and 1960s, unemployment in the countries which came together to form the European Union had averaged little more than 2.0%. By 1985, the percentage claimant count had reached 9.9% and, although the figure had dropped back to 7.7% by 1990, it rose to a peak of 11.1% in 1994,[61] before falling back slowly to 7.7% in late 2001.[62] In Japan, the figure was then 5.3%, and 5.2% in the USA.[63] These figures, however, based, as they are, on those presenting themselves for work but not having any, greatly underestimate the true scale of the problem, especially compared to the position in developed countries during the 1950s and 1960s. This is because they exclude all those who would be willing to work if they could do so for reasonable wages, but who are not actively looking for jobs because they do not believe they can be found. Included in these categories are large numbers of people who were retired early, often against their will, those caught in benefit traps which make it more expensive to work than to stay at home, and others who have become so discouraged that they have dropped out of the labour force altogether. International Labour Organisation statistics indicate that the total number of people who could be attracted back into the active labour force, if the conditions were right, within the EU number about 50% more than those normally appearing in the unemployment figures.[64] Even in the USA, where the social security system makes unemployment a much less attractive option than it is in Europe, almost 5m people previously categorised as 'wanting a job now' have dropped out of the labour force.[65]

As unemployment has risen, so the distribution of wealth and income has become more uneven across the Western world, with poor work opportunities being largely, though not wholly responsible. In the USA, after a gradual reduction in the dispersion of income and wealth during the 1950s and 1960s, the proportion of income going to the rich has vastly increased compared to the poor. By 1998, the top 5% of income earners were receiving 20.7% of all income, compared to 15.6% in 1970 and 14.6% in 1980.[66] As a result, their incomes rose in real terms by about two-thirds, while the median income in the USA barely rose at all.[67] Similar trends have been observed throughout Western Europe, with Britain exhibiting more extreme divergences than the average. In the UK, between 1979 and 1994/95, growth in real income for the richest one-tenth of the population was a little over 60%, while for the poorest tenth it was a rise of 10% before taking housing costs into account, or a fall of 8% if they were included.[68] To a greater or lesser extent, these patterns have been repeated across the whole of the Western world.

As unemployment has increased in the developed world, so, despite successive trade rounds involving tariff reductions on manufactured goods, it has become more difficult in a number of key respects to get the richer countries to agree to open further their economies to imports from the Third World. This is especially true of those which compete with the output from sensitive constituencies such as farmers or regions heavily dependent on the production of goods which can be manufactured much more cheaply in low wage economies. The transition away from these activities, though never easy, is always much more manageable if there are clearly alternative employment options available to those displaced. If, on the other hand, there are poor opportunities almost everywhere else in the economy, resistance to trade liberalisation is bound to be greater, as has been the experience in recent trade rounds. The goods which poor countries need to be able to export to the rich world are those where they have a competitive advantage in cheap labour, and where the production techniques are relatively simple and well known. Unfortunately, these are just the areas where most of the developed world is keenest on maintaining tariff or quota barriers – on food, shoes and garments, for example. The result is then to make it more difficult for poorer countries to break out of the slow growth and high population increase trap in which so many of them find themselves. The implications of such policies on total world population, and the pressure that will consequently be brought to bear on the world's ecology – and sooner rather than later – are all too obvious.

Nor, finally, have monetarist policies scored well on stabilising economies so that, even if their growth rates are lower and unemployment higher than they might otherwise have been, at least their progress is more steady and stable. In fact, since 1973, the ups and downs experienced by the world's developed economies have arguably been more unstable than they were in the 1950s and 1960s. No doubt the goal of all policymakers is to find some mechanism which can be used to iron out automatically the gyrations to which economies are always prone. Control of the money supply turned out in practice, however, to be no more effective than the fiscal 'fine tuning' of the Keynesian era.

Is it fair to say, however, that it is monetarist ideas that have caused the slowdown in world growth rates, with all the consequences which have flowed from it, rather than the counter-proposition that poorer economic performance was caused by other factors, with the intellectual force of monetarism being largely irrelevant? It is true that the trigger for the worsening conditions in the world economy in the 1970s were events such as breakdown in monetary discipline following the abandonment of the Bretton Woods fixed exchange rate regime, and the OPEC action which increased oil prices. It is hard to believe, however, that these events in themselves made monetarist remedies the only solution to the inflationary problems which they presented. Nor, indeed, does the evidence show that the countries which embraced monetarism with the greatest enthusiasm were those which were successful in bringing down inflation either most rapidly or most permanently. On the contrary, the evidence tends to suggest the opposite. Norway, admittedly a small country, largely bucked the monetarist trend, and continued to grow, with almost full employment, throughout the last quarter of the twentieth century, certainly performing much better than other countries of the same size in Europe. Around the Pacific Rim, where monetarism was never as powerful a force as it was in the West, economic performance did not decline significantly after 1973. Excluding Japan, the average annual growth rate in the Asian economies actually accelerated after 1973, rising from 5.2% between 1950 and 1973 to 5.7%[69] between 1973 and 1992. The 1990s saw a sharp fall in performance in most Pacific Rim countries in 1997, after strong growth during the mid-1990s, but the recovery from 1997 has also generally been very rapid.[70]

It is sometimes claimed that the slowdown in growth rates in the developed world is an inevitable consequence of the fact that the standard of living is already high, and that poorer countries always have better opportunities than rich ones to grow fast because there must necessarily be obvious ways for them to catch up with their better-off competitors. This argument cannot, however, be correct. It is not true that richer countries have always tended to grow more slowly than poorer ones, as recent experience in the USA clearly demonstrates. Nor is there the slightest evidence that human wants are being satiated, even in the case of the very rich. Furthermore, most increases in output do not depend on new technological developments. The vast majority result from larger volumes of production of familiar goods and services, of which consumers always seem to want more. Even if there was no new technology to exploit at all, there is every reason to believe that the world economy could go on growing almost as fast as it would have done anyway, as a result of exploiting existing production techniques more extensively.

The real reason for the slowdown in the performance in the world economy, especially in the West, has not therefore to any great extent been due to external factors. The evidence suggests that it is policy changes which have been responsible. Not all of these are attributable to the influence of monetarism, but it is hard to argue that monetarist ideas have not had a major impact on policymakers, persuading them to pursue strategies which have put economic goals in a far different order than this book argues that they deserved to have. Pre-eminent among them has been the aim of conquering inflation. The argument – based squarely on monetarist foundations – has been that if price increases can be brought down on average to no more than 2.0% or 2.5% per annum, then all other economic objectives will fall into place.

This is not, however, what has happened. Nor, indeed, after the heavy inflationary inputs in the 1970s, did those countries which adopted monetarist ideas most enthusiastically even manage to get their inflation rates down more quickly or more permanently than those which continued growing and allowed rising productivity to soak up most of the inflationary pressures. The real reason for the triumph of monetarist over Keynesian ideas during the last quarter of the twentieth century stemmed from the exceptionally serious inflationary problems in the 1970s, which provided a much more compelling justification for a cautious approach to economic management than had prevailed for the previous quarter of a century. The result, however, intended or otherwise, was that the preservation of wealth became more important than its creation. Monetarism reflects, at its best, policies of prudence and care with whose importance few would disagree, and whose necessity is clearly exemplified by the lack of success in economies which have ignored the requirement for them. Pushed too far, however, as the evidence of the last quarter of a century strongly suggests they were, monetarist policies bear much too uncomfortable a resemblance to the quietist, laissez faire policies which have always favoured the rich at the expense of those less fortunate, bringing economic performance overall down to well below its full potential.

The contribution of the right to economics

In the concluding section of Chapter 5, it was argued that the defining influence of the intellectual left on economics, and hence its impact on the way the world economy has developed, has been on how the fruits of economic output should be divided up, and not on how the total should be increased. To a remarkable extent, the same is also true of the intellectual right. Neither school of thought has had achieving higher rates of economic growth as its top priority. Indeed, in both camps, there have been concerns about what much higher levels of output might bring in their wake. The left has shaded off into the Green agenda, which is deeply suspicious of the whole growth process, while much of the right has had an ambivalent approach to the mass culture which has been the inevitable product of increasing affluence. Both have been inclined to express concerns about the materialistic attitudes which they believe are reinforced by concentrating on getting output up, and to worry about the immediate effects on the environment of higher growth rates. Both contain significant traditions which either despise or distrust trade in general and entrepreneurial activity in particular, and which have a distaste for the sometimes messy and occasionally dangerous processes involved in producing the masses of goods and services on which all modern economies depend.

Thinkers and writers on both left and right, therefore, have tended to concentrate much harder on dividing up the cake than making it larger. This may go a long way towards explaining why, compared to developing effective economic growth theory, so much intellectual effort has gone into finding ways of influencing both how the output of the economy is allocated among different sections of the population, and producing justifications for the policies which need to be pursued to achieve these ends. Hardly surprisingly, the left wants to see a more egalitarian split of the national income and wealth, while the right would prefer to see a distribution which more nearly reflects the ability of different categories of people either to generate new value added, or to enjoy the fruits of previous wealth creation.

Viewed in this light, it is not difficult to see why the same themes have recurred across the centuries in the contributions which those on the political right have made to the development of economic theory. There is the same presupposition in favour of *laissez faire* as there was two centuries and more ago, when this term was invented by the Physiocrats in pre-Revolutionary France. There is a distrust of government and its involvement in economic affairs, and a strong tendency to favour a minimalist role for the state, with the correspondingly low levels of taxation which then become feasible. In monetary matters, high priority is given to keeping the price level as stable as possible. Achieving this goal at least periodically through deflationary policies, which involve relatively high rates of interest, is not regarded with particular disfavour. Policies to help the poor through redistributive taxation have often been regarded as wasteful and ineffectual, as well as being unfair to those who have to pay for them. Monetary policy to control the economy is generally preferred to fiscal policies, especially when excess demand might otherwise require increases in taxation.[71] As societies mature, and the centre of gravity shifts away from first-generation wealth creators to subsequent inheritors, whose main concern is to hold on to the wealth they already have rather than to create new sources of it, so power moves from trade and industry to finance. Banks and bankers become more and more powerful compared to those more directly concerned with the creation of new wealth, while the risk-averse and cautious attitude which banking cultivates generates a conservative approach to all aspects of economic policy. Deflating the economy rather than risking increase in inflation becomes the accepted practice. The advantages of a high value to the exchange rate in increasing domestic competition and discouraging wage increases are regarded as significant advantages, as is the benefit to international investment from a high value for the currency. If, in these circumstances, unemployment rises, and the distribution of income and wealth becomes more uneven, this tends to be regarded as both inevitable and not wholly undesirable, as those who have better fortune are allowed to keep and even to enhance the fruits of their good luck.

The reasons why such attitudes are appreciated and supported by a much broader section of most electorates than those who would count themselves among the wealthy are not difficult to find. It is not only those who are well off who benefit from stability, low inflation and financial discipline. Rapid growth and full employment are not totally unmixed blessings, and low rates of inflation positively benefit, at least in the short term, many relatively poor sections of the population such as pensioners and others living on fixed incomes. The impact of the sub-optimal economic performance which this book argues has been the lot of the world over the last two hundred years is very unevenly felt. It is not a major problem for the vast proportion of the population in the developed world who are in steady employment and who already enjoy, by comparison with most of the rest of the world, very high living standards which are still rising.

These attitudes, which monetarist ideas reflect and have helped to reinforce are, however, in the greater scheme of things, a long way away from what the world really needs. The slow growth and wasted opportunities which policies such as these encourage are likely to have serious consequences, especially in the longer run. Complacency and contentment among those who are already well off may be storing up more trouble in the future than they realise, as tensions caused by rising population pressure, escalating disparities in life chances, and pressure on the world's ecology increase. The statistics clearly show that, across the world, there is a positive correlation between reasonably even distributions of wealth, income and life chances on the one hand, and lower crime rates and stronger social cohesion on the other.[72] The resources foregone by slow growth could have been used to deal with longer-term problems such as global warming, finding better ways of disposing of waste and conserving water supplies. Of course in the short term, higher growth rates will worsen these pressures, but all history shows that, with reasonably competent management, they can be made to create solutions faster than they worsen the problems, provided that sufficient of the newly created resources are allocated to dealing with them. Against this background, there is also the biggest single long-term issue with which humanity needs to contend, which is to ensure that the world's population peaks at a manageable level. As we have seen, foregone growth and high levels of unemployment do little to create the climate of opinion which will allow the most disadvantaged countries to trade themselves out of poverty, and to stabilise their populations as their incomes rise.

Despite all of this, it has, on the whole, been the economic thought of the intellectual right which has been in the ascendancy for most of the last two and a half centuries, and a sense of proportion needs to prevail. As The Fraser Institute report *Economic Freedom of the World 1975–1995*[73] clearly shows, it is the economic liberalism which has been mainly the product of right of centre thinkers which has been responsible for much greater and longer-lasting economic success than any other form of political organisation which has been tried. It is very easy for the state to interfere ineffectually or damagingly. History is replete with examples of wasted public expenditure. Reckless expansion does tend to hit the rocks, so a reasonable measure of caution when using fiscal and monetary policies is required. Not all public expenditure is redistributive, building a fairer and less tension-ridden society. Much of it tends to benefit those already well off, while the incidence of taxation can easily reach a long way down the income profile to those earning much less than the average. The provision of public goods and services can too readily be captured by producer interests, who then exploit their positions to exact unjustified costs on everyone else.

The issue, however, is not whether these well-accepted aspects of the right's critiques of collectivism and their contributions to economic policy development are justified and worthwhile. Clearly, in large measure they are. The question is a different one. Would it be possible, without throwing away the disciplined framework of economic relationships which right of centre traditions have done so much to create, to do much better, with higher growth, lower unemployment, and a fairer deal for poor countries and much greater opportunities for a sustainable environment in future? This book argues that it is possible to get the best of both worlds.

9

Economics and the Future

> No great improvements in the lot of mankind are possible, until a great change takes place in the fundamental constitution of their modes of thought.
>
> John Stuart Mill (1806–1873)

During the last hundred years, some conspicuous trends in economics have become apparent. The number of economists has certainly increased vastly, and many more of them are to be found in journalism, business, finance, government and the professions, as well as in the academic world, than was ever the case in the nineteenth century. Many of the techniques used by the economics profession have become much more refined than they were, and also a great deal more sophisticated mathematically. There has been an enormous expansion in the scope and coverage of statistics. The development of computers has made it much easier than it was to handle and process large amounts of data. Yet the impact of economic ideas on the way that policy generally has developed and hence the way that history has unfolded has been remarkably patchy and uneven.

During the twentieth century, there were two huge upheavals in economic ideas, one led by John Maynard Keynes and the other by Milton Friedman. Of course, many other people were associated with these two key figures. The impact of their ideas and writings would not have been nearly so great had each of them not had many convinced, determined and able supporters to help them carry their messages to the world. Nevertheless, without these two key individuals, it is not obvious that the ideas associated with each of them would have had the impact that they did. It may well be the case that others covered the same ground, and that there were significant groups of people who came to more or less the same conclusions at the same time as Keynes and Friedman. No doubt, however, there were other people whose ideas were coalescing round different points of view. The key fact about both Keynes and Friedman – and the same is true of their major predecessors – is not just that they both propounded very powerful sets of practical proposals, backed up by impressive theorising. Their great achievement, in each case, was to get their views generally accepted in their time both in the academic world and in the wider policy-making arena.

Perhaps it is in the nature of things that major changes in perception tend to occur only at intervals, as a result of big upheavals, and that they are much more difficult to introduce incrementally. Certainly, thirty years after monetarist ideas swept the Keynesian Revolution aside, at least in the majority of countries in the Western world, much of their legacy is still in place. It is true that the simple verities with which monetarism started – that there was a rigid relationship between the money supply and the level of inflation a short period afterwards – have been heavily watered down. For example, M3 – the measure of the money supply which, for a decade from the mid-1970s to the mid-1980s, became the lodestar by which British economic policy was run – was discarded, and stopped then even being published in its original form, to be replaced by other measures.[1] Everywhere, politicians eventually resiled from the levels of unemployment and the dislocations to the economy that the very tight monetary conditions and high rates of interest which monetarist policies, implemented *à l'outrance*, demanded.

Nevertheless, much of the monetarist standard of values and priorities still remains firmly in place. Keeping inflation at low levels is widely regarded as the primary economic objective, from which all else will flow. Levels of unemployment, which would have been regarded in the 1950s and 1960s as off the spectrum of acceptability, are now perceived as being a necessary cost to pay to achieve price stability. High rates of interest and tight monetary conditions are treated as an obligatory policy backdrop, their implementation being made more certain by transferring, in most of the developed world, decision-making powers about monetary policy to largely unaccountable central banks. The deleterious impact of such policies on the real economy, particularly manufacturing, is mostly ignored, or treated as an unavoidable consequence of the achievement of more important objectives. The deflationary conditions thus generated produce an increasing dispersion of wealth and income, which those doing best regard with the same toleration as their forebears in the nineteenth century, who believed that the poor will always be with us, and that there was little useful that the state could do to alleviate their condition.

This book argues that this is an extraordinarily myopic view of the world. We can do much better than this. Indeed we will have to make the world's economy perform more effectively if we are going to avoid a major crisis of population and the ecology, let alone, in much of the developed world, problems such as evading an unmanageable increase in the dependency ratio. Yet tackling these broad issues is not, very largely, what economic thinking has been about during recent decades. Apparently trapped in the parameters set by the monetarist legacy, nearly all the new ideas which have materialised assume that the world's major economies, or at least those in the developed West, can do no better than they have over the last quarter of a century. A growth rate of about 2.5% per annum, coupled generally with both much less efficient use of the labour force than used to prevail and widening wealth, income and life chances, is the accepted norm. There is little sign of radical discontent with the status quo, or of a determination to do not just a bit better, but to achieve levels of performance in an altogether different league than those we have seen recently. Yet there is now an increasingly urgent need for this to happen not only in the poorest countries in the world, but also in the developed economies too. This needs to happen for its own sake, but also because the wealth and purchasing power of the developed world needs to provide the way out of poverty for the vast number of human beings who are not nearly so well off.

The fact that there is still a large outstanding agenda does not, however, preclude there having been a huge amount of development in a wide variety of fields of economic study during the last decades of the twentieth century. Inevitably its quality is variable. Much of it is in the form of newspaper articles, and therefore influential in the short term, but in most cases not likely to endure. A further significant proportion has been published in learned journals, and is therefore much more orientated to the economics profession than to the public at large. The writing which seems most likely to make the deepest and most long-lasting impression are books with a clear and powerful enough message both to become significant in academic terms and to be widely read by those interested in current affairs and the formulation of policy. We turn now – necessarily tentatively – to seeing which some of these might have been during the last third of the twentieth century.

Late twentieth century economists

While the change from the Keynesian to the monetarist approach to economic policy has been far the most important to have taken place in economic thinking during the last few decades, this has not, of course, been to the exclusion of a large amount of other work. How much of this will stand the test of time, however, making the names of those who have executed it part of the long history of economics? While there is a broad consensus about the significance of those whose contributions have been sufficiently substantial to merit this accolade during the first half of the twentieth century, thereafter there is increasingly less certainty. Those who have won Nobel prizes in economics, which started being awarded in 1969, certainly provide an important indication, and a full list of the Prize winners is provided later in this chapter. Many of those thus honoured, however, did their most important work a considerable period of time before they were recognised in this way. Furthermore, the Nobel Prize in Economics is, understandably, orientated towards those who have made their mark in the academic world rather than more widely. As a result, albeit with some important exceptions, the principal achievements for which the prize in economics has been awarded have nearly always been in relatively self-contained and complex areas of study. They have not therefore generally been easily accessible to the public at large, characterising the gulf that there is between economics as practised in universities on the one hand, and in the real world on the other. Politicians and civil servants are then left to grapple with practical economic problems, and others to comment on what they do, often in the light of only limited guidance from academic formulations.

Inevitably, the more recent the time-scale, the more difficult it is to see whose work will stand out in the long term. *The Economist* periodically makes an assessment of those regarded within the economic profession as being its most significant rising members. Interestingly, and no doubt reflecting accurately the current state of economics, the most recent listing, published in December 1998, largely consists of people with comparatively narrow specialisation. This being the case, it may significantly reduce their chances of making a major difference to the thrust of economic thinking as a whole. If, to obtain a greater chance of homing in on those who are likely to have a larger overall impact, candidates for consideration include those outside the academic mainstream, this increases the range of potential choice, making selection even more difficult. The people whose names are featured in the paragraphs which follow are therefore not part of a general consensus, but much more the product of personal experience. Allowance must be made for the fact that the selection which follows is biased towards macro-economic policy and that it is even more skewed towards those who have written in English. Here, nevertheless, with all these qualifications, are comments on the work of those writers on economics who seem to have a reasonable claim to have contributed most either to new thinking or to clear exposition, or both, in recent years.

Some of the best work, even if it inevitably has an ephemeral quality to it, has not been done by the academic world but by journalists, many of whom have supplemented their work in newspapers by writing books. The British press has been particularly favourably endowed in this respect, with an exceptionally well-informed and accurate critique of the ways in which British economic policy has unfolded being maintained by Larry Elliott (born 1955) in the *Guardian* and Anatole Kaletsky (born 1952) in *The Times*. Much the same can be said of the writers of *The Economist*, though as nearly all their articles are, as a matter of editorial policy, unsigned, it is not possible to mention them by name.

Sir Samuel Brittan (born 1933) has kept up a similarly high-quality commentary in his articles in the *Financial Times*. Sir Samuel was an early, though critical, convert to the monetarist banner, and has remained throughout a firm defender of liberal capitalism. Typical of his work, he published *Is there an Economic Consensus?*[2] during the period in the 1970s when further moves towards collectivist solutions to Britain's then pressing problems appeared, for a time, to be a real possibility. He reiterated many of the same views in *A Restatement of Economic Liberalism*,[3] published in various editions between 1973 and 1988 providing a significant influence on the policies adopted by Margaret Thatcher's government.

In a different vein, Will Hutton (born 1950), now Director of the Industrial Society, has also been an influential writer. His extremely successful book, *The State We're In*,[4] very much caught the mood of the times, though it is not clear that the policy proposals it contained were sufficiently substantial and workable to warrant the attention they received, and it will be interesting to see how long his influence lasts. It is hard to disagree with his diagnosis that the British are not interested enough in those parts of the economy which pay our way in the world. The issue is whether this affliction is curable without more radical economic policy changes being implemented than those Will Hutton advocated. Economic history demonstrates that changes of heart, on their own, will seldom be enough. Changes in incentives, and the harnessing of self-interest to the public purpose are what is needed, as Adam Smith so perspicaciously pointed out.

As for general commentators from the academic world on the unfolding economic scene, there are four people whose work has been of outstanding quality, at least judged by the wide readership and influence they have achieved. In this case they are all American. Going back furthest is John Kenneth Galbraith (born 1908), Paul M. Warburg Professor of Economics at Harvard University, whose many books have all had a similar thread running through them. Very much a liberal in American terms, he has been a consistent advocate of Keynesian policies and a supporter of public initiative during decades when confidence in action by the state to ameliorate conditions has steadily waned. More than most writers, he has been acutely aware of the capacity of those doing well to twist the ideology of the times to suit their purposes, coining the phrase 'the conventional wisdom' to describe this process. Unlike many economists, Professor Galbraith has a hugely elegant writing style, which establishes a standard seldom achieved by those setting out their views on economic subjects.

While few can rival J.K. Galbraith in this respect, one who can is Paul Krugman (born 1953), Ford International Professor of Economics at the Massachusetts Institute of Technology, another prolific author whose many books have been widely influential.[5] He, too, has the capacity both to teach the reader to look at events in a new light and to reinterpret trends and events through the acuity and thoroughness of his observations, and the forcefulness and clarity with which he expresses them. While both these authors have huge readerships, well deserved in the light of the quality of their writings, it seems strange that neither of them have produced an over-arching view about where economics ought to be going, and how it should get there. The same criticism can also be made against other powerful and influential writers such as Lester Thurow (born 1938), Professor of Economics and Management at the Massachusetts Institute of Technology and Michael E. Porter, Christensen Professor of Business Administration at Harvard Business School, both of whom have been particularly concerned, over the years, about the ability of the US economy to stand up to competition from the rest of the world in the long term. While many of the more detailed points in their books are impressively well made and clearly right, again it is perhaps surprising that neither of them seems to have homed in on the fundamental reasons for the relatively poor growth performance achieved by the USA over the decades since the Second World War. While they have been well aware of the increasing difficulty which much of the US economy has had in competing with the rest of the world, they have been inclined to attribute this to cultural and organisational reasons rather than the cost base being too high, which this book argues is by far the most important explanation. As a result, none of these authors has emphasised how crucial to the history of the USA has been the extent to which production costs for a huge range of goods have been allowed to rise well above the world average, causing the hollowing-out of US manufacturing capacity which has done so much to unbalance the US economy.

Turning to economic history, the most wide ranging books have been by David Landes (born 1924), Emeritus Professor at Harvard University, and Charles P. Kindelberger (born 1910), former Ford International Professor of Economics at the Massachusetts Institute of Technology, again both Americans. If a hinterland of historical knowledge, and interpretation of how and why events developed in the way they did over a long perspective, are key components to understanding the present, books of the quality of David Landes, *The Wealth and Poverty of Nations*[6] and Charles P. Kindelberger's *World Economic Primacy 1500 to 1990*,[7] set standards which it is hard to surpass. On more recent international economic history, one of the most thorough, well researched and persuasive of recent contributions is *Monitoring the World Economy 1820–1992*[8] by Angus Maddison (born 1926), formerly Professor of Economics at the University of Groningen, containing a huge range of comparative statistics, buttressing the many other books which he has written, analysing economic growth and development.

On international economics and monetary development, some of the most influential work has been done by Barry Eichengreen (born 1952), Professor of Economics and Political Science at Berkeley University,

California, exceptionally well summarised in his *Globalizing Capital – A History of the Economic Monetary System.*[9] Similarly impressive is *Economics and World History – Myths and Paradoxes*[10] by Paul Bairoch (1930–1999), formerly Professor of Economic History at the University of Geneva. An interesting and readable book by Peter Jay (born 1937), Economics Editor at the BBC, is his *Road to Riches or the Wealth of Man,*[11] though whether his waltz motif is as illuminating a guide to the development of economic history as he claims seems doubtful. Whatever view one may take about monetarist theorising, *A Monetary History of the United States, 1867–1960*[12] by Milton Friedman and Anna Jacobson Schwartz is an extremely interesting and impressive book. On the wider scene still, as background knowledge to the way ideas about the past generally have developed, making possible the evolution of the political framework within which liberal capitalism operates best, *The End of History and the Last Man*[13] by Francis Fukuyama (born 1952), Professor of Public Policy at George Mason University, is surely one of the most remarkable and significant books written in recent years.

Turning now from economic history to the history of economic thought, much the most readable of all the books available is J.K. Galbraith's *A History of Economics – the Past as the Present.*[14] In heavier and more detailed vein *Economic Theory in Retrospect*[15] by Mark Blaug (born 1927), Emeritus Professor at the Universities of London and Buckingham, must rank highly. So too does *A History of Economic Thought*[16] by Eric Roll (born 1907), a former British senior civil servant. Much more discursive is a long work, *History of Economic Analysis,*[17] written by Joseph A. Schumpeter, and edited by his wife after his death. Perhaps the clearest and most comprehensive book covering this wide canvas is *The Growth of Economic Thought*[18] by Henry William Spiegel (1911–1995), formerly Professor Emeritus of Economics at the Catholic University of America. The problem with all these books, however, is that none of them feels confident about making any very significant assessments of recent economic developments. While understanding their caution, this leaves a gap in the evaluation of late twentieth-century economists which remains to be filled.

During the last fifty years, Britain's exceptionally poor experience with inflation and the confrontational wage negotiation climate for much of the time, have produced a long series of publications about the best way of dealing with these problems. Outstanding among them, have been the books by Richard Layard (born 1934), in his capacity as Director of the Centre for Economic Performance at the London School of Economics, and Roger Bootle (born 1952), Managing Director of Capital Economics Ltd. Richard Layard's work, favouring wages policies and typified by his *How to Beat Unemployment,*[19] sets out the case for controlling the inflationary pressures generated by full employment in this way. His work is very much geared towards the problems which materialise in slow-growing economies exemplified by the UK, however, and therefore does not emphasise the extent to which high productivity growth can soak up inflationary pressures, while increased global competition constrains them. Layard's work is therefore in considerable contrast to the emphasis in *The Death of Inflation*[20] by Roger Bootle. This was one of the first major attempts to grapple systematically with whether the changed environment of the 1990s, when price increases were subdued, was a temporary respite from the battles of the 1970s and 1980s when the fight against inflation dominated the policy agenda, or whether low levels of inflation were here to stay. So far, the course of events predicted by Roger Bootle has been much as he said it would be, of course in the process making the case for incomes policies much less pressing.

Other writers who have had important and original things to say are three more British economists. *The Death of Economics*[21] by Paul Ormerod (born 1950), was widely acclaimed, but arguably his more recent *Butterfly Economics*[22] was more persuasive, particularly in his damning criticism of forecasting, and fine-tuning policies on the basis of projections which had inbuilt tendencies to being unreliable enough to make any such approach unsustainable. This is a modern echo of the work done earlier by Trygve Haavelmo. It strongly reinforces the view that the only way to run economies successfully is to get the fundamentals right to a point where fine-tuning ceases to be a necessary policy component. Wilfred Beckerman (born 1925), now retired but previously Professor of Political Economy in the University of London, and subsequently an Emeritus Fellow of Balliol College, Oxford, seems to have been one of the few economists to have realised how poorly positioned the British economy had been allowed to become, not just when monetarist policies were at their height, but over the longer term, as he explained in his *In Defence of Economic Growth*.[23] Although most people were never persuaded by his Alternative Economic Strategy, which involved trade restraints rather than devaluation, at least he opened up a discussion which still urgently needs to be continued. His book *Small is Stupid: Blowing the Whistle on the Greens*[24] was an exceptionally clear and persuasive argument about the direction in which environmental policies need to be pursued, an approach recently heavily reinforced by a major book by Bjørn Lomborg (born 1965), Associate Professor of Statistics at the University of Aarhus in Denmark, entitled *The Skeptical Environmentalist*,[25] containing a powerful attack on much conventional environmental received wisdom. Finally, at the other end of the political spectrum, Patrick Minford (born 1943), Professor of Economics at the Cardiff Business School, has been one of the more impressive advocates, in such books as *Markets not Stakes*,[26] for the intelligent use of markets rather than other methods of resource allocation. While the opinions on the capacity of the state to influence the economy and to run parts of it directly with success may have been too pejorative, we need to be reminded of the bounds which ought to be applied to initiatives by the state which may not be as successful as their proponents hope they will be. Perhaps even more significant is the importance of economic liberalism both for its own sake in preserving the rights of the individual, and harnessing self-interest to the general interest.

There are two writers who have both had a great deal of influence in analysing how people perceive and react to the economic process, shedding light on how it might be possible to engineer changes in the future. One is Fred Hirsch (born 1931), formerly on the staff of *The Economist* and subsequently Professor of International Studies at Warwick University, whose *Social Limits to Growth*[27] set out for the first time the notion of the importance attached by individuals to the goods they purchased not just for their intrinsic value but because of what their possession conveyed to other people. The concept of 'positional goods' has significant implications for the extent to which it is possible to get the population at large to accept egalitarian policies. In something of the same vein, but even more important in terms of explaining how society really operates was *The Rise and Decline of Nations*[28] by Mancur Olson (1932–1998), Professor of Economics at the University of Maryland. This seminal book, followed up more recently by *Power and Prosperity*,[29] explains with great clarity how stable societies build up webs of interests and perceptions which steadily reinforce more and more effectively the status quo, providing increasing strength to conservative views, while shifting power ever more firmly into the hands of those in established positions. These perceptions throw a great deal of light on the way in which the world economy has developed over the last fifty years, and before, illustrating the process which leads to mature and successful nations losing their entrepreneurial energy, and being overtaken in time by upstarts barely considered as rivals a few decades previously.

Mention should be made of two new schools of thought on macroeconomic policy, whose influence may grow.[30] One is the chartalists, whose central contention is that anything can be used as money provided that the state will accept it in payment of taxes. Various adherents to this school of thought, not least L. Randall Wray (born 1954), Visiting Professor at Bard College, New York, and now on the faculty at the University of Missouri-Kansas City, have used the very different perceptions of money which this view throws up to attack monetarist theorising.[31] They propose that it is much easier to combine low levels of inflation and full employment than is often supposed. They are also critical of monetarist contentions that controlling the money supply is as effective as they claim, holding that the monetary base is, in practice, always supplied by the central bank in the quantity needed, and that attempts to control it are unproductive. Because, as has now become OECD standard practice, capital adequacy ratios have largely replaced minimum reserves against lending for clearing banks, the formal link between monetary base and the amount that clearing banks can lend has been broken. It is, nevertheless, still clear that restrictive monetary policies, high interest rates and high exchange rates slow down economic activity, and bias any country subjected to such policies away from those forms of economic activity which lead most readily to economic growth and rising living standards.

Creditary economists share some of the chartalists' views, but with a rather different emphasis. The creditary economists' main argument is that the study of the money supply is only a small part of the total creation of credit on which modern economies depend. Essentially, any form of debt is capable of being treated as money, provided that the recipients are agreeable. Trade credit is probably the oldest form of debt, and the main purpose of instruments such as bills of exchange – 15 times more common than Bank of England notes in early nineteenth-century Britain[32] – is to convert a trade debt into a document which can readily be used as money. They argue that low interest rates tend to lead to lower prices by encouraging investment in labour-saving machinery, and that in an age of rapid innovation, inflation ought not therefore to be a serious threat. They believe that high interest rates cause rather than reduce inflation, not least because interest charges are a cost, like any other, which needs to be reflected in prices. High interest rates also encourage wage claims from the economically active, who are also the major borrowers.[33]

Finally, careful note needs to be taken of some of the much more radical criticism of economic theory which is welling up within a profession where there is a wide measure of discontent about its thrust and content. *Debunking Economics*[34] by Steve Keen (born 1953) on the faculty of the University of Western Sydney, Australia, in particular, makes very uncomfortable reading for anyone who has been led to believe that economics as presently taught and practised is nearly as soundly based on either logic or empirical verification as is often supposed. Once again, the tendency for ideas about economic issues to be overlaid with prejudice and biased towards the rich and powerful is forcefully exposed as his arguments unfold.

Economics has therefore been full of vitality over the last part of the twentieth century. Much new ground has been covered. As circumstances have changed, and fresh problems have arisen, a great deal of new thinking has been done to find solutions to them. Nagging doubts still remain, however, as to how successful the total enterprise has been. There is far more information than there was before. There are much better statistics. More tools are available in the form of new and relevant ideas which had not been published previously. Yet there is still the lack of an over-arching framework, pulling the whole subject together. Economics in recent years has made progress by filling in niches, not by producing a major synthesis.

Nobel Economics Prize winners[35]

Year	Names	Nationality	Principal Achievement
1969	Ragnar Frisch	Norway	Pioneering econometric studies; planning
	Jan Tinbergen	Netherlands	Pioneering econometric studies; business cycles
1970	Paul A. Samuelson	USA	Mathematical reformulation of economic theory
1971	Simon Kuznets	USA	Income concepts; measurement of growth
1972	Kenneth J. Arrow	USA	Paradox of voting; information theory
	John R. Hicks	UK	Modern micro-economic theory
1973	Wassily Leontief	USA	Input-output analysis
1974	Gunnar Myrdal	Sweden	'American Dilemma'; 'Asian Drama'
	Friedrich von Hayek	UK	Political philosophy and business cycle theory
1975	Leonid Kantorovich	USSR	Linear programming
	Tjalling Koopmans	USA	Linear programming
1976	Milton Friedman	USA	Founder of monetarism; libertarian approach
1977	Bertil Ohlin	Sweden	New approach to international trade theory
	James E. Meade	UK	International economic policy
1978	Herbert A. Simon	USA	Organisation and decision theory; rationality
1979	W. Arthur Lewis	UK	Development studies
	Theodore W. Schultz	USA	Farm economics; human capital
1980	Lawrence Klein	USA	Econometric models and forecasting
1981	James Tobin	USA	Macro-economic and portfolio theory
1982	George J. Stigler	USA	Micro-economic theory; critique of regulation

1983	Gerard Debreu	France	Reformulation of general equilibrium theory
1984	Richard Stone	UK	Development of national accounting systems
1985	Franco Modigliani	USA	Analysis of saving and financial markets
1986	James M. Buchanan	USA	Theories on economic and political decisions
1987	Robert W. Solow	USA	Contributions to the theory of economic growth
1988	Maurice Allais	France	Theory of markets and efficient use of resources
1989	Trygve Haavelmo	Norway	Testing fundamental econometric theories
1990	Harry Markowitz Merton Miller William Sharpe	USA USA USA	Pioneering theories on managing investment portfolios and investment finances
1991	Ronald Coase	USA	Work on value and social problems of companies
1992	Gary S. Becker	USA	Linking economic theory to human behaviour
1993	Robert Fogel Douglas North	USA USA	Creating a new method of studying economic history – cliometrics
1994	John F. Nash John C. Harsanyi Richard Selten	USA USA Germany	Work on 'game theory', which investigates decision making in a competitive environment
1995	Robert E. Lucas Jr	USA	Rational expectations; government policy
1996	James A. Mirrlees William Vickrey	UK USA	Fundamental contributions to the economic theory of incentives with asymmetric information
1997	Robert Merton Myron Scholes	USA USA	Determining a new method of valuing derivatives

1998	Amartya Sen	India and UK	Contributions to welfare economics
1999	Robert A. Mundell	USA	Optimum currency areas
2000	James J. Heckman Daniel L. McFadden	USA USA	Analysing selective samples and discrete choice
2001	George A. Akerlof A. Michael Spence Joseph E. Stiglitz	USA USA USA	Analysis of markets and asymmetric information

Conclusion

The conclusion to which this book leads is that we now need another sea change in the way in which economics is structured and taught, comparable in scale to those achieved by Smith, Keynes and Friedman. All those involved with economic ideas and their impact on the world need to find the strength to drive this change through, to provide policymakers with the intellectual hinterland which they will need to cope with the problems which the twenty-first century is going to bring with it. The challenge which has to be met falls into two parts. The first involves redefinition of the goals which economics should set out to achieve, and the second is to describe convincingly how they should be accomplished in ways which are practical and realistic for policymakers to adopt.

As to the goals, those set out at the beginning of this book bear repeating. We need a clear and unified theory which describes how to achieve and maintain economic growth rates throughout the world of around 3% to 4% in output per head, which may mean considerably higher growth rates for those economies which are poorest and where population numbers are still rising fast. This kind of performance has to be achieved with close to full employment, leaving no more than around 2% to 3% of the willing labour force without a job. These conditions have to be combined with inflation rates which are subdued and stable enough not to cause disruption. They may not be as low as 2% or 2.5%, on the basis of historical experience, but should generally not be more than 4% to 5%. In addition to these targets, two other related goals are required. One is to alleviate extreme poverty both within and between nations, and the second is to ensure that the world economy has a sustainable path ahead of it. The key link between these last two objectives is that by far the most practical way of containing the growth of population within manageable bounds is to make the poorest people on the planet richer as fast as possible, because this is the surest way of reducing the birth rate. In the meantime, the most feasible way of coping with mounting environmental problems is to generate sufficient wealth to make it possible to allocate enough to deal with them, while the number of people in the world is still not so large as to overwhelm all chances of doing so.

How should the world economy be organised to achieve an average growth rate in GDP per head of 3% to 4%? The key concept to grasp is that the only way to higher growth rates in any economy is to push up output per head, or average productivity, and that this is far easier to achieve in some parts of the economy than in others. Table 2.1 on page 16 shows the pattern, which repeats itself throughout the world. Manufacturing, and various forms of activity associated with it, provide far the best opportunities for productivity increases, so if the objective is to get the whole world to grow faster and in a more balanced way, manufacturing opportunities need to be spread around appropriately. This can only be done if the cost base, allowing for whatever levels of investment in plant and machinery and skills in the labour force have been achieved, is arranged to be balanced equitably throughout the world. In particular, it needs to be biased downwards in the case of the poorest countries, if they are to be allowed to grow more rapidly than those currently richer than they are. If this is not done – as clearly is far from being the case at present – manufacturing activity will concentrate in the areas with the lowest cost base, and will desert those with the highest, and the relative performance of the world's economies is then likely to become even more uneven.

The reason why incomes per head in most of the Pacific Rim countries are growing so much faster than those in the West is very largely a cost base issue. For other parts of the world, such as much of Africa, the problem is complicated by other factors such as war, ineffective and venal government, poor education and dire health problems. If these less fortunate countries are going to be allowed to prosper and to raise their living standards, however, in the end it is industrialisation, and the associated productivity increases which will do it. Nothing else will achieve this objective, which is why the reforms necessary to make its attainment possible are so vital.

A sensibly fair and roughly even spread of manufacturing activity throughout the world has another key role to play in ensuring that all the economies in the world can expand fast enough to avoid trade balance problems dragging down those in the weakest situation. Some 65% of all international trade is in manufactured goods,[36] and any well diversified economy will need to make sure that it has a competitive and buoyant export manufacturing sector to ensure that it does not get held back by balance of payments problems. Few countries have sufficient raw materials to fill this gap, and the volume of trade worldwide in services, at about 20% of the total,[37] is much too small in almost all economies to offset significant trade deficits in manufactured goods, though some, such as Britain, have large investment income flows to fill a sizeable part of the gap which might otherwise be there. How is industrialisation to be spread around the world in the way which will optimise the prospects for humanity? The key, as Chapter 2 showed, it is to use internationally co-ordinated macro-economic policy to create both the total demand and the pattern of exchange rates needed to enable the whole world's economy to expand much more rapidly than it has during the last three decades.

Just as was the case in the USA during the Second World War and in Western Europe in the 1950s and 1960s, and as we can see now in many of the Pacific Rim countries, once sustained high rates of economic growth are established, unemployment diminishes rapidly as a problem. There are job opportunities for almost everyone. Furthermore, in all rapidly growing economies, there is a corresponding tendency for standards in education and training among the labour force to be upgraded, partly as a result of state initiatives, especially through the education system, partly by self-help, and partly by on the job training. There is also strong pressure for participation to rise, this being the ratio between the total potential labour force and those actually working. As registered unemployment falls, so more and more people who would otherwise have dropped out of the labour force get attracted back into it again. This is a trend which especially needs encouragement in those parts of the world where there is an aging population, and where the number of people in jobs is otherwise likely to fall markedly in relation to those not working, whom they have to support. As people live longer, but also remain fit, it makes sense to provide them with opportunities to go on working. The greater the extent to which participation ratios can be increased, the more the strain will be taken off the taxation and public expenditure system, which otherwise, particularly in many developed countries where the birth rate is now well below replacement level, is going to be in serious difficulties by not long into the present century.

If full employment is re-established, is there not a danger that inflation will reappear with the same virulence as it did in the 1970s? Given reasonably competent economic management, which is required in any circumstances, there is no reason to believe that it should. The 1970s experience was caused by excessive credit creation, followed by an unsustainable boom. There is no reason why this mistake should be made again. Much more typical was the two-decade-long period between 1950 and 1970 when the increase in the price level in most developed countries averaged around 4% while the growth rate in percentage terms was at least this high, if not higher. Of course there were inflationary pressures during this period, some of them associated with national wage bargaining at a time when international price competition was much less acute than it is nowadays. Rises in the price level did not, however, get out of hand. The key reason why they did not do so was that high productivity increases acted as a sponge to soak them up.

A rather different concern about inflation relates to the changes which would need to be made to exchange rates to distribute more equitably the spread of industrial activity throughout the world, and thence to attempt, over a period of time, to even up living standards between all countries. We have seen that this can only be done if the cost base in those countries where the proportion of economic activity devoted to manufacturing is brought down in relation to those where it is currently concentrating. The economies with low and often falling manufacturing sectors, compared to output as a whole, tend to be among economies in the developed West. They also, however, tend to include many of the poorest countries in the world, whose low growth rates are exacerbated because the birth rate exceeds the expansion in national income. If the performance of economies in both categories is to be improved, they will have to change their monetary policies to bring their exchange rates down, by increasing the money supply and lowering interest rates. Better growth performance in developed countries, to enable the political difficulties of reducing trade barriers to trade with the Third World to be overcome, may be just as important as in the Third World, which needs to be the major beneficiary, simply to relieve widespread poverty and destitution.

Conventional wisdom has it that a combination of looser monetary conditions and a devaluation is bound to increase inflation, and some rises probably will occur. Table 2.3 on page 28, however, provides powerful evidence that it is not devaluations themselves which are inflationary. While higher import prices may push up the price level, lower interest rates, longer production runs and a switch to home sources of supply tend to counteract their impact. If inflation is one or two percentage points higher as a lower cost base pushes up the growth rate, the difference will be largely caused by leading sector inflation. This, it will be recalled, is the averaging process which takes place between the manufacturing sector, where fast growth produces almost no price rises, and the service sector where matching productivity increases are very hard to achieve. As a result, the impact on export competitiveness and growth from a lower exchange rate, tends to be wholly positive. Expansion in national income goes hand in hand with low increases in export prices.

The relief of poverty has two main dimensions, one internal to each individual economy, and the other internationally between them. The extent to which equality should be reduced will always be a matter of political controversy, but nearly everyone would agree that, beyond some point, increasing extremes of deprivation are simply not acceptable. The best single way of reducing inequality within any economy is to get back to conditions which are as close as possible to full employment. This both directly improves life chances for the most disadvantaged, and also increases the capacity of the taxation and benefit system, especially in developed countries, to help those worst off at bearable cost to everyone else. More difficult is the alleviation of conditions in the poorest countries of the world, to lift their populations out of the poverty which in too many cases has stabilised at very low levels of income and expenditure, as rises in the national income are paralleled by increasing numbers of mouths to feed. Aid helps, but, as we have seen, the only real solution is trade and, as always, the establishment of opportunities to raise productivity, especially through manufacturing but also in agriculture, to provide for both the home market and for export. The best contribution that the developed world can make is to open its markets to Third World production. The stronger the economic conditions in the developed countries, the easier this should be to achieve.

As to sustainability, the world is already in a race against time. The world's population, now about 6bn, may well grow to 10bn by the middle of the twenty-first century and may, by then, be as high as 13bn.[38] At present, most of the existing 6bn people have standards of living far below those in the developed world. If 10bn, let alone 13bn people were all to have the same living standards as those in the developed world, on average, have now, the strains on the world's ecology would be immensely increased. Experience suggests that the exhaustion of sources of supply of raw materials will probably not be an insuperable difficulty, and that it should be possible to produce enough food.[39] There will, however, certainly be huge problems to be overcome in supplying this vastly increased population with fresh water, disposing of sewage and rubbish, providing sufficient power, and avoiding global warming getting out of hand. As has been stressed on a number of occasions in this book, the crucial variable is going to be the number of people in the human population when the total plateaus or peaks. The key issue is to raise living standards in the poorest countries fast enough to bring the birth rate down quickly enough, so that the final number is manageable. At the moment, far too little is being done. In Africa alone, despite the AIDS epidemic, the population, estimated at 832m in 2000,[40] has recently been growing at 3% per annum.[41] Far from the gap between the richest and the poorest parts of the world narrowing, it has greatly widened. In 1995 the richest 20% of the world's population had living standards more than 80 times higher than the poorest 20%, compared to a ratio of about 30 to 1 in 1960.[42] Nearly a quarter of humanity – some 1.3bn people – are believed to have been living on less than $1 a day during the 1990s.[43]

The challenge facing economics, then, is to convince both public opinion and those in charge of policy implementation that there are ways of achieving the goals to which all these possibilities point. This is a daunting task, not only because it is never easy to persuade people to adopt new ideas, but also because there is, inevitably, a huge weight of interest against this task being accomplished among those who are content with the way things are. This state of affairs, in turn, reflects much of the development of ideas about how the economy could and should be run from the time when economics began to develop as a subject.

The problem is that the changes which need to be made are not ones which easily appear to be in the best interests of those benefiting most from the current status quo. The richness and stability of the developed Western world has generated a strong consensus around the sorts of economic policies with which a large majority of people are reasonably contented, even if their overall effectiveness is well below what could be attained. The problem is that policies like these are to too great an extent in the interests of wealth holders rather than wealth creators. They benefit old money rather than new; finance rather than industry; services as against manufacturing; the professions *vis à vis* entrepreneurs; and the haves rather than have-nots. The relatively tight monetary policies, with high interest and exchange rates thus generated, produce largely the opposite conditions to those required to break through to the much higher levels of economic performance needed to enable the world's population to unlock the true potential which lies in front of it. As always in the past, it is compellingly simple ideas which will shift public opinion. The issue is whether the prospects of unmanageable claims on the earth's resources, within the lifetime of an increasingly large proportion of the world's inhabitants, will provide a sufficiently powerful trigger to enable the changes in policy which are needed to be made in sufficient time.

For the closer the time gets when the pressures on the world's ecology become critical, the stronger the general interest becomes for everyone to find workable solutions, even if they involve some sacrifice, and more concessions to others, than might previously have been acceptable. The history of economic ideas has been one which has shown a remarkable tendency to regress to the same concepts which underpinned the precepts of the Classical Economists, the Neo-Classicists and the monetarists, interrupted only by the quarter of a century or so during which Keynesian policies were fully in vogue. The success which Keynes achieved in moving policy away from its natural resting place – at least for a time – came from the crisis of the inter-war Depression and the skill with which he advocated changes which were so successful, but only as long as the conditions existed which made their continuing implementation possible. We now need to realise that the approach to economic policy, reflected currently in the way in which most of the Western world, in particular, conducts its economic affairs, is simply not up to the challenges which the twenty-first century is going to present. Is it going to be possible to produce a new consensus capable of making the necessary changes in sufficient time? Only time will tell. By all accounts, however, there is still a long way to go.

Notes

Preface

1 Page 123 in *Globalizing Capital* by Barry Eichengreen. Princeton: 1996, Princeton University Press.
2 Table C-16a in *Monitoring the World Economy 1820–1992* by Angus Maddison. Paris: 1995, OECD.
3 Ibid. same table.
4 Ibid. same table.
5 Ibid. same table.
6 Letter from Geoffrey Gardiner to John Mills dated 21 July 2001.
7 Table 745 in *Statistical Abstract of the United States*. Washington DC: 2000 Edition, US Department of Commerce; and Table B2 in *Economic Report of the President*. 2001 Edition, US Government Printing Office.
8 Table B-47 in *Economic Report of the President*.
9 Table 745 in *Statistical Abstract of the United States*.
10 Table 0601 in *Eurostatistics*. Luxembourg: Successive editions, The European Commission.
11 Table 55, page 160, and Table 65, page 188, in *Labour Force Survey*, Luxembourg: EU Commission, 1999, show total unemployment in the EU 15 in 1998 averaging 17.26m compared to 8.76m inactive people who 'would like to have a job'.
12 *A History of Economics – the Past as Present* by John Kenneth Galbraith. London: 1987, Penguin Books.
13 *A History of Economic Thought* by Eric Roll. London: 1973, Faber and Faber.
14 *Economic Theory in Retrospect* by Mark Blaug. Cambridge: 1996 edition, Cambridge University Press.
15 *The Growth of Economic Thought* by Henry William Spiegel. Washington DC: 1996 edition, Duke University Press.
16 *The Making of Modern Economics* by Mark Skousen. Armonk, New York and London, England: 2001, M.E. Sharpe.
17 *Debunking Economics* by Steve Keen. London and New York: 2001, Zed Books.
18 *The New Palgrave – A Dictionary of Economics* edited by John Eatwell, Murray Milgate and Peter Newman. London: 1998, Macmillan Reference Ltd.
19 *Ten Great Economists* by Joseph A. Schumpeter. London: 1997 reprint, Routledge.
20 *History of Economic Analysis* by Joseph A. Schumpeter. London: Reprinted 1997, Routledge.
21 *Monetarism or Prosperity?* by Bryan Gould, John Mills and Shaun Stewart. London: 1982, Macmillan – now Palgrave Macmillan.
22 Page 18 and 19 in *History of Economic Analysis*.

1 Introduction

1 Table C-16a in *Monitoring the World Economy 1820–1992* by Angus Maddison. Paris: 1995, OECD.
2 Ibid. same table.

3 Letter from Geoffrey Gardiner to John Mills dated 21 July 2001.
4 Tables D-1a and D-1e in *Monitoring the World Economy 1820–1992* supplemented by recent national income statistics for the UK and Taiwan.
5 Economic Report to the President. Washington DC: 2000, United States Printing Office.
6 Page 4 in *A History of Economics – the Past as the Present* by John Kenneth Galbraith. London: 1987, Penguin Books.
7 Table D-1a in *Monitoring the World Economy 1820–1992*.
8 Ibid. Table G-3.
9 Ibid. Table G-3.
10 Ibid. Table G-1.

2 Economic Theory

1 Table 55, page 160, and Table 65, page 188, in *Labour Force Survey*. Luxembourg: EU Commission, 1999.
2 Table 2.5, page 122, in *The State of Working America* by Lawrence Mishel, Jared Bernstein and John Schmitt. Ithaca and London: Cornell University Press, 2001.
3 Article in the *Guardian* by Will Hutton .
4 Page 867 in *Hutchinson's Encyclopedia*. Oxford: Helicon, 1998.
5 Table 3 in the Statistical Annexe to *World Economic Report 1998–99*. Geneva: International Labour Organisation, 1999.
6 Ibid. Table 1.
7 Ibid. same tables.
8 Page 132 in *Economic Theory in Retrospect* by Mark Blaug. Cambridge: Cambridge University Press, 1996 Edition.
9 Page 187 in *Managing the World Economy* by John Mills. London: Palgrave, 2000.
10 Table 1, page 13 in *Employment in Europe*. Luxembourg: The European Commission, 1997.
11 Table 0601 in *Eurostatistics, January 2002 Edition*. Luxembourg: The European Commission, 2002.
12 Table 55, page 160 and Table 65, page 188, in *Labour Force Survey*.
13 Table 101, page 102 in *Employment in Europe*.
14 Table 0604 in *Eurostatistics, January 2002 Edition*.
15 Tables 1 and 4 in the Statistical Annexe to *World Employment Report 1998–99*. Geneva: International Labour Office, 1999.
16 *Employment Policy Institute Economic Report*. Vol. 9, No. 9, November 1995.
17 Table US.10 in *Economic Statistics 1900–1983* by Thelma Liesner. London: *The Economist*, 1985.
18 Ibid. Table G.6.
19 Page 33 in *Employment in Europe*.
20 Table C-16a in *Monitoring the World Economy 1820–1992* by Angus Maddison. Paris: OECD, 1995.
21 Table US.2 in *Economic Statistics 1900–1983* by Thelma Liesner. London; *The Economist*, 1985.
22 Ibid. Table US.9.
23 Page 31 in *Debt and Delusion* by Peter Warburton. London: Allen Lane, The Penguin Press, 1999.
24 Table on pages 280 and 281 in *Sterling: The History of a Currency* by Nicholas Mayhew. London: Allen Lane, The Penguin Press, 2000.

25   Table 3.19 in *Monitoring the World Economy 1820–1992*.
26   Page 198 in *Managing the World Economy*.
27   Ibid. Table C-16a.
28   Answer to a Parliamentary Question.
29   Table 3.19 in *Monitoring the World Economy 1820–1992*.
30   Ibid. Table 3.19.
31   Ibid. Table 3-13a.
32   Ibid. Table 3-18.
33   Ibid. Table 3-17.
34   Page 172 in *International Financial Statistics Yearbook*. Washington DC: IMF, 1998.
35   Tables UK.7, F.3 and G.3 in *Economic Statistics 1900–1983*.
36   Pages 174 to 177 in *Main Economic Indicators*. Paris: OECD, 1999.
37   Table 745 in *Statistical Abstract of the United States*. Washington DC: 2000 Edition, US Department of Commerce.
38   Ibid.
39   *Monitoring Poverty and Social Exclusion 1999* by Catherine Howard *et al*. York: The Rowntree Foundation, 1999.
40   *Breadline Europe* by David Gordon and Peter Townsend. Bristol: The Policy Press, 2000.
41   Page 271 in *Road to Riches or the Wealth of Man* by Peter Jay. London: Weidenfeld and Nicolson, 2000.
42   Table 1 in the Statistical Annexe to *World Employment Report 1998–99*.
43   Ibid.
44   *Guardian*, 30 April 2001.
45   Table A1 in *Trends and Statistics*. Geneva: The World Trade Organisation, 1995.
46   Ibid. Chart III.11 on page 62.
47   Table 1 in the Statistical Annexe to *World Employment Report 1998–99*.
48   Table G-1 in *Monitoring the World Economy 1820–1992*.
49   Ibid. Tables A2 and G1.
50   Chapter 8 in *Development as Freedom* by Amartya Sen. Oxford: Oxford University Press, 1999.
51   Page 13 in *The Economist*, 19 May 2001.
52   Page 106 in *Development as Freedom*.
53   *The Limits to Growth*. Club of Rome Report. Potomac Associates, 1972.
54   Chapter Four in *Small is Stupid: Blowing the Whistle on the Greens* by Wilfred Beckerman. London: Duckworth, 1995.

3 The Pre-Industrial World

1   Page 107 in *Africa: A Biography of a Continent* by John Reader. London: Penguin Books, 1998.
2   Page 100 et seq in *Guns, Germs and Steel* by Jared Diamond. London: Jonathan Cape, 1997.
3   Letter from Geoffrey Gardiner to John Mills dated 21 July 2001.
4   Pages 242 and 276 in *Hutchinson's Encyclopaedia*. Oxford: Helicon, 1998.
5   Unpublished work carried out by Chris Meakin.
6   Letter from Geoffrey Gardiner to John Mills dated 21 July 2001.
7   Page 390 in *Hutchinson's Encyclopaedia*.
8   Letter from Geoffrey Gardiner to John Mills dated 21 July 2001.

9   Page 556 in *Hutchinson's Encyclopedia*.
10 Page 12 in *The Growth of Economic Thought* by Henry William Spiegel. Durham and London: Duke University Press, 1991.
11 Ibid. pages 13 and 14.
12 Page 16 in *A History of Economics – the Past as the Present* by John Kenneth Galbraith. London: Penguin Books, 1987.
13 Page 692 in *The Growth of Economic Thought*.
14 Ibid. page 16.
15 Ibid. page 21.
16 Ibid. page 24.
17 Page 57 in *History of Economic Analysis* by Joseph A. Schumpeter. London: Routledge, 1997 Reprint.
18 Page 25 in *The Growth of Economic Thought*.
19 Ibid. page 25.
20 Page 11 in *A History of Economics – the Past as the Present*.
21 Page 26 in *The Growth of Economic Thought*.
22 Page 12 in *A History of Economics – the Past as the Present*.
23 Ibid. pages 27 to 33.
24 Ibid. pages 34 to 39.
25 Page 70 in *Road to Riches or the Wealth of Man* by Peter Jay. London: Weidenfeld and Nicolson, 2000.
26 Ibid. page 68.
27 Page 18 in *A History of Economics – the Past as the Present*.
28 Page 36 in *A History of Economic Thought* by Eric Roll. London: Faber and Faber, 1973.
29 Letter from Geoffrey Gardiner to John Mills dated 21 July 2001.
30 Page 38 in *A History of Economic Thought*.
31 Page 73 in *Road to Riches or the Wealth of Man*.
32 Page 23 in *A History of Economic Thought*.
33 Page 41 in *The Growth of Economic Thought*.
34 Page 40 in *A History of Economic Thought*.
35 Page 21 in *A History of Economics – the Past as the Present*.
36 Page 258 in *Hutchinson's Encyclopedia*.
37 Ibid. page 77.
38 Page 45 in *The Growth of Economic Thought*.
39 Letter from Geoffrey Gardiner to John Mills dated 21 July 2001.
40 Page 24 in *A History of Economics – the Past as the Present*.
41 Page 42 in *A History of Economic Thought*.
42 Ibid. page 43.
43 Page 69 in *Road to Riches or the Wealth of Man*.
44 Ibid. page 85.
45 Ibid. pages 110 and 111.
46 Ibid. page 117.
47 Ibid. page 87.
48 Ibid. page 117.
49 Ibid. page 127.
50 Letter from Geoffrey Gardiner to John Mills dated 21 July 2001.
51 Page 126 in *Road to Riches or the Wealth of Man*.
52 Page 72 in *History of Economic Analysis*.
53 Page 25 in *A History of Economics – the Past as the Present*.

54   Page 44 in *A History of Economic Thought*.
55   Ibid. page 45.
56   Page 59 in *The Growth of Economic Thought*.
57   Page 35 in *Sterling – The History of a Currency* by Nicholas Mayhew. London: Penguin Group, 1999.
58   Page 49 in *A History of Economic Thought*.
59   Page 89 in *Road to Riches or the Wealth of Man*.
60   Page 23 in *A History of Economics – the Past as the Present*.
61   Page 66 in *The Growth of Economic Thought*.
62   Pages 60 and 61 in *Sterling – The History of a Currency*.
63   Page 78 in *The Growth of Economic Thought*.
64   Page 51 in *A History of Economic Thought*.
65   Ibid. page 81.
66   Page 46 in *A History of Economic Thought*.
67   Page 25 in *A History of Economics – the Past as the Present*.
68   Page 47 in *A History of Economic Thought*.
69   Page 27 in *A History of Economics – the Past as the Present*.
70   Ibid. page 53.
71   Ibid. page 28.
72   Page 52 in *A History of Economic Thought*.
73   Page 28 in *A History of Economics – the Past as the Present*.
74   Page 89 in *The Growth of Economic Thought*.
75   Ibid. page 91.
76   Page 445, Vol. 3 in *The New Palgrave* by John Eatwell *et al.* London: Macmillan Reference Ltd, 1998.
77   Page 31 in *A History of Economics – the Past as the Present*.
78   Ibid. page 32.
79   Ibid. page 33.
80   Ibid. page 42.
81   Page 56 in *A History of Economic Thought*.
82   Ibid. page 57.
83   Page 36 in *A History of Economics – the Past as the Present*.
84   Ibid. page 34.
85   Ibid. page 34.
86   Page 43 in *Sterling – The History of a Currency*.
87   Page 43 in *A History of Economics – the Past as the Present*.
88   Page 11 in *Economic Theory in Retrospect* by Mark Blaug. Cambridge: Cambridge University Press, 1996 Edition.
89   Page 62 in *A History of Economic Thought*.
90   Page 40 in *A History of Economics – the Past as the Present*.
91   Page 65 in *A History of Economic Thought*.
92   Ibid. page 66.
93   Ibid. page 64.
94   Ibid. page 85.
95   Ibid. page 85.
96   Page 14 in *Economic Theory in Retrospect*.
97   Page 67 in *A History of Economic Thought*.
98   Page 11 in *Sterling – The History of a Currency*.
99   Page 44 in *A History of Economics – the Past as the Present*.
100 Page 115 in *The Growth of Economic Thought*.

101   Page 82 in *A History of Economic Thought*.
102   Ibid. page 68.
103   Page 146 in *The Growth of Economic Thought*.
104   Ibid. pages 151 and 152.
105   Page 328 in *History of Economic Analysis*.
106   Letter from Geoffrey Gardiner to John Mills dated 21 July 2001.
107   Pages 22 to 27 in *Money: Whence it Came and Where it Went* by John Kenneth Galbraith. London: André Deutsch, 1975.
108   Page 143, Vol. 3 in *The New Palgrave*.
109   Page 117 in *A History of Economic Thought*.
110   Page 130 in *A History of Economic Thought*.
111   Page 47 in *A History of Economics – the Past as the Present*.
112   Page 239 in *The Growth of Economic Thought*.
113   Ibid. page 52.
114   Page 53 in *A History of Economics – the Past as the Present*.
115   Letter from Geoffrey Gardiner to John Mills dated 21 July 2001.
116   Page 135 in *A History of Economic Thought*.
117   Page 51 in *The Growth of Economic Thought*.
118   Ibid. page 193.
119   Page 49 in *A History of Economics – the Past as the Present*.
120   Page 23, Vol. 4, in *The New Palgrave*.
121   Page 189 in *The Growth of Economic Thought*.
122   Ibid. page 197.
123   Ibid. page 194.
124   Page 49 in *A History of Economics – the Past as the Present*.
125   Page 195 in *The Growth of Economic Thought*.
126   Page 137 in *A History of Economic Thought*.
127   Ibid. page 128.
128   Page 56 in *A History of Economics – the Past as the Present*.

4 Classical Economics

1   Pages 86 and 90 in *A History of Economic Thought* by Eric Roll. London: Faber and Faber, 1973.
2   Page 181 in *Hutchinson's Encyclopedia*. Oxford: Helicon, 1998.
3   Pages 92 and 93 in *A History of Economic Thought*.
4   Page 57 in *A History of Economics – the Past as the Present* by John Kenneth Galbraith. London: Penguin Books, 1987.
5   Page 122 in *The Growth of Economic Thought* by Henry William Spiegel. Durham and London: Duke University Press, Third Edition, 1996.
6   Ibid. page 164.
7   Encyclopedia Britannica website.
8   Pages 159 and 161 in *The Growth of Economic Thought*.
9   Ibid. page 161.
10   Ibid. page 164.
11   Page 100 in *A History of Economic Thought*.
12   Page 126 in *The Growth of Economic Thought*.
13   Page 213 in *History of Economic Analysis* by Joseph A. Schumpeter. London: Routledge, 1997 Reprint.
14   Page 112 in *A History of Economic Thought*.

15 Ibid. page 113.
16 Page 682, Vol. 3, in *The New Palgrave* by John Eatwell *et al.* London: Macmillan Reference Ltd, 1998.
17 Pages 120 and 121 in *A History of Economic Thought*.
18 Page 208 in *The Growth of Economic Thought*.
19 Ibid. page 210.
20 Ibid. page 237.
21 Page 121 in *A History of Economic Thought*.
22 Page 317, Vol. 1, in *The New Palgrave*.
23 Page 222 in *History of Economic Analysis*.
24 Page 31 in *Economic Theory in Retrospect* by Mark Blaug. Cambridge: Cambridge University Press, 1996 Edition.
25 Page 142 in *A History of Economic Thought*.
26 Pages 60 and 61 in *A History of Economics – the Past as the Present*.
27 Ibid. page 58.
28 Ibid. page 61.
29 Ibid. page 63.
30 Ibid. page 64, the quotations being from Book 1, Chapter 2, and Book 4, Chapter 2 in *The Wealth of Nations*.
31 Page 229 in *The Growth of Economic Thought*.
32 Page 64 in *A History of Economics – the Past as the Present*.
33 Ibid. page 65.
34 Ibid. page 66.
35 Page 309 in *History of Economic Analysis*.
36 Ibid. page 590.
37 Page 67 in *A History of Economics – the Past as the Present*.
38 Page 37 in *Economic Theory in Retrospect*.
39 Page 172 in *A History of Economic Thought*.
40 Page 67 in *A History of Economics – the Past as the Present*.
41 Ibid. page 68.
42 Page 246 in *The Growth of Economic Thought*.
43 Page 59 in *A History of Economics – the Past as the Present*.
44 Ibid. page 69, quoting Smith's Introduction.
45 Page 172 in *A History of Economic Thought*.
46 Pages 247 and 259 in *The Growth of Economic Thought*.
47 Page 69 in *A History of Economics – the Past as the Present*.
48 Page 254 in *The Growth of Economic Thought*.
49 Ibid. page 70.
50 Ibid. page 70.
51 Ibid. page 70, quoting Smith, Book 1, Chapter 10, Part 2.
52 Ibid. page 72, quoting Smith, Book 5, Chapter 1, Part 3, Article 1.
53 Page 48 in *Economic Theory in Retrospect*.
54 Page 237 in *The Growth of Economic Thought*.
55 Page 72 in *A History of Economics – the Past as the Present*, quoting Smith, Book 5, Chapter 2, Part 2.
56 Page 171 in *A History of Economic Thought*.
57 Page 240 in *The Growth of Economic Thought*.
58 Page 194 in *History of Economic Analysis*.
59 Page 59 in *A History of Economics – the Past as the Present*.
60 Ibid. page 42.

61 Page 74 in *A History of Economics – the Past as the Present.*
62 Ibid. page 74.
63 Page 249, Vol. 4 in *The New Palgrave.*
64 Ibid. page 249.
65 Page 75 in *A History of Economics – the Past as the Present.*
66 Page 249, Vol. 4, in *The New Palgrave.*
67 Letter from Geoffrey Gardiner to John Mills dated 21 July 2001.
68 Page 75 in *A History of Economics – The Past as the Present.*
69 Ibid. page 76.
70 Page 274 in *The Growth of Economic Thought.*
71 Page 77 in *A History of Economics – The Past as the Present.*
72 Page 266 in *The Growth of Economic Thought.*
73 Page 80 in *A History of Economics – The Past as the Present.*
74 Page 286, Vol. 3, in *The New Palgrave.*
75 Page 271 in *The Growth of Economic Thought.*
76 Ibid. page 275.
77 Ibid. page 273.
78 Ibid. page 276.
79 Page 77 and 78 in *A History of Economics – the Past as the Present.*
80 Pages 581 and 582 in *History of Economic Analysis.*
81 Page 253 in *History of Economic Analysis.*
82 Page 82 in *A History of Economics – The Past as the Present.*
83 Page 286 in *The Growth of Economic Thought.*
84 Page 183, Vol. 4, in *The New Palgrave.*
85 Page 83 in *A History of Economics – The Past as the Present.*
86 Page 344 in *The Growth of Economic Thought.*
87 Pages 82 and 83, quoting Ricardo, in *A History of Economics – the Past as the Present.*
88 Page 321 in *A History of Economic Thought.*
89 Page 83, quoting Ricardo, in *A History of Economics – the Past as the Present.*
90 Ibid. page 83, quoting Ricardo, page 13, but citing Adam Smith.
91 Page 250 in *The Growth of Economic Thought.*
92 Page 83, quoting Ricardo, in *A History of Economics – the Past as the Present.*
93 Ibid. page 84, quoting Ricardo.
94 Ibid. page 84, quoting Ricardo.
95 Ibid. pages 84 and 85, quoting Ricardo.
96 Ibid. page 84, quoting Ricardo.
97 Page 683 in *History of Economic Analysis.*
98 Page 85, quoting Ricardo, in *A History of Economics – the Past as the Present.*
99 Ibid. page 86, quoting Ricardo.
100 Page 189 in *A History of Economic Thought.*
101 Page 321 in *The Growth of Economic Thought.*
102 Page 86 in *A History of Economics – the Past as the Present.*
103 Ibid. page 81, quoting Carlyle's *Latter-Day Pamphlets, No. 1.*
104 Page 299 in *A History of Economic Thought.*
105 Page 233 in *History of Economic Analysis.*
106 Page 117, quoting Alfred Marshall in *Principles of Economics,* Vol. 1, page 70, in *A History of Economics – the Past as the Present.*
107 Page 226, Vol. 1, in *The New Palgrave.*
108 Page 132 in *Economic Theory in Retrospect.*

109 Page 344 in *The Growth of Economic Thought*.
110 Page 194 in *Economic Theory in Retrospect*.
111 Page 351 in *The Growth of Economic Thought*.
112 Ibid. page 349.
113 Pages 105 and 106 in *A History of Economics – the Past as the Present*.
114 Page 351 in *A History of Economic Thought*.
115 Page 357 in *The Growth of Economic Thought*.
116 Ibid. page 359.
117 Page 670, Vol. 1, in *The New Palgrave*.
118 Page 73 in *Economic History of Europe* by Herbert Heaton. New York and London: Harper Bros, 1935.
119 Page 364, quoting J.S. Mill *Principles* page 177, in *A History of Economic Thought*.
120 Page 389 in *The Growth of Economic Thought*.
121 Ibid. page 355.
122 Ibid. page 379.
123 Page 42 in *Globalizing Capital – A History of the International Monetary System* by Barry Eichengreen. Princeton: Princeton University Press, 1996.
124 Page 133 in *Economic Theory in Retrospect*.
125 Page 475, Vol. 3, in *The New Palgrave*.
126 Page 535 in *A History of Economic Thought*.
127 Page 571 in *History of Economic Analysis*.
128 Ibid. page 570.

5 Dissent

1 Page 212 in *A History of Economic Thought* by Eric Roll. London: Faber and Faber, 1973.
2 Page 90 in *A History of Economics – the Past as the Present* by John Kenneth Galbraith. London: Penguin Books, 1987.
3 Page 213 in *A History of Economic Thought*.
4 Page 414 in *The Growth of Economic Thought* by Henry William Spiegel. Durham and London: Duke University Press, Third Edition, 1996.
5 Ibid. page 411.
6 Page 91 in *A History of Economics – the Past as the Present*.
7 Page 415 in *The Growth of Economic Thought*.
8 Page 224 in *A History of Economic Thought*.
9 Page 417 in *The Growth of Economic Thought*.
10 Page 1175 in *Hutchinson's Encyclopedia*. Oxford: Helicon Publishing, 1998.
11 Page 230 in *A History of Economic Thought*.
12 Page 417 in *The Growth of Economic Thought*.
13 Pages 93 and 94 in *A History of Economics – the Past as the Present*.
14 Page 421 in *The Growth of Economic Thought*.
15 Ibid. pages 421 to 426.
16 Page 25, Vol. 4, in *The New Palgrave* by John Eatwell *et al.* London: Macmillan Reference Ltd, 1998.
17 Page 345 in *American Economic History* by John O'Sullivan and Edward F. Keuchel. Princeton and New York: Markus Weiner Publishing, 1989.
18 Page 432 in *The Growth of Economic Thought*.
19 Page 101 in *A History of Economics – the Past as the Present*.

20   Ibid. page 101.
21   Ibid.
22   Page 311 in *A History of Economic Thought*.
23   Ibid.
24   Page 438 in *The Growth of Economic Thought*.
25   Page 323 in *A History of Economic Thought*.
26   Pages 43 to 48 in *The Growth of Economic Thought*.
27   Page 96 in *A History of Economics – the Past as the Present*.
28   Ibid. page 97.
29   Ibid. page 97.
30   Ibid. page 98.
31   Page 240 in *A History of Economic Thought*.
32   Page 306 in *The Growth of Economic Thought*.
33   Page 96 in *A History of Economics – the Past as the Present*.
34   Page 441 in *The Growth of Economic Thought*.
35   Ibid. page 441.
36   Page 98 in *A History of Economics – the Past as the Present*.
37   Pages 242 to 245 in *A History of Economic Thought*.
38   Page 447 in *The Growth of Economic Thought*.
39   Ibid. page 448.
40   Ibid. page 446.
41   Ibid. page 446.
42   Page 134, Vol. 3, in *The New Palgrave*.
43   Page 53 *et seq* in *Karl Marx* by Francis Wheen. London: Fourth Estate Ltd, 1999.
44   Page 442 in *The Growth of Economic Thought*.
45   Ibid. pages 442 to 444.
46   Ibid. page 444.
47   Ibid. page 445.
48   Ibid. pages 498 and 499.
49   Pages 127 and 128 in *A History of Economics – the Past as the Present*.
50   Page 458 in *The Growth of Economic Thought*.
51   Ibid. pages 458 and 459.
52   Page 226 in *Karl Marx*.
53   Page 131 in *A History of Economics – the Past as the Present*.
54   Page 462 in *The Growth of Economic Thought*.
55   Page 132, quoting the 1848 Communist Manifesto, in *A History of Economics – the Past as the Present*.
56   Ibid. page 132, again quoting the Communist Manifesto.
57   Ibid. page 133, quoting Marx.
58   Ibid. page 134, again quoting the Communist Manifesto.
59   Ibid. page 133.
60   Ibid. page 135.
61   Ibid. page 133.
62   Page 472 in *The Growth of Economic Thought*.
63   Page 133 in *A History of Economics – the Past as the Present*.
64   Ibid. pages 136 and 137, quoting Marx.
65   Ibid. page 128.
66   Page 53 *et seq* in *Karl Marx*.
67   Page 253 in *A History of Economic Thought*.
68   Ibid. page 255.

69 Ibid. page 290.
70 Ibid. pages 292 and 293.
71 Page 48 in *The Growth of Economic Thought*.
72 Page 235 in *Economic Theory in Retrospect* by Mark Blaug. Cambridge: Cambridge University Press, 1996 Edition.
73 Page 137 in *A History of Economics – the Past as the Present*.
74 Ibid. page 185.
75 Page 476, quoting Marx, in *Economic Theory in Retrospect*.
76 Page 64 in *Managing the World Economy* by John Mills. London: Palgrave, 2000.
77 Page 594 in *A History of Economic Thought*.
78 Page 484 in *The Growth of Economic Thought*.
79 Ibid. page 485.
80 Page 178 in *A History of Economics – the Past as the Present*.
81 Page 250 in *Economic theory in Retrospect*.
82 Page 594 in *A History of Economic Thought*.
83 Page 249 in *Economic Theory in Retrospect*.
84 Page 659 in *Economic History of Europe* by Herbert Heaton. New York and London: Harper and Brothers, 1936.
85 Page 239 in *Road to Riches or the Wealth of Man* by Peter Jay. London: Weidenfeld and Nicolson, 2000.
86 Ibid. page 239.
87 Page 817 in *Hutchinson's Encyclopedia*.
88 Table C-16c in *Monitoring the World Economy 1820–1992* by Angus Maddison. Paris: OECD, 1995.
89 Ibid. Table 3-4.
90 Ibid. Tables D-1a and D-1c.
91 Ibid. Table B-10c.
92 Page 1088 in *Hutchinson's Encyclopedia*.
93 Table C-16c in *Monitoring the World Economy 1820–1992*.
94 Page 186 in *A History of Economics – the Past as the Present*.
95 Page 251 in *Road to Riches or the Wealth of Man*.
96 Page 1088 in *Hutchinson's Encyclopedia*.
97 Table C-16c in *Monitoring the World Economy 1820–1992*.
98 Ibid. Table C-16c.
99 Page 28 in *The End of History and the Last Man* by Francis Fukuyama. London: Penguin, 1992.
100 Table C-16c in *Monitoring the World Economy 1820–1992*.
101 Ibid. Table D-1c.
102 Page 1088 in *Hutchinson's Encyclopedia*.
103 Page 133 in *Monitoring the World Economy 1820–1992*.
104 Page 503 in *The Growth of Economic Thought*.
105 Ibid. pages 488 and 489.
106 Ibid. pages 486 and 487.
107 Ibid. page 493.
108 Page 945 in *The New Palgrave*.
109 Page 495 in *The Growth of Economic Thought*.
110 Ibid. page 491.
111 Page 185 in *A History of Economics – the Past as the Present*.
112 Page 493 in *The Growth of Economic Thought*.
113 Page 483 in *The Growth of Economic Thought*.

114   Ibid. page 501.
115   Ibid. page 425.
116   Ibid. page 481.
117   Ibid. page 480.
118   Ibid. page 482.
119   Page 343 in *Hutchinson's Encyclopedia*.
120   Page 425 in *The Growth of Economic Thought*.
121   Pages 210 and 211 in *A History of Economics – the Past as the Present*.
122   Ibid. page 211.
123   Page 638 in *Hutchinson's Encyclopedia*.
124   Page 211 in *A History of Economics – the Past as the Present*.
125   Page 497 in *The Growth of Economic Thought*.
126   Ibid.
127   Ibid. page 499.
128   Ibid.
129   Ibid. page 497.
130   Ibid. page 498.
131   Ibid. page 500.
132   Ibid.
133   Page 215 in *A History of Economics – the Past as the Present*.
134   Ibid. page 217.
135   Ibid. page 218.
136   Page 576 in *The Growth of Economic Thought*.
137   Page 212 in *A History of Economics – the Past as the Present*.
138   *Redistribution: A Review of Progress* by John Mills. London: The Labour Economic Finance and Taxations Association, 1974.
139   *Monitoring Poverty and Social Exclusion 1999* by Catherine Howarth *et al*. York: The Rowntree Foundation, 1999.
140   This is the major thesis in *The End of History and the Last Man*.

6 Technical Development

1   Page 171 in *Penguin Dictionary of Economics* by Graham Bannock *et al*. London: Penguin Books, 1998.
2   Page 205 in *The Growth of Economic Thought* by Henry William Spiegel. Durham and London: Duke University Press, Third Edition, 1996.
3   Ibid. page 296.
4   Page 107 in *A History of Economics – the Past as the Present* by John Kenneth Galbraith. London: Penguin Books, 1987.
5   Pages 510 and 511 in *The Growth of Economic Thought*.
6   Page 338 in *A History of Economic Thought* by Eric Roll. London: Faber and Faber, 1973.
7   Ibid. page 339.
8   Ibid. page 339.
9   Ibid. page 340.
10   Ibid. page 343.
11   Page 507 in *The Growth of Economic Thought*.
12   Ibid. page 508.
13   Ibid. page 509.

14 Page 374 in *A History of Economic Thought.*
15 Pages 512 and 513 in *The Growth of Economic Thought.*
16 Ibid. page 516.
17 Ibid. page 530.
18 Ibid. page 548.
19 Ibid. pages 515 and 516.
20 Ibid. page 517.
21 Ibid. pages 530 to 537.
22 Pages 852 and 853, Vol. 4, in *The New Palgrave* by John Eatwell *et al*. London: Macmillan Reference Ltd, 1998.
23 Page 549 in *The Growth of Economic Thought.*
24 Ibid. page 554.
25 Page 917, Vol. 4, in *The New Palgrave.*
26 Pages 618 and 619 in *The Growth of Economic Thought.*
27 Ibid. page 556.
28 Ibid. page 557.
29 Ibid. page 558.
30 Ibid. page 560.
31 Ibid. page 505.
32 Ibid. page 566.
33 Ibid. page 553.
34 Ibid. page 563.
35 Ibid. page 564.
36 Page 395 in *A History of Economic Thought.*
37 Page 404 in *Economic Theory in Retrospect* by Mark Blaug. Cambridge: Cambridge University Press, 1996 Edition.
38 Page 111 in *A History of Economics – the Past as the Present.*
39 Pages 569 and 570 in *The Growth of Economic Thought.*
40 Page 596, Vol. 4, in *The New Palgrave.*
41 Page 579 in *Economic Theory in Retrospect.*
42 Ibid. pages 579 and 580.
43 Ibid. page 579.
44 Chapters 3 and 4 in *Debunking Economics* by Steve Keen. London and New York: Zed Books, 2001.
45 Page 581 in *Economic Theory in Retrospect.*
46 Ibid. page 581.
47 Page 208 in *History of Economic Analysis* by Joseph A. Schumpeter. London: Routledge, 1997 Reprint.
48 Pages 184 and 185 in *A History of Economics – the Past as the Present.*
49 Page 579 in *The Growth of Economic Thought.*
50 Page 184 in *A History of Economics – the Past as the Present.*
51 Page 270, Vol. 1, in *The New Palgrave.*
52 Page 234 in *Penguin Dictionary of Economics* by Graham Bannock *et al*. London: Penguin Books, 1998.
53 Page 428, Vol. 1, in *The New Palgrave.*
54 Page 504 in *A History of Economic Thought.*
55 Ibid. page 502.
56 Pages 69 and 70, Vol. 3, in *The New Palgrave.*
57 Page 281 in *Economic Theory in Retrospect.*
58 Page 571 in *The Growth of Economic Thought.*

59   Pages 206 and 207, Vol. 4, in *The New Palgrave*.
60   Page 587 in *The Growth of Economic Thought*.
61   Ibid. page 585.
62   Letter dated 19 November 2001 from Brian Burkitt.
63   Pages 368 and 372 in *A History of Economic Thought*.
64   Statistics provided by Shaun Stewart.
65   Page 437, Vol. 4, in *The New Palgrave*.
66   Page 296 in *Hutchinson's Encyclopedia*. Oxford: Helicon, 1998.
67   From *In Memoriam*.
68   Page 120 in *A History of Economics – the Past as the Present*.
69   Ibid. page 121, quoting Spencer, page 418 in *The Study of Sociology*.
70   Ibid. page 122, quoting Spencer, page 413 in *Social Statistics*.
71   Ibid. page 123, quoting Sumner, page 90 in *The Challenge of Facts and Other Essays*.
72   Ibid. page 170.
73   Ibid. page 171, quoting Veblen.
74   Ibid. page 172.
75   Ibid. page 172.
76   Ibid. page 173.
77   Ibid. page 174 quoting Veblen, page 1 in *The Theory of the Leisure Class*.
78   Ibid. page 176.
79   Ibid. page 176, quoting Veblen, page 87 in *The Theory of the Leisure Class*.
80   Ibid. page 167, quoting George, page 10 in *Progress and Poverty*.
81   Ibid. page 167.
82   Page 515, Vol. 2, in *The New Palgrave*.
83   Pages 168 and 169 in *A History of Economics – the Past as the Present*.
84   Page 514, Vol. 2, in *The New Palgrave*.
85   Pages 47 and 51 in *Economics and World History* by Paul Bairoch. Chicago: Chicago University Press, 1993.
86   Ibid. page 27.
87   Ibid. page 27.
88   Ibid. page 28, quoting Marshall.
89   Page 647 in *The Growth of Economic Thought*.
90   Ibid. page 648.
91   Page 63 in *Penguin Dictionary of Economics*.
92   Page 649 in *The Growth of Economic Thought*.
93   Ibid. page 655.
94   Page 261 in *A History of Economics – the Past as the Present*.
95   Page 663 in *The Growth of Economic Thought*.
96   Page 509, Vol. 4, in *The New Palgrave*.
97   Page 233 in *Penguin Dictionary of Economics*.
98   Page 655 in *The Growth of Economic Thought*.
99   Page 303 in *Penguin Dictionary of Economics*.
100 Ibid. page 319.
101 Page 571 in *The Growth of Economic Thought*.
102 Page 163 in *Economic Theory in Retrospect*.
103 Page 184 in *Penguin Dictionary of Economics*.
104 Page 586 in *The Growth of Economic Thought*.
105 Page 326, Vol. 4, in *The New Palgrave*.
106 Page 367 in *Penguin Dictionary of Economics*.

107 Page 649 in *The Growth of Economic Thought*.
108 Ibid. page 650.
109 Ibid. page 651.
110 Page 61 in *Penguin Dictionary of Economics*.
111 Page 455, Vol. 1, in *The New Palgrave*.
112 Ibid. page 456, Vol. 1.
113 Page 62 in *Penguin Dictionary of Economics*.
114 Page 457, Vol. 1, in *The New Palgrave*.
115 Page 183 in *Penguin Dictionary of Economics*.
116 Page 655 in *The Growth of Economic Thought*.
117 Page 234, Vol. 4, in *The New Palgrave*.
118 Page 663 in *The Growth of Economic Thought*.
119 Page 243 in *Penguin Dictionary of Economics*.
120 Page 595 in *The Growth of Economic Thought*.
121 Page 620, Vol. 2, in *The New Palgrave*.
122 Page 603 in *The Growth of Economic Thought*.
123 Pages 412 and 413, Vol. 3, in *The New Palgrave*.
124 Ibid. page 203 *et seq.*

7 The Keynesian Revolution

1 Tables US.7, UK.7, F.3 and G.3 in *Economic Statistics 1900–1983* by Thelma Leisner. London: *The Economist*, 1985.
2 Ibid. Table F.2.
3 Ibid. Table G.2.
4 For a full account, see *The Great Inflation* by William Guttmann and Patricia Meehan. Farnborough: Saxon House, 1975.
5 Table UK.10 in *Economic Statistics 1900–1983*.
6 Page 167 in *American Economic History* by John O'Sullivan and Edward F. Keuchel. Princeton and New York: Markus Weiner Publishing, 1989.
7 Tables G.1 and G.2 in *Economic Statistics 1900–1983*.
8 Ibid. Tables G.6 and US.10.
9 Page 85 in *Globalizing Capital – A History of the International Monetary System* by Barry Eichengreen. Princeton: Princeton University Press, 1996.
10 Page 195, quoting Schumpeter in *The Economics of the Recovery Program* page 20, in *A History of Economics – the Past as the Present* by John Kenneth Galbraith. London: Penguin Books, 1987.
11 Page 633 in *The Growth of Economic Thought* by Henry William Spiegel. Durham and London: Duke University Press, Third Edition, 1996.
12 Page 195 in *A History of Economics – the Past as the Present*.
13 Page 1027 in *Hutchinson's Encyclopedia*. Oxford: Helicon, 1998.
14 Page 375, Vol. 1, in *The New Palgrave* by John Eatwell *et al.* London: Macmillan Reference Ltd, 1998.
15 Page 224 in *A History of Economics – the Past as the Present*.
16 Ibid. page 225.
17 Ibid. page 224.
18 Pages 592 and 593 in *The Growth of Economic Thought*.
19 Ibid. page 595.
20 Page 581, Vol. 3, in *The New Palgrave*.

21   Pages 583 to 585 in *The Growth of Economic Thought*.
22   Ibid. page 585.
23   Page 226, quoting Foster and Catchings *The Road to Plenty* page 128, in *A History of Economics – the Past as the Present*.
24   Ibid. page 241.
25   Ibid. page 226.
26   Ibid pages 187 and 188.
27   Page 124, Vol. 3, in *The New Palgrave*.
28   Ibid. page 8, Vol. 3.
29   Table G.6 in *Economic Statistics 1900–1983*.
30   Ibid. Table G.1.
31   Page 85 in *The European Economy 1914–1990* by Derek H. Aldcroft. London: Croom Helm, 1993.
32   Table G.1 in *Economic Statistics 1900–1983*.
33   Ibid. Table G.3
34   Pages 254 and 255, Vol. 4, in *The New Palgrave*.
35   Page 223 in *A History of Economics – the Past as the Present*.
36   Pages 244 and 254 in *Road to Riches or The Wealth of Man* by Peter Jay. London: Weidenfeld and Nicolson, 2000.
37   Letter from Geoffrey Gardiner to John Mills dated 21 July 2001.
38   Page 228 in *A History of Economics – the Past as the Present*.
39   Page 74 in *Maynard Keynes – An Economist's Biography* by D.E. Moggridge. London: Routledge, 1992.
40   Page 19, Vol. 3, in *The New Palgrave*.
41   Page 229 in *A History of Economics – the Past as the Present*.
42   Ibid. page 230.
43   Page 39, Vol. 3, in *The New Palgrave*.
44   Ibid. page 19, Vol. 3.
45   Pages 230 and 231 in *A History of Economics – the Past as the Present*.
46   Ibid. page 231.
47   Page 39, Vol. 3, in *The New Palgrave*.
48   Page 178 in *Dictionary of Economics* by Graham Bannock *et al*. London: Penguin Books, 1998.
49   Page 231 in *A History of Economics – the Past as the Present*.
50   Ibid. page 232, quoting Keynes, *A Treatise on Money*.
51   Page 23, Vol. 3, in *The New Palgrave*.
52   Ibid. page 38, Vol. 3.
53   Ibid. page 38, Vol. 3.
54   Ibid. page 38, Vol. 3.
55   Pages 833 to 836 in *Maynard Keynes – An Economist's Biography*.
56   Page 169 in *Towards True Monetarism* by Geoffrey Gardiner. London, Dulwich Press, 1993.
57   Letter from Geoffrey Gardiner to John Mills dated 21 July 2001.
58   Page 70, quoting Smith, Book 4, Chapter 2, in *A History of Economics – the Past as the Present*.
59   Pages 230 and 231 in *Dictionary of Economics*.
60   Ibid. page 231.
61   Ibid. page 231.
62   Page 522 in *A History of Economic Thought* by Eric Roll. London: Faber and Faber, 1973.

63 Pages 611 and 612 in *The Growth of Economic Thought.*
64 Ibid. page 612.
65 Page 1171 in *History of Economic Analysis* by Joseph A. Schumpeter. London: Routledge, 1997 Reprint.
66 Page 187 in *American Economic History.*
67 Tables US.1 and US.2 in *Economic Statistics 1900–1983.*
68 Page 23, Vol. 3, in *The New Palgrave.*
69 Page 136 in *Hutchinson's Encyclopedia.*
70 Page 227 in *A History of Economics – the Past as the Present.*
71 Ibid. page 239, quoting Hansen in a review of the *General Theory* in the *Journal of Political Economy.*
72 Page 234, Vol. 4, in *The New Palgrave.*
73 Information secured from the William D. Nordhaus website.
74 Page 77 in *Globalizing Capital – A History of the International Monetary System.*
75 Page 241 in *A History of Economics – the Past as the Present.*
76 Ibid. page 241.
77 Ibid. page 245.
78 Ibid. page 246.
79 Page 588, Vol. 3, in *The New Palgrave.*
80 Page 247 in *A History of Economics – the Past as the Present.*
81 Ibid. page 247, quoting Samuelson, *Economics* 12th Edition, page 102.
82 Ibid. pages 253 and 254.
83 Page 33 in *Penguin Dictionary of Economics.*
84 Tables 3–17 and 3–18 in *Monitoring the World Economy 1820–1992* by Angus Maddison. Paris: OECD, 1995.
85 Ibid. Table 3–19.
86 Ibid. Table 3–1.
87 Page 250, quoting Hayek *The Road to Serfdom* page 49, in *A History of Economics – the Past as the Present.*
88 Letter from Geoffrey Gardiner to John Mills dated 21 July 2001.
89 Table UK.7 in *Economic Statistics 1900–1983.*
90 Table 3.19 in *Monitoring the World Economy 1820–1992.*
91 Table UK.1 in *Economic Statistics 1900–1983.*
92 Answer to a Parliamentary Question.
93 Page 217 in *Penguin Dictionary of Economics.*
94 Pages 90 and 91 in *Globalizing Capital – A History of the International Monetary System.*
95 Table 1.3, page 18 in *Taiwan's Economic Success Since 1980* by Chao-Cheng Mai and Chien-Sheng Shih. Cheltenham, UK and Northampton, MA, USA: Edward Elgar, 2001.
96 Table US.14 in *Economic Statistics 1900–1983.*
97 Page 512 in *A History of Economic Thought.*
98 Page 133 in *Globalizing Capital – A History of the International Monetary System.*
99 Page 308 in *Penguin Dictionary of Economics.*
100 Page 172 in *International Financial Statistics Yearbook.* Washington DC: IMF, 1998.
101 Table 3.1 in *Monitoring the World Economy 1820–1992.*
102 Ibid. Table 3.1.
103 Page 496, quoting Keynes *General Theory* page 31, in *A History of Economic Thought.*

104 Page 283, quoting Keynes *Essays in Persuasion* page 366, in *A History of Economics – the Past as the Present*.
105 Ibid. page 283, quoting Keynes *Essays in Persuasion* page 373.
106 Table 3–18 in *Monitoring the World Economy 1820–1992*.
107 Pages 325 and 326, Vol. 4, in *The New Palgrave*.
108 Ibid. page 181, Vol. 1.
109 Letter from Geoffrey Gardiner to John Mills dated 21 July 2001.
110 Page 3, Vol. 3, in *The New Palgrave*.
111 Ibid. page 414, Vol. 3.
112 Ibid. page 728, Vol. 1.
113 Ibid. page 455, Vol. 2.

8 Hard Money

1 Pages 156 and 157, quoting Bryan, in *A History of Economics – the Past as the Present* by John Kenneth Galbraith. London: Penguin Books, 1987.
2 Ibid. page 141.
3 Page 22 in *Penguin Dictionary of Economics* by Graham Bannock *et al.* London: Penguin Books, 1998.
4 Page 176, Vol 2, in *The New Palgrave* by John Eatwell *et al.* London: Macmillan Reference Ltd, 1998.
5 Pages 151 and 152 in *A History of Economics – the Past as the Present*.
6 Ibid. page 152.
7 Ibid. pages 152 and 153.
8 Page 594 in *The Growth of Economic Thought* by Henry William Spiegel. Durham and London: Duke University Press, Third Edition, 1996.
9 Ibid. page 628.
10 Page 481, Vol. 3, in *The New Palgrave*.
11 Page 194 in *A History of Economics – the Past as the Present*.
12 Page 537 in *The Growth of Economic Thought*.
13 Page 257, Vol. 1, in *The New Palgrave*.
14 Pages 537–542 in *The Growth of Economic Thought*.
15 Ibid. page 539.
16 Page 123, Vol. 3, in *The New Palgrave*.
17 Page 812, Vol. 4, in *The New Palgrave*.
18 Page 642 in *The Growth of Economic Thought*.
19 Pages 333–335 and 415, Vol. 4, in *The New Palgrave*.
20 Ibid. pages 812 and 813, Vol. 4.
21 Ibid. pages 94 and 95, Vol. 1.
22 Ibid. page 413 *et seq*, Vol. 1.
23 Ibid. page 264, Vol. 4.
24 Page 279 in *A History of Economics – the Past as the Present*.
25 Page 545, quoting Schumpeter, in *The Growth of Economic Thought*.
26 Page 238 in *A History of Economics – the Past as the Present*.
27 Pages 543 and 545 in *The Growth of Economic Thought*.
28 Ibid. page 545.
29 Page 250 in *A History of Economics – the Past as the Present*.
30 Page 267, Vol. 3, in *The New Palgrave*.
31 Page 582 in *The Growth of Economic Thought*.

32 Chapters 2 and 3 in *Debunking Economics* by David Keen. London and New York: Zed Books, 2001.
33 Pages 422 *et seq*, Vol. 2, in *The New Palgrave*.
34 Page 18 *et seq* in *The Scourge of Monetarism* by Nicholas Kaldor. Oxford: Oxford University Press, 1986 reprint.
35 Page 719 in *Hutchinson's Encyclopedia*. Oxford: Helicon, 1998. M3 is defined for the UK as notes and coins in circulation, plus the operational balance of clearing banks with the Bank of England, plus current account deposits and deposit accounts, plus all other deposits held by UK citizens and companies in the UK.
36 Tables B-1 and B-68 in *Economic Report of the President*. Washington DC: US Government Printing Office, 1999.
37 Table 5.2, page 228 in *Economic Trends 1996/97 Annual Supplement*. London: Office for National Statistics, 1997.
38 Pages 88 and 89 in *International Financial Statistics*. Washington DC: The International Monetary Fund, 1998.
39 Letter from Geoffrey Gardiner to John Mills dated 21 July 2001.
40 Page 492, Vol. 3, in *The New Palgrave*.
41 Page 270 in *A History of Economics – the Past as the Present*.
42 Article by Larry Elliott in the *Guardian*. London: 15 February 2001.
43 Table 13.9, page 132 in *Financial Statistics*. London, Central Statistical Office, March 1983.
44 Table US.15 in *Economic Statistics 1900–1983* by Thelma Liesner. London: *The Economist*, 1985.
45 Ibid. Table UK.1.
46 Ibid. Table UK.10.
47 Ibid. Table US.1.
48 Ibid. Table US.10.
49 Table G-2 in *Monitoring the World Economy 1820–1992* by Angus Maddison. Paris: OECD, 1995.
50 Ibid. Table G-3.
51 Ibid. Table G-2.
52 Ibid. Table G-3.
53 Ibid. Table G-2.
54 Ibid. Table G-3.
55 Ibid. Table G-2.
56 Ibid. Table G-3.
57 Ibid. Table C-16a.
58 Ibid. Table D-1a.
59 Ibid. Table C-16a.
60 Ibid. Table D-1a.
61 Table on page 117 in *Employment in Europe*. Luxembourg: The European Commission, 1997.
62 Table 0601 in *Eurostatistics*. Luxembourg: The European Commission, January 2002.
63 Ibid. Table 0601.
64 Table 55, page 160, and Table 65, page 188, in *Labour Force Survey*, Luxembourg: EU Commission, 1999.
65 Table 668 in *Statistical Abstract of the United States*. Washington DC: US Department of Commerce, 2000.
66 Ibid. Table 745.

67 Ibid. Table 739.
68 Page 4 in *Breadline Europe*, quoting Hills 1998, edited by David Gordon and Peter Townsend. Bristol: The Policy Press, 2000.
69 Table 3-17 in *Monitoring the World Economy 1820–1992*.
70 Various tables in *International Statistics Yearbook*. Washington DC: IMF, 1998.
71 Page 273 in *A History of Economics – the Past as the Present*.
72 Table 2-9 in *Monitoring the World Economy 1820–1992*.
73 *Economic Freedom of the World 1975–1995* by James Gwartney, Robert Lawson and Walter Block. 1997: Vancouver: The Fraser Institute.

9 Economics and the Future

1 Chapter 36 in *The View from No.11* by Nigel Lawson. London: Transworld Publishers Ltd, 1992.
2 *Is there an Economic Consensus?* by Samuel Brittan. London: Macmillan, 1973.
3 *A Restatement of Economic Liberalism* by Samuel Brittan. London: Macmillan, 1988.
4 *The State We're In* by Will Hutton. London: Jonathan Cape, 1995.
5 These books are listed in the bibliography.
6 *The Wealth and Poverty of Nations* by David Landes. London: Little Brown, 1998.
7 *World Economic Primacy 1500–1990* by Charles P. Kindelberger. New York and Oxford: Oxford University Press, 1996.
8 *Monitoring the World Economy 1820–1992* by Angus Maddison. Paris: OECD, 1995.
9 *Globalizing Capital – A History of the Economic Monetary System* by Barry Eichengreen. Princeton: Princeton University Press, 1996.
10 *Economics and World History – Myths and Paradoxes* by Paul Bairoch. Chicago: Chicago University Press, 1993.
11 *The Road to Riches or the Wealth of Man* by Peter Jay. London: Weidenfeld and Nicolson, 2000.
12 *A Monetary History of the United States, 1867–1960* by Milton Friedman and Anna Jacobson Schwartz. Princeton: Princeton University Press, 1993 Edition.
13 *The End of History and the Last Man* by Francis Fukuyama. London: Penguin, 1992.
14 *A History of Economics – the Past as the Present* by John Kenneth Galbraith. London: Penguin Books, 1987.
15 *Economic Theory in Retrospect* by Mark Blaug. Cambridge: Cambridge University Press, 1996 Edition.
16 *A History of Economic Thought* by Eric Roll. London: Faber and Faber, 1973.
17 *History of Economic Analysis* by Joseph A. Schumpeter. London: Routledge, 1997 Reprint.
18 *The Growth of Economic Thought* by Henry William Spiegel. Durham and London: Duke University Press, Third Edition, 1996.
19 *How to Beat Unemployment* by Richard Layard. Oxford: Oxford University Press, 1986.
20 *The Death of Inflation* by Roger Bootle. London: Nicholas Brealey, 1996.
21 *The Death of Economics* by Paul Ormerod. London: Faber and Faber, 1994.
22 *Butterfly Economics* by Paul Ormerod. London: Faber and Faber, 1998.
23 *In Defence of Economic Growth* by Wilfred Beckerman. London: Jonathan Cape, 1974.

24 *Small is Stupid: Blowing the Whistle on the Greens* by Wilfred Beckerman. London: Duckworth, 1995.

25 *The Skeptical Environmentalist* by Bjørn Lomborg. Cambridge: Cambridge University Press, 2001.

26 *Markets not Stakes* by Patrick Minford. London: Orion Business Books, 1998.

27 *Social Limits to Growth* by Fred Hirsch. Cambridge, Mass: Harvard University Press, 1976.

28 *The Rise and Decline of Nations* by Mancur Olson. New Haven and London: Yale University Press, 1982.

29 *Power and Prosperity* by Mancur Olson. New York: Basic Books, 2000.

30 Letter from Geoffrey Gardiner to John Mills dated 21 July 2001.

31 *Understanding Modern Money: The Key to Full Employment and Price Stability* by L. Randall Wray. Cheltenham: Edward Elgar, 1998.

32 Letter from Geoffrey Gardiner to John Mills dated 21 July 2001.

33 Letter from Geoffrey Gardiner to John Mills dated 21 July 2001.

34 *Debunking Economics* by Steve Keen. London and New York: Zed Books, 2001.

35 Information drawn from page 663 in *The Growth of Economic Thought*; page 1181 in *Hutchinson's Encyclopedia*. Oxford: Helicon, 1998, and the Nobel Internet website.

36 Page 37 in *OECD Main Indicators, July 1999*. Paris: OECD, 1999.

37 Ibid. page 37.

38 Page 863 in *Hutchinson's Encyclopedia*.

39 Page 206 in *Development as Freedom* by Amartya Sen. Oxford: Oxford University Press, 1999.

40 Page 271 in *Road to Riches or the Wealth of Man*.

41 Table A–2 in *Monitoring the World Economy 1820–1992*.

42 Page 271 in *Road to Riches or the Wealth of Man*.

43 Ibid. page 271.

BIBLIOGRAPHY

Aldcroft, Derek H. *The European Economy 1914–90*, London: Routledge, 1993.
Aldcroft, Derek H. and Ville, Simon P. *The European Economy 1750–1914*, Manchester: Manchester University Press, 1994.
Ayres, Robert U. *Technological Forecasting and Long Range Planning*, New York etc: McGraw Hill Book Company, 1969.
Bainbridge, Timothy and Teasdale, Anthony *The Penguin Companion to the European Union*, London: Penguin, 1996.
Bairoch, Paul *Economics and World History – Myths and Paradoxes*, Chicago: Chicago University Press, 1993.
Bannock, Graham, Baxter, R.E. and Davis, Evan *Penguin Dictionary of Economics*, London: Penguin Books, 1998.
Barro, Robert J. *Determinants of Economic Growth*, Boston: Massachusetts Institute of Technology, 1999.
Beckerman, Wilfrid *In Defence of Economic Growth*, London: Jonathan Cape, 1974.
Beckerman, Wilfrid *Small is Stupid: Blowing the Whistle on the Greens*, London: Duckworth, 1995.
Beloff, Lord *Britain and the European Union: Dialogue of the Deaf*, London: Macmillan, 1996.
Bernstein, Peter L. *Against the Gods – The Remarkable Story of Risk*, New York: John Wiley & Sons, 1996.
Blaug, Mark *Economic History and the History of Economics*, New York etc: Harvester Wheatsheaf, 1986.
Blaug, Mark *Economic Theory in Retrospect*, Cambridge: Cambridge University Press, 1996.
Blinder, Alan S. *Hard Hearts Soft Heads*, Reading, Mass.: Addison-Wesley, 1987.
Block, Fred L. *The Origins of International Economic Disorder*, Berkeley, Los Angeles and London: University of California Press, 1977.
Booker, Christopher and North, Richard *The Castle of Lies*, London: Duckworth, 1996.
Boorstin, Daniel J. *The Discoverers*, New York and London: Penguin, 1983.
Bootle, Roger *The Death of Inflation*, London: Nicholas Brealey, 1996.
Bragg, Melvyn *On Giants' Shoulders: Great Scientists and Their Discoveries*, London: Hodder and Stoughton, 1998.
Brandt Commission *North–South Co-operation for World Recovery*, London and Sydney: Pan Books, 1983.
Brazelton, W. Robert *Designing US Economic Policy*, London and New York: Palgrave, 2001.
Brittan, Samuel *The Price of Economic Freedom*, London: Macmillan, 1970.
Brittan, Samuel *Is there an Economic Consensus?*, London: Macmillan, 1973.
Brittan, Samuel *A Restatement of Economic Liberalism*, London: Macmillan, 1988.
Brittan, Samuel *Capitalism with a Human Face*, London: Fontana Press, 1995.
Broadberry, S.N. *The Productivity Race*, Cambridge: Cambridge University Press, 1997.
Buchan, James *Frozen Desire – An Inquiry into the Meaning of Money*, London: Picador, 1997.

Burkitt, Brian and Baimbridge, Mark *What 1992 Really Means*, London: British Anti-Common Market Campaign, 1989.

Burkitt, Brian, Baimbridge, Mark and Whyman, Philip *There is an Alternative*, London: Campaign for an Independent Britain, 1996.

Caves, Richard E. *Britain's Economic Prospects*, Washington: The Brookings Institution, 1968.

Chafe, William H. *The Unfinished Journey: America Since World War II*, New York and Oxford: Oxford University Press, 1995.

Chowdhury, Anis and Islam, Iyanatul *The Newly Industrialising Economies of East Asia*, London and New York: Routledge, 1995.

Coates, Ken and Santer, Jacques *Dear Commissioner – An Exchange of Letters*, Nottingham: Spokesman Books, 1996.

Connolly, Bernard *The Rotten Heart of Europe*, London: Faber and Faber, 1995.

Crosland, C.A.R. *The Future of Socialism*, London: Jonathan Cape, 1956.

Davies, Norman *Europe – A History*, Oxford: Oxford University Press, 1996.

Denison, Edward F. *Why Growth Rates Differ*, Washington DC: The Brookings Institution, 1969.

Denison, Edward F. *Accounting for United States Growth 1929–1969*, Washington DC: The Brookings Institution, 1974.

Denison, Edward F. *Accounting for Slower Economic Growth*. Washington DC: The Brookings Institution, 1979.

Denman, Roy *Missed Chances: Britain and Europe in the Twentieth Century*, London: Cassell, 1996.

Diamond, Jared *Guns, Germs and Steel*, London: Jonathan Cape, 1997.

Eatwell, John, Milgate, Murray and Newman, Pete *The New Palgrave: A Dictionary of Economics*, London: Macmillan Reference Ltd, 1998.

Eichengreen, Barry *Globalizing Capital – A History of the International Monetary System*, Princeton: Princeton University Press, 1996.

Einzig, Paul *The Case Against Joining the Common Market*, London: Macmillan, 1971.

Elliott, Larry and Atkinson, Dan *The Age of Insecurity*, London: Verso, 1998.

Eltis, Walter *Growth and Distribution*, London: Macmillan, 1973.

Feldstein, Martin *The Risk of Economic Crisis*, Chicago and London: The University of Chicago Press, 1991.

Ferris, Paul *Men and Money: Financial Europe Today*, London: Hutchinson, 1968.

Foreman-Peck, James *A History of the World Economy since 1850*, New York etc: Harvester Wheatsheaf, 1995.

Friedman, Irving S. *Inflation: A World-wide Disaster*, London: Hamish Hamilton, 1973.

Friedman, Irving S. and Schwartz, Anna Jacobson *A Monetary History of the United States, 1867–1960*, New York: National Bureau of Economic Research, 1963, reprinted 1993.

Fukuyama, Francis *The End of History and the Last Man*, London: Penguin, 1992.

Galbraith, J.K. *The Affluent Society*, London: Hamish Hamilton, 1960.

Galbraith, J.K. *American Capitalism*, London: Hamish Hamilton, 1961.

Galbraith, J.K. *The New Industrial State*, London: Hamish Hamilton, 1968.

Galbraith, J.K. *Economics and the Public Purpose*, London: André Deutsch, 1974.

Galbraith, J.K. *Money – Whence It Came, Where It Went*, London: André Deutsch, 1975.

Galbraith, J.K. *A History of Economics – the Past as the Present*, London: Penguin Books, 1987.

Galbraith, J.K. *The Culture of Contentment*, London: Sinclair-Stevenson Ltd, 1992.

Galbraith, J.K. *The Good Society: The Humane Agenda*, London: Sinclair-Stevenson Ltd, 1996.

Gardiner, Geoffrey *Towards True Monetarism*, London: The Dulwich Press, 1993.

Giddens, Anthony *The Third Way*, Cambridge: Polity Press, 1998.

Goldsmith, James *The Trap*, London: Macmillan, 1994.

Gordon, David and Townsend, Peter *Breadline Europe: The Measurement of Poverty*, Bristol: The Policy Press, 2000.

Gray, John *False Dawn*, London: Granta Books, 1998.

Grieve Smith, John *Full Employment: A Pledge Betrayed*, London: Macmillan, 1997.

Gunther, John *Inside Europe Today*, London: Hamish Hamilton, 1961.

Guttmann, William and Meehan, Patricia *The Great Inflation*, Farnborough: Saxon House, 1975.

Hallett, Graham *The Social Economy of West Germany*, London: Macmillan, 1973.

Hama, Noriko *Disintegrating Europe*, London: Adamantine Press, 1996.

Harvey-Jones, John *Getting it Together*, London: Heinemann, 1991.

Hayek, F.A. *The Road to Serfdom*, London and Henley: Routledge & Kegan Paul, 1944.

Heaton, Herbert *Economic History of Europe*, New York and London: Harper and brothers, 1936.

Henderson, Callum *Asia Falling*, New York: McGraw-Hill, 1998.

Henig, Stanley *Political Parties in the European Community*, London: George Allen & Unwin, 1979.

Herman, Valentine and Lodge, Juliet *The European Parliament and the European Community*, London: Macmillan, 1978.

Hicks, John *Capital and Growth*, Oxford: Clarendon Press, 1965.

Hicks, John *A Theory of Economic History*, Oxford: Clarendon Press, 1969.

Hirsch, Fred *Money International*, London: Allen Lane, 1967.

Hirsch, Fred *Social Limits to Growth*, Cambridge, Mass.: Harvard University Press, 1976.

Holland, Stuart *Out of Crisis: A Project for European Recovery*, Nottingham: Spokesman Books, 1983.

Holt, Stephen *Six European States*, London: Hamish Hamilton, 1970.

Howarth, Catherine *et al.* *Monitoring Poverty and Social Exclusion 1999*, York: The Rowntree Trust, 1999.

Hutchinson's Encyclopedia, Oxford: Helicon Press, 1998.

Hutton, Will *The State We're In*, London: Jonathan Cape, 1995.

Isard, Peter *Exchange Rate Economics*, Cambridge: Cambridge University Press, 1995.

Ito, Takatoshi *The Japanese Economy*, Cambridge, Mass. and London, England: The MIT Press, 1996.

Jamieson, Bill *Britain beyond Europe*, London: Duckworth, 1994.

Jay, Douglas *Sterling: A Plea for Moderation*, London: Sidgwick & Jackson, 1985.

Jay, Peter *Employment, Regions and Currencies*, London: Eurofacts, 1996.

Jay, Peter *Road to Riches or the Wealth of Man*, London: Weidenfeld and Nicolson, 2000.

Johnson, Christopher *In with the Euro, Out with the Pound*, London: Penguin, 1996.

Johnson, Paul *A History of the American People*, London: Weidenfeld and Nicolson, 1997.

Jones, E.L. *The European Miracle*, Cambridge: Cambridge University Press, 1993.

Keen, Steve *Debunking Economics*, London and New York: Zed Books, 2001.

Kemp, Tom *Industrialization in Nineteenth Century Europe*, London: Longman, 1994.

Kenny, Anthony *A Brief History of Western Philosophy*, Oxford: Blackwell, 1998.

Keynes, John Maynard *The Economic Consequences of Mr Churchill*, London: Hogarth Press, 1925.

Keynes, John Maynard *The General Theory of Employment, Interest and Money*, London: Macmillan 1957 edition. First published 1936.

Kindleberger, Charles P. *World Economic Primacy 1500 to 1990*, New York and Oxford: Oxford University Press, 1996.

Krugman, Paul R. *The Age of Diminished Expectations*, Cambridge, Mass. and London, England: The MIT Press, 1990.

Krugman, Paul R. *Peddling Prosperity*, New York and London: Norton, 1994.

Krugman, Paul R. *Rethinking International Trade*, Cambridge Mass. and London: The MIT Press, 1994.

Krugman, Paul R. *Strategic Trade Policy and the New International Economics*, Cambridge, Mass. and London, England: The MIT Press, 1995.

Krugman, Paul R. *The Self-Organizing Economy*, Malden, Mass. and Oxford: Blackwell, 1996.

Krugman, Paul R. *Pop Internationalism*, Cambridge Mass. and London, England: The MIT Press, 1997.

Krugman, Paul R. *The Return of Depression Economics*, London: Allen Lane, The Penguin Press, 1999.

Kuznets, Simon *Modern Economic Growth*, London: Yale University Press, 1965.

Lamont, Norman *Sovereign Britain*, London: Duckworth, 1995.

Landes, David *The Wealth and Poverty of Nations*, London: Little Brown, 1998.

Lang, Tim and Hines, Colin *The New Protectionism*, London, Earthscan, 1993,

Layard, Richard *How to Beat Unemployment*, Oxford: Oxford University Press, 1986.

Leach, Rodney *Monetary Union – A Perilous Gamble*, London: Eurofacts, 1996.

Liesner, Thelma *Economic Statistics 1900–1983*, London, *The Economist*, 1985.

Lingle, Christopher *The Rise & Decline of the Asian Century*, Hong Kong: Asia 2000, 1997.

Lipton, Michael *Assessing Economic Performance*, London: Staples Press, 1968.

Little, I.M.D. *A Critique of Welfare Economics*, Oxford: Oxford University Press, 1957.

Lomborg, Bjørn *The Skeptical Environmentalist*, Cambridge: Cambridge University Press, 2001.

Maddison, Angus *Economic Growth in the West*, London: George Allen & Unwin, 1964.

Maddison, Angus *Economic Growth in Japan and the USSR*, London: George Allen & Unwin Ltd, 1969.

Maddison, Angus *Dynamic Forces in Capitalist Development*, Oxford: Oxford University Press, 1991.

Maddison, Angus *Monitoring the World Economy 1820–1992*, Paris: OECD, 1995.

Maddox, John *What Remains to be Discovered*, London: Macmillan, 1998.

Mai, Chao-Cheng and Shih, Chien-Sheng *Taiwan's Economic Success Since 1980*, New York and Cheltenham: Edward Elgar, 2001.

Marris, Robin *How to Save the Underclass*, London: Macmillan, 1996.

Marsh, David *Reculer pour mieux sauter*, London: Prospect, 1997.

Mayhew, Nicholas *Sterling – The History of a Currency*, London: Penguin Group, 1999.

Maynard, Geoffrey and van Ryckeghem, W. *A World of Inflation*, London: Batsford, 1976.

Mayne, Richard *The Recovery of Europe*, London: Weidenfeld and Nicolson, 1970.

Meade, James E. *The Intelligent Radical's Guide to Economic Policy*, London: George Allen & Unwin Ltd, 1975.

Michie, Jonathan and Grieve Smith, John *Unemployment in Europe*, London: Harcourt Brace, 1994.

Minford, Patrick *Markets not Stakes*, London: Orion Business Books, 1998.

Mishan, E.J. *21 Popular Economic Fallacies*, London: Allen Lane, 1969.

Mishel, Lawrence, Bernstein, Jared and Schmitt, John *The State of Working America 2000/2001*, New York: Cornell University Press, 2001.

Moggridge, D.E. *Maynard Keynes – An Economist's Biography*, London: Routledge, 1995.

Monti, Mario *The Single Market and Tomorrow's Europe*, London: Kogan Page, 1996.

Nevin, Edward *The Economics of Europe*, London: Macmillan, 1994.

North, Douglass C. *The Economic Growth of the United States 1790–1860*, New York and London: W.W. Norton, 1966.

Nove, Alec *The Soviet Economy*, London: George Allen & Unwin, 1961.

OECD *The Residual Factor and Economic Growth*, Paris: OECD, 1971.

Okita, Saburo *The Developing Economies and Japan*, Tokyo: University of Tokyo Press, 1980.

O'Leary, James J. *Stagnation or Healthy Growth? The Economic Challenge to the United States in the Nineties*, Lanham, New York, London: University Press of America, 1992.

Olson, Mancur *The Rise and Decline of Nations*, New Haven and London: Yale University Press, 1982.

Ormerod, Paul *The Death of Economics*, London: Faber and Faber, 1995.

Ormerod, Paul *Butterfly Economics*, London: Faber and Faber, 1998.

O'Sullivan, John and Keuchel, Edward F. *American Economic History: From Abundance to Constraint*, Princeton, N.J.: Markus Wiener Publishing Inc, 1989.

Patten, Chris *East and West*, London: Macmillan, 1998.

P.E.P. *Economic Planning and Policies in Britain, France and Germany*, London: George Allen & Unwin, 1968.

Pilbeam, Keith *International Finance*, London: Macmillan, 1994.

Pinder, John *The Economics of Europe*, London: Charles Knight, 1971.

Pinker, Stephen *How the Mind Works*, London: Allen Lane the Penguin Press, 1997.

Porter, Michael E. *et al. Can Japan Compete?*, London: Macmillan Press Ltd – now Palgrave Macmillan, 2000.

Postan, M.M. *An Economic History of Western Europe 1945–1964*, London: Methuen, 1967.

Reader, John *Africa: A Biography of the Continent*, London: Penguin Books, 1998.

Robbins, Lord *Money, Trade and International Relations*, London: Macmillan, 1971.

Roberts, J.M. *The Hutchinson History of the World*, London: Hutchinson, 1976.

Roberts, J.M. *A History of Europe*, Oxford: Helicon, 1996.

Rohwer, Jim *Asia Arising*, London: Nicholas Brealey Publishing, 1996.

Roll, Eric *A History of Economic Thought*, London: Faber and Faber, 1973.

Rome, Club of *The Limits to Growth*, London: Potomac Associates, 1972.

Roney, Alex *EC/EU Fact Book*, London: Chamber of Commerce and Industry/Kogan Page, 1995.

Rostow, W.W. *The Stages of Economic Growth*, Cambridge: Cambridge University Press, 1960.

Rostow, W.W. *Why the Poor Get Richer and the Rich Slow Down*, London: Macmillan, 1980.

Salter, W.E.G. *Productivity and Technical Change*, Cambridge: Cambridge University Press, 1969.

Sampson, Anthony *The New Europeans*, London: Hodder and Stoughton, 1968.

Schumpeter, Joseph A. *Capital, Socialism and Democracy*, London: George Allen & Unwin, 1943.

Schumpeter, Joseph A. *History of Economic Analysis*, London: Routledge, 1997 reprint.

Schumpeter, Joseph A. *Ten Great Economists*, London: Routledge, 1997 reprint.

Sen, Amartya *On Ethics & Economics*, Oxford: Blackwell, 1995.

Sen, Amartya *Development as Freedom*, Oxford: Oxford University Press, 1999.

Shonfield, Andrew *In Defence of the Mixed Economy*, Oxford: Oxford University Press, 1984.

Singh, Jyoti Shankar *A New International Economic Order*, New York and London: Praeger Publishers, 1935.

Skousen, Mark *The Making of Modern Economics*, Armonk, New York and London, England: M.E. Sharpe, 2001.

Slichter, Sumner H. *Economic Growth in the United States*, Westport, Connecticut: Greenwood Press, 1961.

Smith, Adam *The Wealth of Nations Books I–III*, London: Penguin Books, republished 1997; original published in 1776.

Soros, George *The Crisis of Global Capitalism*, London: Little, Brown and Company, 1998.

Spence, Jonathan *The Chan's Great Continent*, London: Allen Lane The Penguin Press, 1998.

Spiegel, Henry William *The Growth of Economic Thought*, Durham and London: Duke University Press, 1996.

Stein, Herbert *The Fiscal Revolution in America*, Chicago and London: University of Chicago Press, 1969.

Stewart, Michael *Keynes in the 1990s: A Return to Economic Sanity*, London: Penguin, 1993.

Stone, P.B. *Japan Surges Ahead*, London: Weidenfeld and Nicolson, 1969.

Thurow, Lester C. *The Zero-Sum Society*, New York: Basic Books, 1980.

Tsoukalis, Loukas *The New European Economy*, Oxford: Oxford University Press, 1993.

US Council of Economic Advisers *Economic Report of the President*, Washington, DC: US Government Printing Office, 1999.

van Doren, Charles *A History of Knowledge*, New York: Ballantine Books, 1991.

Warburton, Peter *Debt and Delusion*, London: Allen Lane The Penguin Press, 1999.

Wheen, Francis *Karl Marx*, London: Fourth Estate Ltd, 1999.

Wilson, Edward O. *Consilience: The Unity of Knowledge*, London: Little Brown and Company, 1998.

Wray, L. Randall *Understanding Modern Money*, Northampton, Mass.: Edward Elgar Publishing, Inc, 1998.

Index

The subjects listed in the index do not include references to Britain, Europe, France, Germany, the United States and World Wars I and II, because references to them occur so frequently in the text.